Irrelevant Elections?

Irrelevant Elections?

THE QUALITY OF
LOCAL DEMOCRACY IN BRITAIN

WILLIAM L. MILLER

CLARENDON PRESS · OXFORD
1988

Oxford University Press, Walton Street, Oxford OX2 6DP
Oxford New York Toronto
Delhi Bombay Calcutta Madras Karachi
Petaling Jaya Singapore Hong Kong Tokyo
Nairobi Dar es Salaam Cape Town
Melbourne Auckland

and associated companies in
Berlin Ibadan

Oxford is a trade mark of Oxford University Press

Published in the United States
by Oxford University Press, New York

British Library Cataloguing in Publication Data

Miller, William L. (William Lockley), 1943–
Irrelevant elections? : the quality of
local democracy in Britain.
1. Great Britain. Local government.
Political aspects
I. Title
352.041
ISBN 0–19–827572–2

Library of Congress Cataloging in Publication Data
Miller, William Lockley, 1943–
Irrelevant elections? : the quality of local democracy in Britain
William L. Miller.
p. cm.
Includes index.
1. Local elections—Great Britain—Public opinion.   2. Voting—
Great Britain—Public opinion.   3. Public opinion—Great Britain.
I. Title.
JS3215.M55   1988   324.6941—dc19   87–36563
ISBN 0–19–827572–2

Typeset by Hope Services, Abingdon, Oxon
Printed in Great Britain
at the University Printing House, Oxford
by David Stanford
Printer to the University

Preface

In one respect at least, any discussion of British local democracy recalls a discussion of democracy in Eastern Europe or Latin America: it is as important to justify it as to describe it. We cannot take its existence for granted. And even if it exists, we cannot take its quality for granted. We know that local elections exist, but the mere existence of elections is not, by itself, sufficient evidence of a healthy democracy. We need to know what kind of elections they are and how they fit into the web of public attitudes and official actions.

This book is based upon a panel survey of 745 members of the British electorate, each of them interviewed twice—the first time at the end of November 1985, the second time just after the local government elections in May 1986. The survey was funded by the Economic and Social Research Council and builds upon previous work which I did for the Widdicombe Committee. The panel differs from previous surveys especially in revealing the contrast between intentions in November and behaviour in the following May.

The basic questions about local elections and democracy are introduced in Chapter 1 and answered in Chapter 17. Chapters 2 to 16 review the literature and present a detailed analysis of the panel survey. I have included numerous highly detailed tables for those who wish to cross-check my conclusions or develop their own theories. In addition, I have made very extensive use of computer-drawn graphics. These graphics do not add anything to the information presented in the tables: they subtract. The graphics are intended to emphasize the main points made in the text and tables. They tell the essential story by themselves. For further, more detailed information each graphic refers the reader to the corresponding table or tables.

It is a little presumptious of an author to advise his readers on how to approach his book, but this text is packed with detail, and the best way to get an overview of its argument and findings is to read Chapter 1; then to flick through the pages looking at the graphics in Chapters 2 to 16, consulting tables and text only when the meaning of the graphic is obscure; and finally to read Chapter 17. By then the shape of the wood should be clear and it will be safe to venture amongst the trees!

Glasgow   W. L. Miller
1987

Contents

Figures

Tables

Introduction

1 The Problem of Irrelevant Elections

The purposes and functions of elections are manifold,[1] but at its best the British political system is expected to provide government which is 'representative and responsible'—the title of Birch's classic text on the British constitution.[2] The phrase denotes government that is representative of the governed and responsible to them. It implies a connection between the inputs and outputs of government, between electoral choice and public policy, which is likely to influence both the quantity and quality of electoral behaviour. Where the connection is weak, we may expect that the quantity of electoral behaviour will be low—relatively few people will bother to vote; and we may also expect that the quality of electoral behaviour will be poor—voting patterns will lack meaning, significance, or relevance.

Although some writers on British central government have asked 'Do parties make a difference?'[3] the general assumption has been that central government has a large measure of effective autonomy and that British governments can be held responsible by their electorates for the events and conditions of the time. Butler and Stokes refer to the 'popular acceptance' of the 'idea that the (central) government is accountable for good and bad times'.[4] The nature of that accountability may be quite complex in terms of both realities and perceptions, but the general notion that the real or supposed policy outputs of British central government will have an impact on its popularity and eventual electoral success underlies many studies of central government policy.[5]

Do Local Elections Imply Local Democracy?

In sharp contrast, most analysts of British local government have highlighted its lack of autonomy, and its insulation from its electorate.[6] Caught between the requirements imposed from above by central government and the social needs and resources of the local area, there has been real doubt as to whether local government has any effective political autonomy at all. Moreover, while the general public is reputed to overestimate central government's freedom of action, it is reputed to underestimate or even disregard altogether local government's freedom of action. Central government's own actions have not been calculated to clarify local government responsibilities; rather, they have spread confusion in the public mind.[7]

On this perspective, British local government is indeed both representative and responsible. But it is *representative of its local electorate* (at least in a formal sense) yet *responsible to central government*. So local government is not likely to figure very large in the public imagination, even when people are invited to vote in a local election; they are likely to stay at home or vote in accordance with their attitude to central government, which dominates their image of politics. In short, there is no connection between local elections and local politics—other than accidental interference: paradoxically, *local* elections are part of *national* politics, not local politics.

That is, of course, only one viewpoint. Without disputing the constraints under which local government operates, we might note: first, that these constraints are primarily financial, and non-financial decsions may be important at least to some voters, in some localities, at some times; second, that elections are inherently seductive—they appear to offer choice, and though this may not deceive the voters' minds, it may deceive their emotions. So despite increasingly tight constaints on local government it is possible that some electors may retain a local orientation at local elections.

Nevertheless the traditional view of local government elections is summed up in Newton's phrase, 'the annual general election'.[8] Most analysts have assumed that local government election results are a largely accidental by-product of central government's popularity at local election time. If local elections have a political message, it is assumed to be a message aimed at central government. If policies need changing to avoid electoral retribution, it is central government policies which are put under scrutiny. If local elections indicate that *government* is unpopular, it is assumed to be *central government* that has offended the electorate.

Thus the impact of policy outputs on elections, which has long been a fashionable topic in analyses of central government, has been neglected in studies of local government. Conversely, the question of whether parties really do make a difference to policy outputs has been the major focus of local government policy studies. The writings of James Alt neatly illustrate this focus on particular causal directions at different levels of government. In his early work on local government he sought to explain budget decisions on the basis of the social and political characteristics of the local authority—an *election results cause policy outputs* model. In his later work he turned his attention to central government and sought to explain its political popularity on the basis of public attitudes towards economic conditions—a *policy outputs cause election results* model.[9]

The impact of local elections on policy outputs has been the prime concern not just in case-studies of local decision-making processes[10] but especially in cross-sectional statistical studies that compare one local authority with another. Typically these latter predict a variety of local expenditure variables from a range of indicators of local needs, local resources, and local political complexion. Using multiple regressions they seek to determine whether the political predictors add anything to the explanation of budget decisions, once account has been taken of the needs and resources of the area. They ask, in the title of Sharpe and Newton's book on British local government, 'Does politics matter?'[11]

In one sense, however, that title is misleading. Sharpe and Newton's actual question is whether the party balance on the local council affects its behaviour, which is ultimately a question about the policy impact of local elections. In this book we ask whether those local election results reflect local or national politics—'does local politics matter even for the outcome of local elections, let alone the policy outputs of local government?' More starkly still our question is, '*does local politics exist at all?*'

There is so much doubt about whether the political complexion of a local authority has any effect on policy that it has generated a great deal of research. Of course, if that research showed that local politics had a major effect on policy then voters, in their own interests, would be wise to take local as well as national considerations into account when deciding their behaviour in local elections. But the perceptions of ordinary electors are not shaped by obscure academic research reports, and it is the electors' perceptions, right or wrong, that influence electoral behaviour.

Irrelevant Elections

Now if the majority of electors ignore local elections altogether and refuse to vote, while most of those that do vote use the local election to pass judgement upon central government, we can argue that local elections are meaningless and irrelevant—both for local government and for central government. The message that local elections then send to local government is almost completely irrelevant because few voters are evaluating local government's performance when they vote. And the message they send to central government is not much better in quality since the majority of electors simply do not participate in local elections, and amongst the minority who do a few, at least, may be influenced by their attitudes towards their local council.

Using elections to one office in order to send a message to another is unsatisfactory because it weakens the link (weak enough already) between politicians' actions and their electoral success: it destroys politicians' responsibility to their electorates. And inevitably the message lacks clarity: it resembles the noise we get from a radio when two stations broadcast on much the same frequency, or the confusion that comes when two telephone wires get crossed. The mingling of signals makes it difficult to interpret either one. So local elections heavily influenced by national political concerns may be a very poor way of controlling or influencing either local or national government.

The problem of meaningless and irrelevant elections is a general one, however. British local government is the subject of this present investigation, but it is perhaps not the worst and certainly not the only example of an irrelevant electoral process. Elections to the European Parliament seem to have little to do with Europe and much to do with internal politics in the different states of the European Community.[12] Similarly the composition of the national legislature in the USA is, to a considerable extent, the by-product of local political battles that have little relevance to national political questions. Former Speaker of the House, Tip O'Neill, exaggerated but did not mislead when he claimed that in the USA 'all politics is local'.[13] In both the European and American examples politics may be more local than the election, in contrast to the case of British local government where the elections are more local than the politics, but the lack of fit between the scale of politics and the scale of elections is essentially the same.

The Extent of Local Democracy

The basic concern of this book is to assess whether local elections reflect local or national politics, and, if they reflect both to some degree, then to assess to what extent they reflect local and national influences.

What are people's perceptions of, and attitudes towards local government autonomy and local government performance? Do they have sufficiently stable views on these questions for us to dignify them with the word 'attitudes'? We must remember that some of the classic studies on the electorate's views about national politics concluded that they had 'non-attitudes'—that is, they answered survey interviewers' questions, but appeared to do so in a random and thoughtless fashion.[14] More recent work suggests that electors do have relatively stable 'attitudes' on some of the issues in national politics.[15] But what about local politics? If people are concerned only with national politics then they may still have lightly held (and soon discarded) 'non-attitudes' about local government.

Who votes in local elections? Do low turn-out rates imply an electorate divided into a majority who ignore local elections and a sizeable minority who regularly vote in them? Or do low turn-out rates simply reflect intermittent local election participation by the electorate as a whole? Why do some people vote in local elections when others do not? Are they motivated by an interest in local politics or by an interest in national politics? How well do local election voters represent the larger electorate? Are there social biases in local electoral participation? And does it matter—do social biases produce political biases as well?

What influences voters' choices in local elections? Do they simply vote their national political preference at the time? What kinds of people, if any, vote differently in national and local elections? And how many of each kind are there?

Do attitudes and patterns of attitudes towards local government vary from place to place? Or from time to time? In particular, are attitudes different at local election time in May? Are they different only in places with an election, or does election-time fever affect all localities, whether or not there is an election locally? Does living under a politically unsympathetic council affect people's attitudes to local government? Is local government more popular in some regions than in others?

These are the detailed questions to be addressed in this book, before we attempt to evaluate the quality of local democracy in contemporary Britain.

The Local Election Panel

To answer these questions we shall look at a major panel survey of attitudes towards local government and local politics. It is important, at the outset, to understand some of the design characteristics of this survey, which is the most elaborate survey of the local electorate ever carried out in Britain. A technical description is given in Appendix I.

The most important feature of this survey is its panel design—that is, it is based upon *two* interviews with each respondent, one in the late autumn of 1985 and the second in the late spring of 1986.

For the first wave of interviews, 1,145 respondents were interviewed in late November 1985. This round of interviews was done for the Widdicombe Committee of Inquiry into Local Government. The survey was a (clustered) random sample of mainland Britain using 112 sampling points. However, Scotland was over-sampled in order to produce sufficient numbers of respondents for comparisons between Scotland, which has its own local government system, and the rest of Britain. Tables in this book are based upon weighted analyses, in which the Scots respondents have been downweighted to their proper proportion of the British electorate. Thus the only effect of the over-sampling in Scotland is to make figures for Scotland more reliable than they would be if fewer Scots had been interviewed. No bias results.

It seems likely that midway between annual rounds of local elections and just a month before Christmas people's thoughts would be upon domestic matters rather than upon local government. This wave of interviews shows us the local electorate at a non-election time.

The next local elections took place in May 1986. At that time there were local elections throughout Scotland (for regional and island councils), throughout London (for borough councils and, in central London, for the Inner London Education Authority also), throughout the former metropolitan counties (for the district councils) and in some parts of the shire counties (for district councils). Immediately after the 1986 local elections, we attempted to reinterview all the respondents that had been interviewed the previous November. Altogether 745 reinterviews were achieved. Of these 745 people, 505 lived in areas where there was a local election in May 1986. This wave of interviews shows us the local electorate at a local election time, when their attention may have been less on domestic concerns and more on politics. We shall see.

For simplicity and comparability, the text of this book is based entirely upon the panel sample of 745. Appendix II compares the panel with the full November cross-section of 1,145 and shows that the panel is very closely representative of the full November sample. It is very slightly biased towards the more interested and informed, but the bias is so slight that it is unnecessary to distinguish here between the answers given by the full November cross-section and the answers given (in November) by the panel respondents.

Compared to a single-wave study like that originally done for the Widdicombe Committee[16] this panel design has two advantages. First, we can look at attitudes and relationships when they matter most—at election time, rather than Christmas time. Second, we can analyse change dynamically. We can follow the evolution of individuals' attitudes and behaviour through from November 1985 to May 1986, from the political calm of Christmas to the political squall of a local election. We can see whether those who said in November that they would vote in a local election actually did so when they had the opportunity in May. We can see whether they held the same opinions in November and May; whether the election context led to sharper and more coherent attitude patterns than existed in the weeks before Christmas; and whether the impact of the election contest affected everyone in May, or only those who lived in an area where there a local election. That impact—or lack of it—will be a further guide to whether local elections in Britain have any meaning.

Notes

1. See M. Harrop and W. L. Miller, *Elections and Voters: A Comparative Introduction* (London: Macmillan, 1987), especially ch. 9.
2. A. H. Birch, *Representative and Responsible Government* (London: Allen and Unwin, 1964).
3. R. Rose, *Do Parties Make a Difference?* (London: Macmillan, 1980).
4. D. Butler and D. Stokes, *Political Change in Britain* (London: Macmillan, 1974).
5. C. A. E. Goodhart and R. J. Bhansali, 'Political Economy', *Political Studies* 18 (1970), 43–106. Later examples include W. L. Miller and M. Mackie, 'The Electoral Cycle and the Asymmetry of Government and Opposition Popularity', *Political Studies* 21 (1973), 263–79; D. Butler and D. Stokes, *Political Change in Britain* (London: Macmillan, 1974); J. Alt, *The Politics of Economic Decline* (Cambridge: Cambridge University Press, 1979); P. Whiteley (ed.), *Models of Political Economy* (London: Sage, 1980); A. Lewis, 'Attitudes to Public Expenditure and their Relationship to Voting Preferences', *Political Studies* 28 (1980), 284–92; C. A. Pissarides, 'British Government Popularity and Economic Performance', *Economic Journal* 90 (1980), 569–81; P. Moseley, 'The British Economy as Represented by the Popular Press', *Studies in Public Policy No. 105* (Glasgow: Strathclyde University, 1982); J. Hudson, 'Prime Ministerial Popularity in the UK 1960–81', *Political Studies* 32 (1984), 86–97.

6. See, for example, B. Keith-Lucas, 'What Price Local Democracy?', *New Society*, 12 Aug. 1976, 340–1.

7. R. A. W. Rhodes, 'Continuity and Change in British Central-local Relations 1979–83', *British Journal of Political Science* 14 (1964), 261–83.

8. K. Newton, *Second City Politics* (Oxford: Oxford University Press, 1976).

9. J. Alt, 'Some Social and Political Correlates of County Borough Expenditures', *British Journal of Political Science* 1 (1971), 49–62; J. Alt, 'Politics and Expenditure Models', *Policy and Politics* 5 (1977), 83–92; J. Alt, *The Politics of Economic Decline* (Cambridge: Cambridge University Press, 1979).

10. Case-studies are reported in J. G. Bulpitt, *Party Politics in English Local Government* (London: Longmans, 1967); H. V. Wiseman, *Local Government at Work* (London: Routledge, 1967); J. Dearlove, *The Politics of Policy in Local Government* (Cambridge: Cambridge University Press, 1973); K. Newton, *Second City Politics* (Oxford: Oxford University Press, 1976); W. H. Cox, *Cities: The Public Dimension* (Harmondsworth: Penguin, 1976); P. Saunders, *Urban Politics: A Sociological Interpretation* (London: Hutchinson, 1980).

11. Examples of these attempts to answer the question 'does politics matter?' include F. R. Oliver and J. Stanyer, 'Some Aspects of the Financial Behaviour of County Boroughs', *Public Administration* 47 (1969), 169–84; N. T. Boaden, *Urban Policy-Making* (Cambridge: Cambridge University Press, 1971); N. T. Boaden and R. R. Alford, 'Sources of Diversity in English Local Government Decisions', *Public Administration* 47 (1969), 203–23; J. Alt, 'Some Social and Political Correlates of County Borough Expenditures', *British Journal of Political Science* 1 (1971), 49–62; B. P. Davies, A. Barton, I. McMillan, and V. Williamson, *Variations in Services for the Aged* (London: Bell, 1971); B. P. Davies, A. Barton, and I. McMillan, *Variations in Children's Services among British Urban Authorities* (London: Bell, 1972); R. J. Nicholson and N. Topham, 'The Determinants of Investment in Housing by Local Authorities: An Econometric Approach', *Journal of the Royal Statistical Society Series A* 134 (1971), 272–303; R. J. Nicholson and N. Topham, 'Investment Decisions and the Size of Local Authorities', *Policy and Politics* 1 (1972), 23–44; R. J. Nicholson and N. Topham, 'Urban Road Provision in England and Wales 1962–68', *Policy and Politics* 4 (1976), 3–29; D. N. King, 'Why Do Local Authorities' Rate Poundages Differ?', *Public Administration* 51 (1973), 3; D. E. Ashford, 'Resources, Spending and Party Politics in British Local Government', *Administration and Society* 7 (1975), 286–311; D. E. Ashford, R. Berne, and R. Schramm, 'The Expenditure Financing Decision in British Local Government', *Policy and Politics* 5 (1976), 5–24; J. Alt, 'Politics and Expenditure Models', *Policy and Politics* 5 (1977), 83–92; J. A. Schofield, 'Determinants of Urban Service Expenditures', *Local Government Studies* 4 (1978), 65–79; J. N. Danziger, *Making Budgets:*

Public Resource Allocation (Beverley Hills: Sage, 1978); S. Pinch, 'Patterns of Local Authority Housing Allocation in Greater London', *Transactions of the Institute of British Geographers* 3 (1978), 35–54; C. D. Foster, R. A. Jackman, and M. Perlman, *Local Government Finance in a Unitary State* (London: Allen and Unwin, 1980); L. J. Sharpe, 'Does Politics Matter? An Interim Summary with Findings' in K. Newton (ed.), *Urban Political Economy* (London: Pinter, 1981); B. Davies and O. Coles, 'Electoral Support, Bureaucratic Criteria, Cost Variations, and Intra-authority Allocations', *Political Studies* 29 (1981), 414–24; T. J. Karran, 'Borough Politics and County Government: Administrative Styles in the Old Structure', *Policy and Politics* 10 (1982), 317–42; K. Hoggart, 'Explaining Policy Outputs: English County Boroughs 1949–74', *Local Government Studies* 9 (1983), 57–68; G. A. Boyne, 'Output Disaggregation and the Quest for the Impact of Local Politics', *Political Studies* 32 (1984), 451–60; L. J. Sharpe and K. Newton, *Does Politics Matter? The Determinants of Public Policy* (Oxford: Clarendon Press, 1984). The question is tested in a Continental European setting by M. Aitken and R. Depre, 'Politics and Policy in Belgian cities', *Policy and Politics* 4 (1976); and by T. Hansen and F. K. Jellberg, 'Municipal Expenditures in Norway: Autonomy and Constraints in Local Government Activity', *Policy and Politics* 4 (1976), 25–50; and in an American setting by R. I. Hofferbert, *The Study of Public Policy* (Indianapolis: Bobs-Merrill, 1974); I. Sharkansky, *Spending in the American States* (Chicago: Rand McNally, 1968); I. Sharkansky (ed.), *Policy Analysis in Political Science* (Chicago: Markham, 1970).

12. J. Blumler and A. Fox, *The European Voter* (London: Policy Studies Institute, 1982).

13. Although Kramer (1971) and Tufte (1978) have suggested that congressional election results do, in aggregate, respond to national influences to some extent, the contrary view is put strongly by Mann (1978), Mann and Wolfinger (1980), Fiorina (1977), and Fenno (1978). Jacobson (1983) presents an ingenious and well-documented argument that explains why the aggregate of congressional results follows national trends despite the intensely local character of congressional election campaigns. We shall return to Jacobson's theory in later chapters. See G. Kramer, 'Short-term Fluctuations in US Voting Behaviour 1896–1964', *American Political Science Review* 65 (1971), 131–43; E. Tufte, *Political Control of the Economy* (Princeton: Princeton University Press, 1978); T. Mann, *Unsafe at Any Margin: Interpreting Congressional Elections* (Washington: American Enterprise Institute, 1978); T. Mann and R. Wolfinger, 'Candidates and Partisan Congressional Elections', *American Political Science Review* 74 (1980), 617–32; M. Fiorina, *Congress: Keystone of the Washington Establishment* (New York: Yale University Press, 1977); R. Fenno, *Home Style: House Members in their Districts* (Boston: Little Brown, 1978);

G. C. Jacobson, *The Politics of Congressional Elections* (Boston: Little Brown, 1983).

14. The classic thesis of non-attitudes is given in P. E. Converse, 'The Nature of Belief Systems in Mass Publics', in D. E. Apter (ed.), *Ideology and Discontent* (New York: Free Press, 1964), 206–61.

15. For a review of revisionist claims see D. R. Kinder, 'Diversity and Complexity in American Public Opinion', in A. W. Finifter (ed.), *Political Science: The State of the Discipline* (Washington: American Political Science Association, 1983).

16. The November wave of interviews was done for the Widdicombe Committee and is reported in K. Young, 'Attitudes to Local Government' and W. L. Miller, 'Local Electoral Behaviour' which together constitute *Research Volume III of The Committee of Inquiry into the Conduct of Local Authority Business. Cmnd. 9800.* (London: HMSO, 1986). Where there are differences between that volume and this text, this text should be taken as definitive.

Part I
Local Politics

2 Does Anybody Know or Care about Local Politics?

'Local government is big business. Councils spend over £47,000 million a year. This amounts to 30 per cent of all state spending and about one eighth of the National Income.'[1] But does anybody care? After all, bank clerks process billions of pounds every year but no one spends very long thinking about their power and influence. Why not?—because they are merely engaged in a routine process, without policy discretion. Similarly, the vast sums of moneys processed by local government may utterly fail to impress, if the electorate believe (rightly or wrongly) that local government is a mere agent of central government and not a significant policy-maker. Indeed, they may see the essential problems of local government (like those of bank-clerking) as problems of maintaining efficiency and avoiding corruption rather than as problems of policy and politics. So despite local government's vast expenditures and vast areas of responsibility, it may still fail to interest the bulk of the electorate.

On the other hand, the electorate have some direct contact with local government: they face rates demands; they use the services provided by local government; they are subject to local government planning decisions; and they are sometimes aggrieved by the actions of their local council. Further, they have indirect contact with their local council through reports in the local press and on local radio or television.

Contact with Local Government

According to figures issued by the Department of the Environment only two-thirds of people live in households that pay rates in full; another 18 per cent pay partially rebated rates; and 16 per cent live in households that are either not liable for rates or enjoy a full rebate.[2] However, that is not the way the electorate sees it.

When our panel respondents were asked the bald question: 'Do you know if your household pays rates?' almost everyone claimed to be a

Table 2.1. Contact with local government

	Nov. %	May %
Read/watch local media		
Read evening paper	32	31
Read local weekly	67	71
Watch local TV news	79	81
Listen to local radio news	38	43
Pay rates		
Pay in full	78	79
Partial rebate	11	11
Full rebate/no rates	11	10
% who say they pay rates		
(before probe about rebates)	95	96
Complaints and personal contacts:		
Ever wanted to complain about something the		
local council has done or failed to do?	45	n.a.
Actually complained?	27	n.a.
Contacted councillor by phone, visit or letter	20*	27
Contacted officials by phone, visit or letter	49*	60

*These figures for November are based upon a sequence of questions about complaints and contacts; so they are not completely strictly comparable with those from the May wave of interviews.

ratepayer—95 per cent in November and 96 per cent in the following May said their household paid rates, while only 3 per cent said they did not. A further question about whether their household enjoyed a partial or full rebate brought the responses a little more into line with Department of Environment figures, though four out of five still claimed to pay full rates. But it is politically significant that it took a further probing question both in November and *even at the second interview* in May to reduce the number of self-described ratepayers beneath 95 per cent. Whatever their net cash outflows, nearly all electors think of themselves as ratepayers and on that ground alone we might expect them to feel some interest in local government.

In November (but not in May) we asked whether respondents had 'ever wanted to complain about something their local district council had done or failed to do?'; 45 per cent said they had wanted to, and 27 per cent claimed they had actually done so. A further question revealed that many who would not admit to complaining to councillors or officials none the less agreed that they had contacted them by visit, phone, or letter. In the May survey we omitted the question about complaints and simply asked everyone whether they had contacted councillors or officials about district council business; 27 per cent said they had contacted their councillors and 60 per cent said they had contacted their local council offices.

Less personally, we may presume that many electors heard something in the mass media about local council affairs. Four-fifths said they watched local TV news, two-fifths listened to local radio news, while a third read an evening paper—and evening papers are exclusively local papers. Most significant of all perhaps, two-thirds of respondents read a local weekly paper. In terms of their spatial span of circulation and coverage, TV (even local TV) is the least local, while the local weekly press is the most specifically local.

Interest in Local Government

Direct and indirect contact should perhaps encourage interest in local government, but it is no guarantee of interest. We put several questions which reveal how much interest people actually have in local politics. First, we asked quite explicitly, 'how much interest do you have in what's going on in *national* politics?' and 'how often do you discuss *national* politics with other people?' Then we asked the same two questions about *local* politics. Elsewhere in the interviews we asked: 'Is there any issue in politics, national or local, that you feel strongly about? What is that? . . . (and) Is this a problem mainly for local councils or mainly for central government to deal with?' Finally, at yet another point in the interview we asked: 'Are there any local issues which would be important to you in deciding how to vote in a local election? What are they?'

A majority of respondents said they had 'not much interest' or 'none at all' in local politics—64 per cent in November and the same in May. Of course, few people are intensely interested in politics of any kind; but when asked about national politics only 46 per cent in November and 43 per cent in May said they had 'not much interest' or 'none at all'.

Similarly with the reported level of political discussion—a majority of 54 per cent in both November and May said they 'rarely' or 'never' discussed local politics. By contrast only 39 per cent in November and 37 per cent in May said the same about national politics. It is particularly striking that the local election campaigns in April and May 1986 had no effect upon the reported levels of interest in and discussion of local politics. In so far as there was a change between the

Table 2.2. Interest and discussion

	Nov. %	May %
Interest in national politics:		
Great deal	15	18
Fair amount	39	40
Not much	33	32
None at all	13	11
Interest in local politics:		
Great deal	7	7
Fair amount	29	29
Not much	48	50
None at all	16	14
Discuss national politics:		
Often	30	30
Occasionally	31	33
Rarely	20	19
Never	19	18
Discuss local politics:		
Often	15	14
Occasionally	31	32
Rarely	30	33
Never	24	21
Issues of importance are a matter for:		
DK/none	45	34
Local councils	7	8
Central government	38	49
Both	9	10
Local issues influencing the vote:		
None	57	50
Rates	11	9
Rents	7	7
Education	14	15
Unemployment	7	11
Planning	5	5
Refuse	4	5
Social services	5	4
Health	6	5
Other	10	13

DK = Don't know

pre-Christmas rush and local election time it was interest in and discussion of *national* politics, *not local*, that seemed to rise—though the rise was slight. (But since, in a panel survey, we interview the same people on two occasions, even slight trends are more likely to be real,

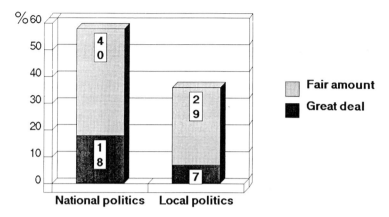

Fig. 2.1. Interest in politics (May) (*see Table 2.2*)

though small, and less likely to be due to accidents of sampling than if we were comparing two different surveys.)

Turning to issues, 57 per cent said in November that there were no local issues that would influence their vote in local elections. This dropped to 50 per cent in May, but the only 'local issue' that was mentioned much more in May than in November was unemployment which may be local in its incidence, but is not primarily a responsibility of local government.

Our more general question about whether there were any issues in politics 'national or local' that people felt strongly about confirmed the impression that local issues were not very important either in November or in May.

People were more concerned about political issues at the time of the local elections; the number who said there was no issue they felt strongly about dropped from 45 per cent to 34 per cent. But the rising importance of issues was clearly more significant for national politics than for local. The number who said that the issue that concerned them was mainly a problem for local councils rose only from 7 per cent to 8 per cent; and the number who said it concerned both local councils and central government rose only from 9 per cent to 10 per cent. The bulk of the increased concern about issues related to matters which the respondents said were mainly a problem for *central* government: concern about these issues rose from 38 per cent to 49 per cent.

The evidence clearly shows that interest in local politics is low and, in particular, it is much lower than interest in national politics. Perhaps however we need to stress that there is a difference between a low level of interest and no interest at all. About a third of the electorate expressed at least a 'fair amount' of interest in local politics; and a sixth of the electorate felt strongly about some issue that was, in their view, at least partly the responsibility of local government. Substantial numbers of electors said that local issues of education, rates, rents, unemployment, or other matters influenced their vote in local elections. So even though interest in local politics is low, even though it may be subordinate to an interest in national politics, that does not mean that local politics is totally non-existent or has no effect at all upon local elections. We should not expect it to have a very large effect, but we should expect it to have some.

Knowledge about Local Government

Interest and knowledge are interrelated. Altogether, we put sixteen questions about knowledge of local politics to our panel in both November and May. Ten of these investigated whether respondents knew which tier of local government (if any) provided particular services. Young has analysed the responses in November and concluded that his 'findings point to a reasonably well-informed electorate'.[3] Knowledge of service provision was far from exact—

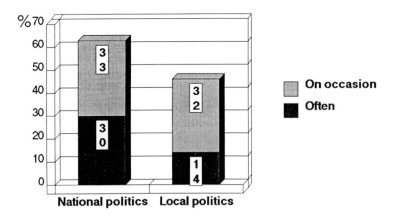

Fig. 2.2. Discuss politics (May) (*see Table 2.2*)

Table 2.3. Knowledge about local government

	Nov. %	May %
Know county/regional council name:		
Correct	55	64
Wrong	13	16
DK	32	21
Know city/district/borough council name:		
Correct	73	80
Wrong	4	5
DK	24	15
Know name of any councillor for ward:		
Correct	31	42*
Wrong	9	6*
DK	60	53*
Know councillor's party:		
Correct	58	74*
Wrong	12	6*
DK	31	20*
Know party controlling county:		
Correct	57	n.a.
Wrong	20	n.a.
DK	23	n.a.
Know party controlling district:		
Correct	61	81*
Wrong	16	10*
DK	23	9*

*Based on interviews in areas where elections were held in May; and refers to tier of local government that was up for election then—that is, upper tier in Scotland, lower tier elsewhere.

though the two-tier structure of British local government, plus the numerous exceptions and variations in different parts of the country, is designed to confuse experts and academic researchers, let alone the general public. The major mistake concerned hospitals, which a plurality of respondents thought were provided by the county or regional council (they are provided in fact by quasi-independent Health Authorities, some of whose members are drawn from the councils). However, the real administrative confusion is so great that we hesitate to use the service responsibility figures as a true guide to public knowledge.

Some simpler indicators are more valid. Respondents were asked to name their county or regional council, their city, borough, or district council, (any of) their local ward councillors, their local councillor's party, and the party in control of their county and district councils. Young points out that some of these questions tap rather impersonal awareness of the kind that goes with attention to the media, while others tap very localized, highly personal knowledge. Specifically, different factors may underlie knowledge of institutions and parties on the one hand, compared to knowledge of individuals on the other.

Regional and county council names were not very well known: only 55 per cent got them right in November, rising to 64 per cent in May. City, borough, or district council names were better known: 73 per cent got them right in November and 80 per cent in May. About 60 per cent knew which party (if any) controlled their county and district councils in November and, where elections took place in May, 81 per cent knew which party now controlled the council. Similarly 58 per cent knew the party of their local councillor in November and, where elections occurred, 74 per cent knew the party of their newly elected councillor in May. But councillors as named individuals were much less well-known. Only 31 per cent of the electorate knew their councillor's name in November and only 42 per cent could name their newly elected councillor in May.

Three things are clear: first, the level of knowledge is substantial, but far from total; second, knowledge about councillors is much lower than about parties and councils; third, knowledge—unlike interest—rose sharply at election time. Young has pointed to a fourth conclusion: knowledge of councillors is not only lower, but is spread rather differently from other forms of knowledge. Generally, the more home-centred respondents (women, lower social classes, those not working) have markedly low levels of knowledge about parties and institutions, but average or above average levels of knowledge about councillors. This may reflect a very narrowly local form of knowledge, ward-centred, rather than district- or county-centred.

Opposing the Councils

So far, we have looked at interest in and knowledge about local politics. What about active participation? We asked respondents what they 'would do' if their local council was proposing a scheme that they thought was really wrong. They were provided with a list of possibilities, and they were also asked to say which action they thought would be most effective.

Table 2.4. How to oppose a local council

If local council proposed a scheme you thought was really wrong which would				
	you do		be the most effective action	
	Nov. %	May %	Nov. %	May %
Contact:				
Councillor	51	53	16	15
Council offices	28	21	4	3
Ombudsman	8	12	3	5
MP	48	55	23	27
Auditor	2	2	1	0
Press/radio/TV	26	30	16	18
Other people	3	2	1	0
Petition	56	56	12	9
Demonstrate	9	7	2	2
Go to court	5	5	4	2
Vote against council	19	18	4	4
Other	n.a.	2	1	1
None of these	4	3	6	4
DK	2	2	6	6

Over half said they would contact their local councillor; about the same said they would contact their MP; and a similar number would sign a petition. Over a quarter would contact the press. About a fifth would contact council officials and a similar number would vote against the council. This hierarchy of responses roughly reflects perceptions of the relative effectiveness of different actions. Very few respondents thought that voting or arguing with council officials would do much good. More thought that contacting the press or contacting their elected councillor would be effective. By a substantial margin, contacting their MP was the most popular choice of effective action. In short, while the idea of contacting elected local representatives has some support, many more people think it would be best to go over the head of the local authority and appeal to the press or to their parliamentary representative. Local election voting was not seen to be a useful way of controlling local government.

Local and National Orientations

Searching for further evidence that local politics exists we asked about people's motivations in local election voting: did they vote for the

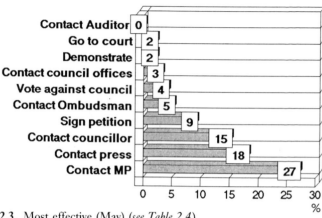

Fig. 2.3. Most effective (May) (*see Table 2.4*)

candidate or the party? Did they do so more often in local than in national elections? And were they more influenced by local or national issues when casting their vote in a local election? The answers need to be checked against actual behaviour (which we shall do in a later chapter). None the less, even taken at face value, the answers are illuminating.

Table 2.5. Local orientation in voting

	Nov. %	May %
Vote for candidate or party?		
In national elections:		
Candidate	12	8
Party	81	86
Both equally	4	4
DK/DNV	3	3
In local elections:		
Candidate	33	31
Party	56	58
Both equally	5	6
DK/DNV	6	5
Local vote more influenced by local or national issues?		
Local	56	56
National	24	28
Both equally	12	11
DK	8	5

DNV = Did not vote

While over 80 per cent of respondents claimed to vote 'for the party, not the candidate' in national elections, less than 60 per cent claimed that about local elections. Moreover, over half claimed that their local election voting choice was determined 'more by local issues than by national issues'. Here then is remarkable evidence of a vigorous local politics underlying local elections.

But we must be sceptical about these claims. How can so many base their local election vote on choice of candidate rather than party, when so few can recall their elected councillor's name at non-election times? Certainly name recognition is fairly high on election day, but that suggests only a transient and superficial aquaintance with the councillors as individual personalities (still less with their electoral opponents).

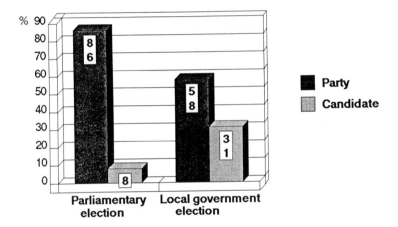

Fig. 2.4. Vote for candidate or party (May) (*see Table 2.5*)

And how can local issues be so influential when so many cannot even name a local issue, and when so very few quote local issues as the ones they feel strongly about? Undoubtedly, the electors are much less locally orientated in their politics than they claim to be. None the less, they do claim a very high degree of local orientation. Even if they exaggerate when asked these questions about their voting motivations, we might expect that substantial numbers are indeed influenced, to some degree, by local politics. We shall submit this proposition to a harsh test in later chapters. For the moment, we note the incontrovertible fact that the electorate likes to think of itself as locally orientated in local government elections.

Notes

1. T. Byrne, *Local Government in Britain* (Harmondsworth: Penguin, 1986), 193.
2. K. Young, 'Attitudes to Local Government', *Research Volume III of the Committee of Inquiry into the Conduct of Local Authority Business. Cmnd 9800* (London: HMSO, 1986), 20.
3. Ibid. 31.

3 Does Anybody Want Local Democracy?

In the last chapter we looked at attitudes towards local politics; in this chapter we look at attitudes towards local democracy—that is, towards a system of local government based upon *elections*. And we focus not on whether people know about it or are interested in it but on whether they are satisfied with its performance. Above all, we ask whether they *want* a local government system controlled from below, by the local electorate that it serves.

Local Democracy

It is worth reminding ourselves first, that the local provision of services does not require any system of local government and second, that local government does not imply local democracy.

Services can be provided by national agencies. In the town of Hull, the telephone service is provided by local government, but in the rest of Britain telephone services are provided by national agencies such as British Telecom, and more recently, Mercury. Similarly gas, electricity, and postal services are provided by essentially national agencies. There is no intrinsic reason why this should be so. Indeed, in the past many of these services were provided by local government. When Attlee's reforming post-war Government *nationalized* the 'commanding heights of the economy', the term nationalization combined two separate meanings. Some undertakings were *socialized*, that is they were transferred from private to public (or 'social') ownership; but many were simply transferred from local government to central government —they were already socialized long before they were nationalized. Conversely, the Thatcher Government's *privatization* schemes of the 1980s were aptly described because most enterprises (not all) were *privatized without being denationalized*—that is, enterprises were transferred from public to private ownership but not from central to local. Thus, while Attlee's Government transferred gas from local public ownership to a national public monopoly, Thatcher's Government did not restore the previous system: it simply went on to transfer ownership from a public monopoly to a private monopoly. As a general rule we may say that there are very few services that could not be run by local governments yet very few that must be run by them. It is a matter of political choice and administrative convenience.

Next we need to draw a distinction between local government and local democracy. Even though a service is provided by local authorities of some kind, these need not be democratically controlled from below. They can be independent self-perpetuating corporations operating with minimal interference from above or below (like the old local government councils before the nineteenth-century reforms). Or they can be bodies largely appointed and controlled by central government. Classic examples of modern independent public corporations are the BBC and the universities which operate under Royal Charters. Even when they are still largely independent according to their charters, central government now exerts considerable influence through a few key appointments and more especially through its control of grants and funds. Elected local government controls the polytechnics but not the Scottish central institutions (directly controlled by central government) nor the universities. A good example of a system of local government directly appointed and controlled by central government is the misnamed National Health Service. The Attlee Government removed 1,700 hospitals from the control of elected local governments, but instead of putting them under a national corporation it put them under a set of appointed regional hospital boards. In the mid 1970s most of elected local government's remaining health services were transferred to appointed local boards. On a larger scale the most outstanding example of appointed local government in Britain is the Scottish Office. Directly or indirectly this controls most government activities in Scotland and only in Scotland—so it is certainly 'local' government of a kind (remember that the population of Scotland is much smaller than the population of the old London GLC area). Although the Scottish Office devises special arrangements for the government of Scotland it does not consult the Scottish electorate about them. All the political posts in the Scottish Office are filled by central government appointees, exclusively chosen from the party that has a majority at Westminster, no matter how few seats the party holds in Scotland (currently only ten out of seventy-two).

Finally, even elective local government does not imply one particular system of elected local authorities. Schools were run by elected school or education boards in England until 1902, and in Scotland until 1928. In the nineteenth century there were separately elected boards for poor relief, for public health, and for roads in addition to elected school boards. So electoral control can be exercised service by service through separate boards. In the United States electoral control is often exercised service by service through separate referendums on the financing of different services or on other policy questions. British local referendums on alcohol sales are the nearest equivalent. Since the mid 1970s however, the electoral input to British local government has been largely confined (not totally) to elections for two tiers of general purpose local authorities; an upper tier called regions in Scotland and counties in England and Wales; and a lower tier called boroughs, districts, or cities in various parts of the country. In 1985 the Thatcher Government responded to its opponent's control of the metropolitan counties (and the Greater London Council) by abolishing them all, though it then created a new elective upper tier in central London—the Inner London Education Authority, popularly known as ILEA.

Popular awareness of local government is sufficiently low that most electors probably know very little of this range of historical precedents. We asked them about their attitudes towards the system as it was in 1985, that is a two-tier system of counties ('regions' in Scotland) and districts, both directly elected.

Elective Local Government

To the frustrated student, researcher, or politician an outstanding feature of local government is its complexity. Uniform structures and responsibilities have never been achieved; responsibilities overlap between counties and districts and they change frequently as central government reorganizes local government in major or minor ways almost annually. As an example, consider this: development control and planning is a responsibility of the districts in England and Wales; in Scotland the responsibility is shared between the regions and the districts—except in the Dumfries and Galloway Region and the Highland Region where it is a purely regional responsibility. So there is no uniform system within Britain, nor even within Scotland, indeed not even within rural Scotland since Grampian Region and Borders Region do things differently.[1]

Such complexities do not seem to inhibit voting. Voters find it much easier to make up their minds how to vote than to understand the system their votes are meant to control. In the panel only 32 per cent in

Table 3.1. Attitudes to local democracy

How strongly do you agree or disagree with the following statements about
local council elections?

	Nov. %	May %
The way that people vote at local elections is the main thing that decides how things are run:		
Agree strongly/agree	61	62
Neither	12	13
Disagree strongly/disagree	21	21
DK	7	4
Local council elections are sometimes so complicated that I really don't know who to vote for:		
Agree strongly/agree	32	28
Neither	8	6
Disagree strongly/disagree	59	66
DK	3	1
So many other people vote in local elections that it's not important whether I vote or not:		
Agree strongly/agree	15	12
Neither	5	4
Disagree strongly/disagree	77	82
DK	2	2

Note: Because of rounding, percentages may not add up to exactly 100%.

November, still less—only 28 per cent—in May, agreed that 'local
council elections are sometimes so complicated that I really don't know
who to vote for'.

Indeed their commitment to the idea of voting was remarkably high.
They firmly rejected the view that 'so many other people vote in local
elections that it's not important whether I vote or not' by 77 per cent to
15 per cent in November and by an even larger margin of 82 to 12 per
cent in May. By substantial if somewhat lower margins, they affirmed
the view that 'the way people vote at local elections is the main thing
that decides how things are run in this area' (supported by 61 per cent
to 21 per cent in November, and 62 per cent to 21 per cent in May).

Partisan Local Government

As we shall see later, the voters' choice is constrained by party loyalties
whenever the electoral battle is a party contest. A large majority of
respondents felt that over the last decade local councils had become

more dominated by party politics, and by a large majority they claimed to prefer local government run on non-party lines. Political scientists would say that without party cues to help in the voting decision and without party discipline to make councillors abide by their election-time manifestos, the problems of making realistic choices at the polling station would become much more severe: voters would simply lack enough information to make meaningful choices. But that was not the view of the majority of the electorate who opted strongly for a more personal politics at local level.

Satisfaction

Their dislike of party-dominated local government notwithstanding, the panel were remarkably content with the operation of the current system. They were asked how satisfied they were with seven local services: education, housing, street-cleaning, home helps, refuse collection, planning, and the fire service.

Generally they tended either to be satisfied or 'not know' about the service. (Particularly large numbers had no view about home helps and planning, presumably because these affect very specific groups.) Few

Table 3.2. Parties in local government

	Nov. %	May %
Do you think that in the last 10 years or so local councils have become more or less dominated by party politics, or has it not changed?		
More party dominated	63	64
Less	3	2
No change	24	26
DK	11	9
In most areas, all councillors came from one of the political parties and councils are organized on party lines. There are some areas where most councillors are independent and the council is not organized on party lines. Which do you personally think is the better system?		
Party system	33	36
Non-party system	55	52
DK	13	12

Table 3.3. Satisfaction with services and contacts

	Nov. %	May %
Schools:		
Very/fairly satisfied	55	55
Neither	11	10
Very/fairly dissatisfied	17	17
DK	17	18
Housing:		
Very/fairly satisfied	40	44
Neither	19	16
Very/fairly dissatisfied	17	18
DK	26	23
Street-cleaning:		
Very/fairly satisfied	68	72
Neither	5	5
Very/fairly dissatisfied	28	23
DK	0	1
Home helps:		
Very/fairly satisfied	41	46
Neither	14	14
Very/fairly dissatisfied	8	8
DK	38	33
Refuse:		
Very/fairly satisfied	87	86
Neither	2	2
Very/fairly dissatisfied	10	11
DK	0	1
Planning:		
Very/fairly satisfied	33	36
Neither	15	15
Very/fairly dissatisfied	11	9
DK	41	40
Fire service:		
Very/fairly satisfied	80	81
Neither	5	6
Very/fairly dissatisfied	1	0
DK	14	12

Ever contacted one of your councillors/council departments on the (district) council by visit, phone, or letter? How satisfied were you with the way your councillor dealt with the matter?

May only

	Councillor %	Council dept. %
Very/fairly satisfied	19	39
Neither	1	2
Very/fairly dissatisfied	7	18
No contact	74	40

were dissatisfied: the percentage dissatisfied ranged from only 8 per cent on home helps to a maximum of 28 per cent on street-cleaning.

Similarly few electors were dissatisfied with their contacts with councillors or council departments. Many, of course, had not made such contacts at all, but only 7 per cent were dissatisfied with a councillor and 18 per cent with a council office as a result of contact by visit, phone, or letter. The difference between these two levels of dissatisfaction very largely reflects higher rates of contact with council offices than with councillors.

The Scope of Elected Local Government

Another guide to people's broad satisfaction with the present system of elected local authorities is provided by questions about the services that local government 'should' or 'should not' be allowed to provide. The panel were asked about roads, housing, and parks, which are at present part of their mandatory responsibilities; and also about playgroups, grants to voluntary organizations, and spending on job-creation, which are not legally required activities of local government.

The panel's views were positive on all these services, though the pattern of their responses showed a pale reflection of the legal position—where services were not already mandatory, larger numbers of respondents said local government should be allowed to provide them without being required to do so. Negligible numbers were opposed to local government provision of roads, housing, parks, and playgroups. About a tenth opposed spending on job-creation and a fifth opposed grants to voluntary organizations. Generally therefore, the public gave strong support to widening rather than constricting the scope of elected local government.

Comparative Satisfaction with Local and Central Government

A comparison with attitudes towards central government may be helpful. The panel were asked: 'on the whole do you think the XXX runs things well?', inserting the name of the county council, then the name of the district council, and (in May only) 'the government' in turn. There was little difference between assessments of the county and district councils, or between November and May. But there was a massive difference between levels of approval for local and central government. In May, 75 per cent thought both county and district

Table 3.4. Scope of local government

People have different views on what local councils should or should not do. For each of these, can you say if councils should be required to do them, or should they be able to do them if they wish, or should they not be allowed to do them?

	Nov. %	May %
Maintain roads:		
Have to	78	76
Allowed	15	18
Forbidden	6	6
DK	2	1
Provide play groups:		
Have to	49	53
Allowed	42	40
Forbidden	6	4
DK	3	3
Give grants to voluntary organizations:		
Have to	17	16
Allowed	59	58
Forbidden	19	21
DK	5	5
Provide council housing:		
Have to	81	81
Allowed	14	17
Forbidden	2	2
DK	2	1
Provide parks:		
Have to	78	80
Allowed	19	18
Forbidden	2	2
DK	2	1
Try to create jobs:		
Have to	59	54
Allowed	28	33
Forbidden	9	10
DK	4	2

councils had run things 'very or fairly well'. By contrast, only 44 per cent felt the same about central government.

For the past decade, central and local government have been locked in a public quarrel over local government finance. Central government has accused local government of overspending, and local government has accused central government of reducing central grants to local authorities in order to cover up central government's own overspending

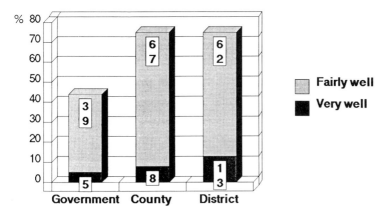

Fig. 3.1. How well do they run things? (May) (*see Table 3.5*)

Table 3.5. Comparative satisfaction

	Nov. %	May %
On the whole do you think the (county) council runs things:		
Very well	9	8
Fairly well	64	67
Not at all well	16	17
DK	10	8
On the whole do you think the (district) council runs things:		
Very well	11	13
Fairly well	61	62
Not at all well	21	20
DK	7	5
On the whole do you think the government runs the country:		
Very well	n.a.	5
Fairly well	n.a.	39
Not at all well	n.a.	51
DK	n.a.	5
Local councils often say they are short of money. Do you think this is mainly because of council overspending, or mainly because councils don't get enough help from the government?		
Council overspending	29	30
Lack of government help	45	50
Both equally	17	14
Other	3	3
DK	6	3

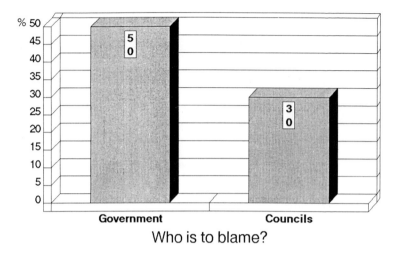

Fig. 3.2. Blame for cash problems (May) (*see Table 3.5*)

and so focus the taxpayers' resentment upon local rather than national government. What did our panel think? By a majority of 45 per cent to 29 per cent in November, rising to 50 per cent against 30 per cent in May, they blamed central government.

Local Autonomy

This brings us to basic questions about the autonomy of local government: does it have any? should it have more or less? We asked, 'how much control do you think the local councils have over the levels of local rates and services?' Opinion was evenly balanced: in November 38 per cent thought that councils had more say, 32 per cent central government; in May there were fewer 'don't knows' so both figures rose a little, to 41 per cent and 36 per cent respectively, but the balance remained unchanged.

This is a rather odd finding when so many more blame central rather than local government for local financial problems. Perhaps it reflects a degree of wishful thinking, since two other questions reveal strong support for the maintenance and even extension of local government autonomy.

When we asked whether local councils should be subject to more or less central government control there was a lot of support for no

Table 3.6. Local autonomy

	Nov. %	May %
How much control do you think the local councils here have over the levels of local rates and local services?		
Almost completely controlled by councils	23	25
Councils more say	15	16
Control shared equally	16	15
Government more say	20	23
Almost completely controlled by government	12	11
DK	15	11
Do you think local councils ought to be controlled by central government more, less, or about the same as now?		
A lot more government control	6	4
A little more government control	9	8
About the same	46	48
A little less government control	16	19
A lot less government control	18	18
DK	6	4
How good or bad an idea would it be for the people who run local government to be appointed by central government instead of being elected by local people?		
Very good idea to appoint	4	3
Fairly good	8	9
Neither	5	5
Fairly bad	23	22
Very bad	58	58
DK	3	4

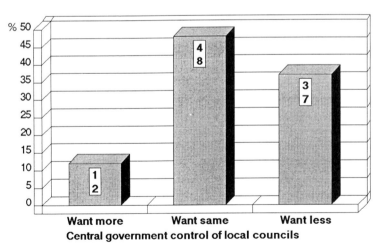

Fig. 3.3. Want central control? (May) (*see Table 3.6*)

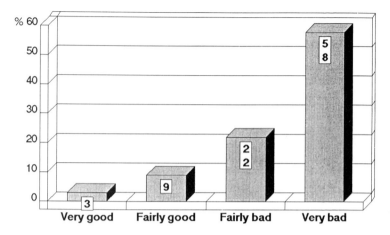

Fig. 3.4 Appoint local councils? (May) (*see Table 3.6*)

change but, amongst those who did want change, the balance was strongly in favour of less government control: in November 34 per cent wanted less and only 15 per cent more; by May the balance had tipped even more in that direction—37 per cent wanted less central control and only 12 per cent wanted more.

Finally we put the ultimate question, the one we discussed at the beginning of this chapter: should local government be elected or should it be appointed by central government? The idea of appointed local government was overwhelmingly rejected. In November only 12 per cent supported an appointed system and 81 per cent rejected it. The figures were almost identical in May. Moreover, fully 58 per cent said that the idea of a non-elected system of local government was not merely bad but *very* bad. Support for the idea of local democracy runs very high indeed. Despite the fact that so few electors exercise their right to vote in local elections, it is a right that they value.

Notes

1. T. Byrne *Local Government in Britain* (Harmondsworth: Penguin, 1986), 314–16.

4 Do People Have Meaningful Attitudes about Local Politics?

A fundamental problem with survey research is reflected in the old saying, 'ask a silly question and you'll get a silly answer'. We hope that the questions we put into our survey questionnaires are not just 'silly'; but the problem remains that if we ask questions we are likely to get answers *whether or not* these answers mean anything very much to the survey respondent. Faced with an interviewer, the respondent inevitably feels under some pressure to say something in reply to the questions that are fired at him (or her). So a survey may elicit a mass of replies to attitude questions yet still not *mean* very much. This is particularly worrying when we are investigating attitudes towards local politics because we suspect that local politics are relatively (at least) unimportant to the ordinary man in the street and we dare not assume that the replies to questions about local politics are more than random responses to irrelevant questions.

The Interrogator's Strategy

There are several useful approaches to dealing with this problem of random response. We could encourage respondents to give 'don't know' replies by emphasizing in the question wording that they should only give an answer if they have already thought about the subject in question. For example, instead of asking (as we did) 'On the whole do you think your district council runs things very well, fairly well, or not at all well?', we could have asked, 'Do you think much about how well your district council is running things?' and then only put our question about 'how well' to those who confessed to thinking about this topic. That approach would certainly have increased the number of 'don't knows' in the sample, though it might have ensured that those who did answer the 'how well' question gave more meaningful replies. We could do something similar by restricting our analysis of attitudes about local politics to those who expressed a high level of interest in local politics—that is, we could throw away some replies whose meaningfulness was suspect.

Unfortunately there is no guarantee that those who claim they have thought about the topic actually have done so, and no certainty that those who modestly disclaim deep thought have actually given the topic any less thought than anyone else. If we suspect the meaningfulness of our respondents' replies we really cannot ask the respondents themselves to tell us whether their own replies are meaningful.

So instead we shall adopt what might be called the *interrogator's strategy*, modelled upon the practice in the best detective and spy stories—we ask the questions more than once, we ask them in slightly different forms, and we look for evidence of inconsistency. That is the best we can do to check the meaningfulness of replies without using data from outside our interviews themselves. Take age, for example. We might ask someone their age. To check the honesty and accuracy of the reply we could go and check official records like birth certificates. But if we wished to check the reply using only interview questions themselves then we could ask the person's age several times at different points in the interview or we could ask for age in years at one point and date of birth at another. If all these answers were consistent it would not prove that the respondent really was the age they claimed to be, but it would at least show that they had very definite views about how old they wished us to think them: objectively right or wrong, their answers would certainly be meaningful, not ill-considered random responses. And indeed, unless we had special reasons to disbelieve them, the very consistency of their replies would suggest that they were telling the truth as they saw it. 'O, what a tangled web we weave, When first we practise to deceive!' wrote Scott. No logical necessity guarantees that deceit will show up as inconsistency, but it takes a lot of care and effort to maintain consistency in deceit.

The classic use of consistency checks to divide survey replies into *attitudes* and *non-attitudes* is Converse's study of political attitudes in America during the 1950s.[1] He argued that if replies to different questions do not hang together in some way, and if replies to the same question put to the same individual on different occasions do not correlate, then these replies reveal what he called 'non-attitudes' rather than attitudes—by which he meant that survey respondents were merely giving random replies to questions about issues that they cared little about. In his study of the American electorate, Converse used questions on the major issues of American domestic and foreign policy. We might imagine that 'non-attitudes' would be much more prevalent on more mundane questions about British local government. We shall see.

The idea of putting the same question twice to the same person is simple enough. But if we are to use the consistency of the replies to assess their meaningfulness then we must be careful about the time-lapse between putting the question a first time and a second. If the time-lapse is too short then the respondent may simply remember his first reply rather than think through the question again. Conversely, if the time-lapse is too long then on questions about attitudes (as distinct from questions about facts) there may be a genuine change of attitude and then inconsistency need not imply lack of meaning. Within the context of a forty-five-minute interview we judged that it would not be worth while to repeat a question as a consistency check. However, the six-month lapse between November 1985 and May 1986 seems almost ideal for such checks: it is too long for respondents to remember their previous replies in detail and yet too short for us to expect major genuine changes in basic attitudes towards local politics—though obviously long enough for some genuine change in matters like voting intentions.

In our panel we asked 47 questions twice, once in November and once in May. We shall use these for *continuity* checks. And in both waves we asked a number of questions which were similar, though not identical, in wording. These will allow us to do 27 *consistency* checks of a less precise kind, since perfectly matched answers are less likely on different questions than with repeated use of the same question.

Measuring Continuity and Consistency

Before we look at the results of these checks, we need to devise some measure or measures of continuity or consistency: when the match is less than perfect we need some measure of how good or how bad it is. The most obvious measure turns out to be misleading. We might think that continuity could be measured by the percentage of our panel respondents who gave the same answer to a question on each of two occasions. Alas this will not do.

Let us take as an example the question whether panel respondents thought that local elections for the whole council should be held every four years or whether it would be better to elect part of the council every year. Excluding those with no opinion in November or May we find the following pattern:

		May		
		Every 4 yrs	Annual	TOTAL
November	Every 4 yrs	237 (36%)	112 (17%)	349 (53%)
	Annual	105 (16%)	204 (31%)	309 (47%)
	TOTAL	342 (52%)	316 (48%)	658 (100%)

The figures in brackets represent % of the full (weighted) sample of 658 who expressed opinions in both November and May.

From this table we see that 36% + 31% = 67% of respondents gave the same reply on both occasions—which seems a high figure. However, we also notice that in both November and May the division of opinion was close to 50 : 50—half opting for four-yearly elections, half for annual elections. Suppose that their replies were entirely random: that in November each person tossed a coin (heads for four year, tails for annual) and then in May each person once again tossed a coin. What sort of table would that generate? It would be like this:

		May		
		Every 4 yrs	Annual	TOTAL
November	Every 4 yrs	25%	25%	50%
	Annual	25%	25%	50%
	TOTAL	50%	50%	100%

and purely by chance 25% + 25% = 50%, that is fully half, of the panel would give the same reply on both occasions. So the 67% who actually gave the same replies were not all that much more numerous than we should expect in a coin-tossing electorate! But matters could be worse. We asked another question about whether people watched local news broadcasts on TV. Most did. Their answers produced this table:

In this case 71% + 11% = 82% gave the same answer on both occasions. But this time we see that approximately four-fifths watched

		May		
		Watched	Did not	TOTAL
November	Watched	528 (71%)	59 (8%)	587 (79%)
	Did not	74 (10%)	82 (11%)	156 (21%)
	TOTAL	602 (81%)	141 (19%)	743 (100%)

TV in November, and the same in May. Now suppose that everyone has an 80% chance of saying 'yes' to this question. Suppose that in November each respondent spun a roulette wheel on which four-fifths of the positions were marked 'yes' and one-fifth 'no' and when the ball came to rest they gave the corresponding answer. And suppose that in May each respondent simply spun the wheel again to generate another answer. What sort of table would that generate? It would look like this:

		May Watched	Did not	TOTAL
November	Watched	64%	16%	80%
	Did not	16%	4%	20%
	TOTAL	80%	20%	100%

(The way to calculate the entries in the body of this table is to multiply together the appropriate row and column marginal percentages.) We see that 64% + 4% = 68% would give the same answer on both occasions purely by chance. So although the 82% who actually did give the same answer is high, it is not all that much higher than chance alone would have produced in a television-watching and roulette-playing electorate!

What would be a good measure of the degree of continuity beyond that produced by chance alone? We suggest a *continuity coefficient* or *consistency coefficient*, C, defined as follows:

$$C = \frac{(A - E)}{(100 - E)} \times 100\%$$

where A is the Actual percentage who give the same answer twice and E is the percentage we would Expect to give the same answer twice for purely random reasons.

When our measure C is applied to a two-by-two table it produces the same value as R, the familiar (Pearson) correlation coefficient unless the overall balance of opinion on the attitude in question has changed. (See the note at the end of this chapter for the outline of a mathematical proof.) In that case it provides a useful interpretation of the correlation coefficient. When there are more than two possible replies to a question C and R can, and do, assume widely different values. Each measure has its virtues and we shall use both. C has the advantage that it focuses purely upon exact continuity or consistency. It can be applied to categorical as well as ordinal or interval data while R cannot. For example, C can be used to assess the continuity in replies to a voting question that has answers 'Too Young/Did Not Vote/Conservative/Labour/Alliance/Other', while it would be inappropriate to calculate R for such a question.

On the other hand, it is sometimes a disadvantage to focus, as C does, purely on exact continuity. For example, when we have a scale rather than a set of distinct answer categories—'Agree strongly/Agree/Neither/Disagree/Disagree strongly' then we may be inclined to accept that any respondent who gave one answer in November and the adjacent, but not exactly the same, answer in May was none the less exhibiting a high, though not perfect, degree of continuity. In this case R takes account of closely similar but not identical answers, while C does not. We may feel that C is too stringent a measure for assessing the continuity of response with such scale questions.

Continuity of Attitudes to Local Government

Near-perfect stability

Thanks no doubt to the accuracy of the interviewers and the keypunchers who input the data to the computer, we have no recorded cases of sex change. So sex heads the list of continuity rankings. Recorded ages changed a little but only a little—4 per cent moved to an older age-group and less than 1 per cent (but not quite zero!) moved to a younger age-group between November and May. These variables really show the accuracy of respondents when faced with a straight factual question about themselves. Almost perfect continuity on these variables suggests that the interviewers and data processors were very accurate and that respondents did not give meaningless replies to factual questions on which they were well-informed. Consequently any lack of continuity in replies to other questions is a property of the questions themselves rather than the respondents, the interviewers, or the data processors.

Choice between Labour and Conservative party identification was only marginally less stable than age. So was house tenure. General election voting preferences between Labour and Conservative were slightly less stable than party identifications. A little less stable still were choice of morning newspaper and employment category: during the six months of our survey there was a small switch out of full-time employment and into part-time employment (4 per cent, though not

Table 4.1 Near-perfect stability

Correlation coefficient R	Index of consistency C	Variables Names (categories)	Actual % same	Statistically expected % same
100	100	Sex (M/F)	100	50
98	96	Age (Y/M/O)	97	33
93	94	Party identification: Two party (Con./Lab.)	97	50
n.a.	93	Tenure (own/council/housing assoc/priv rent/other)	97	56
90	90	GE vote preference: Two party (Con./Lab.)	95	50
n.a.	85	Morning paper (12 titles and none)	88	19
n.a.	80	Employment (FT/PT/UNEM/ not WK)	87	36

the same 4 per cent, in each case). Now each of these characteristics (other than sex) could actually have changed over a six-month period. People grow older, they move house, change job, cancel newspapers, and change their minds about the parties. In all these cases we may be measuring real change rather than inaccurate or ill-considered replies.

High stability

The next item on our continuity list is respondents' memories of their 1983 general election vote, which had a continuity coefficient C of only 77 per cent. In this case any change between November and May reflects inaccuracy since the reality is history and unchangeable. However in this case we used a six-category measure of voting and

Table 4.2. High stability

Correlation coefficient R	Index of consistency C	Variables Names (categories)	Actual % same	Statistically expected % same
n.a.	77	GE vote 1983 (TY/DNV/C/L/A/O)	83	25
74	74	Reads local evening paper (Y/N)	89	57
n.a.	74	Party identification (C/L/A/O/none)	82	31
n.a.	66	GE vote preference (C/L/A/O/WNV/ undecided/refused)	76	29

most of the changes that occurred were between remembering voting for a party and remembering abstaining—only 1 per cent remembered voting Labour at one interview and Conservative at the other. Our multi-party version of the current party identification question and current general election preference were somewhat less stable (C = 74 per cent and 66 per cent respectively) than memories of 1983.

None of the other questions in our set of forty-seven showed high levels of continuity. That is to say, attitudes towards local government were a good deal less stable than attitudes towards parties.

Low stability

Continuity was low (C and R both under 40 per cent) on knowledge of district and county names and on knowledge of the local councillor's name or party; on answers to the question whether respondents voted for the party or the candidate; on whether they voted on local or national issues in local elections; and on what were the important issues either nationally or locally. Continuity was similarly unimpressive on several questions about the organisation of local elections—on whether councillors should be appointed rather than elected; on whether local elections should elect the whole council every four years or a part of the council every year; on perceptions of central government control; on perceptions of whether local elections had become more or less dominated by parties; and on perceptions of whether voters decide the way things are run locally.

To say that opinion on these matters was very unstable is not to say anything about how many people would support one side at a given time. For example a large majority at both times thought that local elections had become more dominated by party in recent years; but substantial numbers changed their minds in both directions (cancelling out in aggregate) between November and May. We conclude that although the majority view can be associated with the electorate as a whole, particular views on this question cannot be associated with particular individuals. Individuals express a prevalent view rather than their own, and divisions of respondents according to their answers on this question are not very meaningful.

In a few cases, low levels of continuity probably reflected real change rather than random instability. The knowledge questions, in particular, score low on continuity primarily because there was so much gain in knowledge. Averaging over four knowledge questions, over twice as

Table 4.3. Low stability

Correlation coefficient R	Index of consistency C	Variables Names (categories)	Actual % same	Statistically expected % same
39	35	Vote for candidate or party in local elections (C/both/P)	66	48
38	33	Vote on national or local issues (L/both/N)	64	46
n.a.	37	Priority local issue (9 issues and 'none')	59	35
36	23	Government should appoint councils (1–5)	56	43
35	33	Know councillor's name (Y/N)	69	54
n.a.	35	Priority national issue (10 issues and 'none')	50	23
34	34	Preferred frequency of local elections (every 4 yrs/annual)	67	50
32	31	Know district name (Y/N)	75	64
31	31	Know county name (Y/N)	66	51
30	15	Alienation scale: 'votes decide' (1–5)	47	38
29	28	Perception of partisan councils (more/no change/less)	69	57
26	15	Perception of government control (1–5)	33	21
25	25	Know councillor's party (Y/N)	67	56
24	25	Vote for candidate or party in general elections (C/both/P)	82	76
13	17	Responsible for most important issue (council/both/ government)	65	58

many people gained knowledge between November and May as lost it. So a large part of the instability on these items was meaningful change rather than random response.

Moderate stability

Almost half of our repeated questions showed medium levels of continuity—neither as stable as party identification nor as unstable as attitudes towards appointing councillors. On these questions the level of continuity suggests that we *can* associate particular viewpoints with particular individuals even though we recognise that these viewpoints may not be held too tenaciously.

Interest and discussion of local politics were fairly stable with

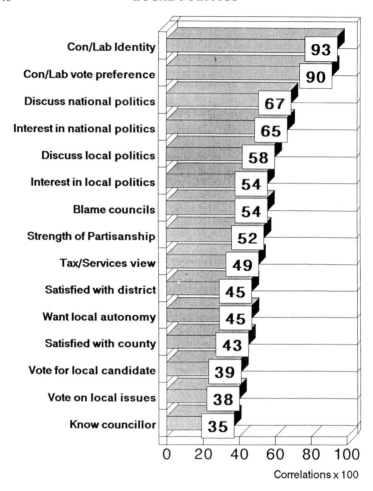

Fig. 4.1. Continuity correlations (*see Tables 4.1–4.4*)

continuity correlations of 54 per cent and 58 per cent respectively. Assignment of blame for local financial difficulties to either the councils or central government also had a continuity correlation of 54 per cent.

Satisfaction with the county council (R = 43 per cent) and district council (R = 45 per cent), a desire for less government control over local councils (R = 45 per cent), and support for a partisan system of local government (R = 42 per cent) were all moderately stable. Responses to the alienation scale questions—'the people you vote for say they'll do things for you, but once they're in they forget what they've said' or 'local elections are sometimes so complicated that I really don't know who to vote for' or 'so many people vote in local council elections that its not important whether I vote or not'—were even more stable; and attitudes towards compulsory voting in local elections (R = 54 per cent) more stable still.

Since it does address an important question about local autonomy let us see what a continuity correlation of 45 per cent implies in detail for the question: 'Do you think local councils ought to be controlled by central government more, less, or about the same amount as now?' The pattern of answers is shown in Table 4.5.

Fully 52 per cent chose the same answer on this five-point scale in

Table 4.4. Moderate stability

Correlation coefficient R	Index of consistency C	Variables Names (categories)	Actual % same	Statistically expected % same
67	46	Discuss national politics (nev/rar/occ/oft)	60	26
65	46	Interest in national politics (GD/FA/NM/none)	62	30
61	56	Number of morning papers read	76	45
58	45	Discuss local politics (nev/rar/occ/oft)	50	27
54	42	Blame council or government (C/both/G)	65	40
54	32	Interest in local politics (GD/FA/NM/none)	56	35
54	54	Approve compulsory voting (Y/N)	77	50
54	60	Pay rates (N/partial/Y)	86	65
		Alienation scales:		
51	30	'So many' (1–5)	55	36
50	26	'Broken promises' (1–5)	47	28
49	29	'Too complex' (1–5)	53	34
45	40	Satisfied with district (V/F/N)	70	50
45	29	Want more government control (1–5)	52	32
45	45	Watch local TV news (Y/N)	82	67
44	44	Read local weekly paper (Y/N)	76	57
43	42	Satisfied with County (V/F/N)	75	57
42	40	Prefer partisan local councils	72	53
40	40	Listen to local radio news (Y/N)	71	52

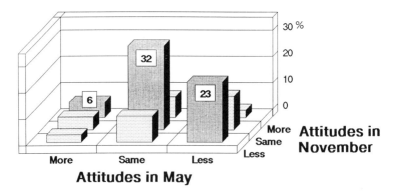

Fig. 4.2 Want more central control? (*see Table 4.5*)

Table 4.5. Continuity in attitudes towards local autonomy

Should central government control be:

| | May | | | | |
	Lot more	Little more	Same	Little less	Lot less
November					
Lot more	2	1	3	1	0
Little more	1	2	5	1	1
Same	1	4	32	8	5
Little less	1	1	6	6	3
Lot less	0	1	4	4	10
					100%

Note: entries are percentages of the full sample and sum to 100%.

November and May; and 84 per cent chose either exactly the same answer or an adjacent answer. Only 3 per cent switched from wanting more central control to less, and the same number from less to more. Although this level of continuity is a long way short of absolute stability we suggest that it does imply meaningful replies by our respondents. People really do have attitudes towards local government.

Continuity on National Political Issues

The stability of British electors' attitudes on local government issues compares well with Converse's findings on the stability of American attitudes to national political issues. But his findings were based on the late 1950s and used a different measure of continuity. Happily, we can directly compare the stability of national and local political attitudes in contemporary Britain, using our own panel data. In a survey about local government we naturally had few questions on national political issues, fewer still that we asked twice. However one that we did ask twice was the key question of taxes versus services (using a four-point scale ranging from more of both to less of both). Its continuity correlation was 49 per cent—similar to that for the attitudes towards local councils and local elections. Strength of (national) party identification had much the same level of stability (R = 52 per cent). So did general election turnout intentions (R = 46 per cent). By the criteria of continuity, therefore, attitudes towards local politics were as meaningful as attitudes towards the national political issue of taxes versus services and as meaningful as the strength (though not the direction) of national party identification.

Table 4.6. Moderate stability on national political questions

Correlation coefficient R	Index of consistency C	Variables Names (categories)	Actual % same	Statistically expected % same
52	50	Strength of party identification (V/F/not V/none)	65	30
49	39	Tax versus services: (cut lot/cut/keep/incr)	57	30
46	30	Turn-out intention in general election scale (1–6)	61	44

Levels of interest in, and discussion of, national politics were more stable (R = 65 per cent and 67 per cent respectively) than interest in, and discussion of, local politics (R = 54 per cent and 58 per cent respectively) but these differences in stabilities were only large enough to indicate a quantitative, rather than qualitative, difference.

Consistency and Coherence of Attitudes towards Local Government

Continuity is one form of consistency. The correlation between attitudes on different, but related questions is another. Because the questions are different we should not normally expect an exact

Table 4.7. High coherence

Correlation coefficient R	Index of consistency C	Variables	When asked
n.a.	91	Vote choice: in previous district election/ in previous county election	Nov.
n.a.	74	Vote choice: in previous district election/ in 1986 local elections	Nov./May
n.a.	72	Vote choice: in previous county election/ in 1986 local elections	Nov./May
64	n.a.	Interest in national politics/ discussion of national politics	Nov.
63	n.a.	Interest in local politics/ discussion of local politics	Nov.
62	n.a.	Interest in national politics/ discussion of national politics	May
62	n.a.	Turn-out: in previous district election/ in previous county elections	Nov.
60	n.a.	Interest in local politics/ discussion of local politics	May

match—even the number of answer categories may vary, and C will normally be inapplicable. An exception is when the two questions have identical answer categories, for example two questions about voting in different elections.

High Coherence

Memories of past votes in county and district elections head the list. Next comes the correlation between past and current voting choices in

Table 4.8. Low coherence

Correlation coefficient R	Index of consistency C	Variable	When asked
21	n.a.	Blame councils or government/ satisfaction with county	May
17	n.a.	Blame councils or government/ satisfaction with district	May
13	n.a.	Blame councils or government/ satisfaction with county	Nov.
10	n.a.	Blame councils or government/ satisfaction with district	Nov.

local elections. Interest in politics (whether national or local) correlates well with frequency of discussion about politics—the correlations range from 60 to 64 per cent.

Low Coherence

Blaming the councils for their own financial difficulties correlates moderately well with satisfaction with central government (R = 36 per cent) but correlates badly with satisfaction with local government (R = between 10 and 21 per cent), which suggests that national rather than local political attitudes have the dominant influence on whether people blame the councils or central government for local problems.

Moderate Coherence

Satisfaction with the county council correlates at about 45 per cent with satisfaction with the district council. In our May wave of interviews we put the tax versus services question in two very different forms. The correlation between the answers to these two tax versus services questions is about the same as the correlation between satisfaction with county and district councils.

The view that there should be more central control of local government correlates moderately well with the view that central government should appoint local officials (R = 30 per cent in May, 36 per cent in November); with blaming councils rather than central government for financial difficulties (R = 31 per cent in November, 36 per cent in May); and with the view that local councils rather than central government control the levels of rates and local services (R = 33 per cent in November, 32 per cent in May).

These are certainly no more than modest correlations but they are enough to suggest a degree of coherence and consistency as well as continuity in public attitudes towards local councils. Significantly the correlations between various questions about local government, and the continuity correlations still more so, generally exceed the levels of correlations between attitudes to various national political issues reported in Butler and Stokes's classic study of national politics in Britain, *Political Change in Britain*.[2]

Table 4.9. Moderate coherence

Correlation coefficient R	Index of consistency C	Variables	When asked
45	n.a.	Satisfaction: with district council/with county council	Nov.
45	n.a.	*Tax versus services: 4-point scale/ 11-point scale	May
44	n.a.	Satisfaction: with district council/with county council	May
43	n.a.	*Tax versus services: 4-point scale/ 3-point scale	May
37	n.a.	Vote for candidate or party: in local election/ in general election	Nov.
36	n.a.	Blame council or government/satisfaction with government	May
36	n.a.	Government should appoint/government should control	Nov.
33	n.a.	Government does control/government should control (negative correlation)	Nov.
32	n.a.	Government does control/government should control (negative correlation)	May
31	n.a.	Blame councils or government/ government should control	Nov.
30	n.a.	Government should appoint/government should control	May
29	n.a.	Blame councils or government/government should control	May
29	n.a.	Vote for candidate or party: in local elections/ in general elections	May
29	n.a.	Turn-out: in previous district election/ in 1986 local elections	Nov./May
28	n.a.	Turn-out: in previous county election/ in 1986 local elections	Nov./May

*Three tax-versus services scales appear in this table. They were defined as follows: the 4-point scale offered respondents the options of (1) cut government spending quite a lot so that taxes can be cut; (2) cut government spending a little so that taxes remain the same; (3) keep government spending as it is and raise taxes a little; (4) increase government spending and raise taxes quite a lot. The 11-point scale offered respondents a line of 11 lettered points with one end marked 'more taxes and services', the other end marked 'tax and service cuts', and the mid-point marked 'no change'. The 3-point scale is a transformation of the 11-point scale, based on whether respondents picked the 'no change' point, or one of the 'more' points, or one of the 'cut' points. One reason for reducing the 11-point scale to a 3-point one is that almost a third of respondents picked the 'no change' point.

A Stratified Local Electorate?

Finally we can return to one of the approaches we discussed at the start of this chapter. Although we have produced evidence that local political attitudes are generally meaningful, that they are not entirely

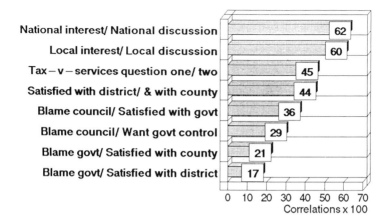

National interest/ National discussion — 62
Local interest/ Local discussion — 60
Tax – v – services question one/ two — 45
Satisfied with district/ & with county — 44
Blame council/ Satisfied with govt — 36
Blame council/ Want govt control — 29
Blame govt/ Satisfied with county — 21
Blame govt/ Satisfied with district — 17

0 10 20 30 40 50 60 70
Correlations x 100

Fig. 4.3. Coherence correlations (*see Tables 4.7–4.9*)

random replies by indifferent respondents, it is none the less still possible that those with a particular interest in local politics may display still higher levels of continuity and consistency in their attitudes. Within the electorate, there may be a core or stratum with a particular interest and concern for local politics, and particularly coherent and stable attitudes towards local government. Alas our evidence is mixed.

We divided respondents up into those with a high interest in local politics—defined as stating in both November and May that they had a 'great deal' or 'fair amount' of interest; those with a low interest—defined as stating in both November and May that they had 'not much' or 'none at all'; and those whose level of interest in local politics varied. Table 4.10 shows that on five out of six key questions, continuity was slightly greater amongst those with *low* interest, though on the sixth question (about local autonomy) continuity of opinion was much higher amongst those with a *high* level of interest in local politics.

However there was more evidence that high interest affected coherence and consistency across different questions. Amongst those with a high interest in local politics, assignment of blame between government and councils correlated particularly well with satisfaction with the county council, with satisfaction with the district council, (negatively) with satisfaction with the government, and (negatively) with a desire for more government control of local councils.

On the other hand the correlation between satisfaction with county

Table 4.10. Continuity and consistency amongst those with high and low interest in local politics

Amongst those whose interest in local politics is	Correlation coefficient R	
	High	Low
Stabilities over time:		
Blame councils or government	55	57
Satisfaction with county	39	45
Satisfaction with district	44	47
Government should appoint councils	36	37
Perception of government control	31	33
Want more government control	62	40
Coherences between different questions:		
Blame government/satisfied with county (Nov.)	27	8
Blame government/satisfied with county (May)	41	17
Blame government/satisfied with district (Nov.)	26	5
Blame government/satisfied with district (May)	23	15
Blame government/satisfied with government (May)	48	30
Want more government control/blame councils (Nov.)	43	29
Want more government control/blame councils (May)	29	27
Want more government control/satisfied with government (May)	46	27
Satisfied with county/satisfied with district (Nov.)	39	48
Satisfied with county/satisfied with district (May)	36	53

and district councils was higher amongst those with a low level of interest in local politics—though perhaps that may reflect the inability of the uninterested to distinguish between the different tiers of local government.

Overall then, we have discovered a substantial degree of coherence and stability in individuals' attitudes to local government. This suggests that attitudes towards local councils are meaningful: they are not non-attitudes. We have found less evidence to support the view that a particular subset of electors have particularly meaningful attitudes on local government.

Notes

1. The classic statement of the thesis of non-attitudes is P. E. Converse, 'The Nature of Belief Systems in Mass Publics', in D. E. Apter (ed.), *Ideology and Discontent* (New York: Free Press, 1964), 206–61.
2. D. Butler and D. Stokes, *Political Change in Britain* (London: Macmillan, 1974), 320–2.

Note: The relationship between our continuity/consistency coefficient C, and the correlation coefficient R, for a 2 by 2 table.

It is sufficient to consider the table with all cells expressed as proportions of the total sample. There are only three degrees of freedom. For convenience let us denote two of the marginals as $\bar{x}$ and $\bar{y}$ and one of the cells as d. All the other cells and marginals can be calculated from these. Again, for convenience in calculating the correlation coefficient let us code the first and second rows and columns as zero and one. We then have:

	ACTUAL TABLE				'EXPECTED' CELL ENTRIES		
	X Variable				X Variable		
	0	1			0	1	
Y Var 0	$1-\bar{x}-\bar{y}+d$	$\bar{x}-d$	$1-\bar{y}$	Y Var 0	$(1-\bar{x})(1-\bar{y})$	$\bar{x}(1-\bar{y})$	$1-\bar{y}$
Y Var 1	$\bar{y}-d$	d	$\bar{y}$	Y Var 1	$(1-\bar{x})\bar{y}$	$\bar{x}\bar{y}$	y
	$1-\bar{x}$	$\bar{x}$	1		$1-\bar{x}$	$\bar{x}$	1

Our Consistency Coefficient is defined as:

$$C = \frac{A - E}{1 - E}$$

where A and E refer to the actual and statistically expected contents of the diagonal cells.

Now $A - E = [(1-\bar{x}-\bar{y}+d) - (1-\bar{x})(1-\bar{y})] + [d - \bar{x}\bar{y}]$
$= 2(d - \bar{x}\bar{y})$

And $1 - E = 1 - (1-\bar{x})(1-\bar{y}) - \bar{x}\bar{y}$
$= \bar{x} + \bar{y} - 2\bar{x}\bar{y}$

So $C = \dfrac{2(d - \bar{x}\bar{y})}{\bar{x} + \bar{y} - 2\bar{x}\bar{y}}$

and if $\bar{x} = \bar{y}$ (that is, if the balance of opinion does not shift over time) then:

$C = \dfrac{d - \bar{x}^2}{\bar{x} - \bar{x}^2}$

The Correlation Coefficient is defined as:

$R = \dfrac{\sum (x - \bar{x})(y - \bar{y})}{\sqrt{\{\sum (x - \bar{x})^2 \cdot \sum (y - \bar{y})^2\}}}$

Applying this formula to the table gives:

$\sum (x - \bar{x})(y - \bar{y}) = d - \bar{x}\bar{y}$

$\sum (x - \bar{x})^2 = \bar{x}(1 - \bar{x})$

$\sum (y - \bar{y})^2 = \bar{y}(1 - \bar{y})$

Whence

$R = \dfrac{d - \bar{x}\bar{y}}{\sqrt{\{\bar{x}\bar{y}(1 - \bar{x})(1 - \bar{y})\}}}$

And if $\bar{x} = \bar{y}$ then this becomes:

$R = \dfrac{d - \bar{x}^2}{\sqrt{\bar{x}^2 (1 - \bar{x})^2}}$

$= \dfrac{d - \bar{x}^2}{\bar{x} - \bar{x}^2}$

Hence C and R are exactly equal when there is no net trend in opinion and $x = y$. They are approximately equal when the net trend is small.

Part II

Voter Participation in Local Elections

5 Why Do People Vote in Local Elections?
Some Theoretical Models

Turn-out rates in British local elections are low. Newton shows that the turn-out rate (defined as the percentage of the registered electorate casting a valid vote) in English county boroughs was around 50 per cent in the late 1940s but declined to around 40 per cent by the mid 1950s and stabilized at that level.[1] The reform of the local government system in the mid 1970s was partly intended to encourage more participation, but did not do so.

Clearly, turn-outs in Scotland and Wales were higher than in England, but it was still a reasonable approximation to say that the typical local government turn-out was around 40 per cent. Turn-out almost doubled in 1979 because the local elections were held on the same day as the general election but it is now back to the norm—at the 1985 English county elections, for example, it was 41 per cent and at the English metropolitan borough elections in 1986 it was 39 per cent.[2]

Even these figures have to be qualified however. In Scotland and Wales about one-fifth of councillors were returned unopposed. Unopposed returns were less frequent in English non-metropolitan areas and very rare indeed in English metropolitan areas. If we are interested in *actual* electoral turnout, as distinct from the *propensity* to vote, the figures given in Table 5.1 significantly overstate Scottish and Welsh turnouts. Revised figures are shown in Table 5.2.

A second qualification concerns the electoral register. All these turnout figures express turnout as the number of voters divided by the number of names on the electoral register. In Britain, unlike the United States, registration is the responsibility of government, not the responsibility of the citizen. Overall, the quality of the British electoral register is therefore very high but it is still not perfect, and its quality varies sharply across social groups, local authority areas, and time.

According to Todd and Butcher's analysis of a 1981 OPCS survey, 'at the time of council elections (i.e. in May) about 89 per cent of eligible people are registered and still living at their qualifying address and a further three per cent still live within the same (parliamentary)

Table 5.1. Average turn-out rates in local elections, 1973–1978

	% turn-out in contested areas
Upper tier authorities:	
Greater London Council	40
English metropolitan counties	39
English shire counties	42
Welsh counties	53
Scottish regions	48
Lower tier authorities:	
London boroughs	40
English metropolitan districts	36
English shire districts	42
Welsh districts	52
Scottish districts	50

Source: T. Byrne, *Local Government in Britain* (Harmondsworth: Penguin, 1986), 102–3.

Table 5.2. Average turn-out rates as percentage of full electorate in contested and non-contested areas

Local authority	% turn-out in contested areas	% actual turn-out in whole national area
Scottish regions	48	43
Scottish districts	50	43
Welsh counties	53	44
Welsh districts	52	44

constituency'.[3] Effective non-registration therefore runs at between 8 per cent and 11 per cent in the country as a whole. But it is between 11 and 14 per cent in Wales, and between 16 and 19 per cent in Inner London.[4] It is also significantly higher amongst the young, the geographically mobile, commonwealth immigrants, and ethnic groups.

Within Inner London non-registation in May of each year runs at 32 per cent amongst those aged under 30 years; at 34 per cent amongst New Commonwealth citizens (who are, of course, legally entitled to vote in British elections); at 27 per cent amongst Blacks and 30 per cent amongst Asians (irrespective of citizenship); at 37 per cent amongst the unemployed; and at 50 per cent amongst the young unemployed (aged under 30 years). These are Todd and Butcher's OPCS (Office of Population Censuses and Surveys) figures for a new register, adjusted for the date of local council elections, by adding 3 per cent to their base-line figures.

In parliamentary elections the under-registration of certain groups in limited areas may not have a significant effect on the overall national outcome, if only because they constitute a small proportion of the national electorate. However, their concentration in particular localities has more serious implications for local government. In some local authorities the electoral register is very different from the eligible population: in the Royal Borough of Kensington and Chelsea, for example, the OPCS study suggests that about a quarter of those otherwise eligible to vote in a local election cannot do so because they are not on the register.

Despite social and ethnic variations, the key influences on registration seem to be age and mobility. Even in Inner London, the non-registration rate amongst residents of two years standing who are also aged over 30 years is only about 10 per cent at council election time. But these stable residents make up less than two-thirds of the eligible local population.

Absolute figures for turn-out are not easily interpretable since the achievable maximum level is not obvious: near 100 per cent turn-out would simply indicate massive fraud, for example. So we need a point of comparison. Turn-out in British parliamentary elections was unusually high in the 1950 and 1951 elections. Since then it has averaged 76 per cent, never falling beneath 72 per cent nor rising above 79 per cent. So local election turn-out is usually a little more than half that in parliamentary elections. The only exception occurred in 1979 when a snap general election led to simultaneous local and parliamentary elections in the English and Welsh districts (though not in London or Scotland). Turn-out figures in contested local elections rose from 36 per cent (in 1978) to 74 per cent (in 1979) in the English metropolitan districts, from 42 per cent to 76 per cent in the English shire districts, and from 53 per cent to 77 per cent in the Welsh districts. In the parliamentary election turn-out was 76 per cent in England and 79 per cent in Wales. Clearly there are no strong incentives to avoid voting in local government elections provided the elector has already reached the polling station. Given the high level of support for the idea of local democracy that we found in Chapter 3, this is not a surprising conclusion. Lack of positive motivation, not actual antagonism, must therefore explain the difference between turn-outs in local government and parliamentary elections.

When members of our panel who expressed a firmer intention to vote in a parliamentary election than in a local election were asked why they were less inclined to vote in local elections, their answers revealed scant evidence of antagonism towards local government. The most frequently cited reasons were that central government and parliamentary elections were more important, that national issues aroused more feeling, and that central government itself exercised control over local government.

It is tempting to dismiss the significance of low turn-outs in local elections altogether, but the fall-off between typical parliamentary turn-out levels and local election turn-outs is so large that those who vote in local elections could be very unrepresentative not merely of the eligible population, or of the registered electorate, but even of those who vote regularly in parliamentary elections. There is a clear electoral cycle to local election results: when a party is in office at Westminster it tends to do badly in local elections, especially in the mid-term of a parliament. That could be because people change their voting choices from year to year. But turn-out levels in local elections are so low that the same effect could be produced simply by variations in morale and differential turn-out. The local government electorate may not change very rapidly from year to year, but the 40 per cent subset who vote in one year could well be quite different from the subset who turn out to vote the next year. We shall investigate this question in the next chapter.

In passing, note that other comparisons are possible. Turn-out in British local government elections is not a great deal less than at American presidential elections; and it is somewhat more than the turn-out for off-year congressional elections in America or for European Parliament elections in the UK. About half of American adults vote in presidential elections and only a third in US (off-year) congressional or British European Parliament elections. Moreover, while turn-out in American national elections is much lower now than in the last century, turn-out in British local government elections was never high. Complaints about apathy towards local government elections were frequent in the 1920s, 1930s, and 1940s, and nineteenth-century local elections were characterized by abysmally low rates of both contest and turn-out.[5]

Previous Studies of Voter Turn-out in Britain

Since the war, there has been a growing tendency for specially low turn-outs in working-class, urban areas.[6] But amongst individuals the extent of social bias has remained slight. Crewe, Fox, and Alt used data from the 1966–74 series of British Election Panel Studies for a thorough analysis of turn-out in parliamentary elections. Over a sequence of four elections they found that only 1 per cent of survey respondents were persistent non-voters. Non-voting in parliamentary elections was intermittent. Altogether 28 per cent of respondents missed at least one of the four votes, but their non-voting was fairly haphazard. Strong social biases did not show up, and the percentage of regular voters was slightly *higher* (not lower) in the working class than in the middle class. Crewe and his associates discovered 'two particularly sturdy sources of irregular voting: relative youth, and a weak or absent party identification'. Both exerted independent effects but strength of 'partisanship appears to have a greater bearing than age on turn-out regularity'.[7]

The biases produced by these effects were somewhat complex. In every election, non-voters who were poorly motivated and had no interest in politics tended to be Labour supporters, but those more accidental non-voters with higher levels of interest in politics tended more towards the party that was most popular at the time. If this second group of non-voters had voted, they would therefore have made little difference to the result. So the net effect of non-voting was a very small persistent bias against Labour.

Dyer and Jordan took advantage of a legal requirement in Britain that allowed them to inspect the voting registers marked up by polling station officials. Thus they avoided one problem with surveys of non-voting: the tendency for people to claim they have voted when they have not. Dyer and Jordan's painstaking study revealed the importance of party in two respects: first, psychological identification with a party and second, party activity, especially canvassing. Without these party-based means of mobilizing working-class people—one psychological, one organizational—there would have been a marked turn-out bias against working-class people and marked bias against the Labour Party. A recent analysis of constituency voting patterns by Mughan (1986) obviously cannot deal with questions of motivation and identification directly since it is not based upon interview data. But it confirms the conclusions of these earlier studies by identifying the marginality of a constituency and the current national standing of the parties (in opinion polls) as the major determinants of constituency turn-out in general elections, since marginality is likely to be related to party activity and national standing to the strength of party identification.[8]

Nothing so comprehensive has yet been published on turn-out patterns in British local government. Byrne lists findings from a variety of local participation studies, none of them very recent.[9] Maud and Redcliffe-Maud both present the results of large scale surveys on local government participation but neither has much to say about voting.[10] The Redcliffe-Maud survey neglects voting entirely and the Maud survey report devotes only three pages to voting. It notes that 75 per cent of survey respondents claimed to have voted in the recent district elections though the official turn-out rate had only been 42 per cent. Bealey *et al.* and Birch had also noted similar over-reporting of local government turn-out by survey respondents.[11]

Beyond that, the Maud survey's only findings on local government voting were: (1) that young people voted less than the middle-aged or old and (2) that actual voting was related—though rather loosely—to having positive attitudes towards voting. These positive attitudes correlated with age, education, and higher socio-economic groups. Positive attitudes to voting also correlated with sex although the Maud report noted that voting, itself, did not.

A number of other surveys, usually local in scope, supplemented by an analysis of ward level election results give more direct information about local voting.[12] These confirm that sex has little effect on turn-out and that in Britain, in sharp contrast to the USA, class also has little effect. The middle-aged are specially likely to vote, as are those who live in owner-occupied housing (or even council housing—private renters are least likely to vote), those who have a low rate of geographic mobility, and those with a strong sense of party identification.

Contextual and institutional factors are also influential. Though there is some conflict over the evidence,[13] several studies have pointed to the importance of parties, party conflict, and party activity in increasing turn-out levels.[14] Fletcher confined his research to a study of city ward election results; so he could not be expected to detect psychological influences on turn-out. None the less his conclusion boldly states: 'the only factors that appear to have influenced (local) turn-out are those connected with the keenness of inter-party conflict'. He instances marginality, the presence of a Liberal to make the contest three-way rather than two-way, and the existence of a national trend running against the party defending the particular ward and adds: 'although there may be other factors influencing turn-out in local elections—the overwhelming influence is the closeness of party conflict'. (Mughan's more recent study of general election turn-out patterns in parliamentary constituencies reaches similar conclusions.)

There is a tendency in rural areas towards a lack of contest because the incumbent councillor is personally known to his electors who may not wish to give offence by opposing him[15], but in areas where uncontested seats are the norm such contests as do occur may produce a high turn-out.[16] Turn-out tends to be less in larger authorities and areas with a relatively transient population,[17] which fits Verba and Nie's 'decline of community model': 'as communities grow in size, and, more important, as they lose those characteristics of boundedness that distinguish the independent city from the suburb, participation (in local politics, not in national politics) declines'.[18]

Because the average level of turn-out in local government elections is so low there is evidence that special efforts by party canvassers can certainly increase turn-out and sometimes swing elections results. Fletcher suggests that differential turn-out effects produce larger swings in local elections than in national—though the relative size of wards compared to constituencies would also tend to produce the same effect. Consequently, he claimed, the rule of thumb that parliamentary constituencies with a party lead of 5 per cent were marginal, in the sense of being likely to change hands, went with a rather different rule for local government wards: wards with party majorities of under 20 per cent were marginal in his view.[19] Whatever the national average swing, swings in individual wards might deviate from it by a large amount. Similar findings in the context of American congressional elections led Mann to title his book *Unsafe at Any Margin*.[20] The influence of party campaigns on local turn-out has been reported in studies of Harrow, Ashford, Wolverhampton, West Hartlepool, Newcastle, Lancaster, and Dundee.[21]

Once again Newton puts the contrary view that in Birmingham at least 'turn-out in marginal wards has little or nothing to do with the closeness of the party competition, the involvement of the electorate in a closely fought campaign, or the efficiency of local party machinery'.[22] However his own study of Birmingham shows that turn-out was higher in marginal wards, though he regarded the correlation as too weak to be significant.[23]

Newton correlates ward turn-outs in Birmingham over the 1949–71 period with a variety of spatial and temporal variables. Most of the correlations are too small to achieve statistical significance. None the less it is worth mentioning some of these small correlations while cautioning against over-interpretation. Turn-out was higher when polling days were sunny, lower when they were wet; turn-out was higher in marginal wards; turn-out increased as the next (parliamentary) general election came closer; turn-out was lower in wards with transient populations. But the only finding that Newton himself chooses to stress is the large correlation between low turn-out in Birmingham local elections, and the level of 'don't knows' in the national Gallup Polls: 'When political issues are not clear cut and there is no strong preference for one of the parties, one would expect a relatively high percentage of don't knows and a low turn-out. This is the case in local elections. The finding serves to underline the conclusion that the main determinants of (local) turn-out are not to be found within the community but rather in the country as a whole.'[24]

Other work has also pointed to the domination of national politics over local turn-out. Butler and Stokes centred their study of parliamentary voting round the concept of psychological identification with the national parties.[25] It was measured by two questions:

(1) The *partisan direction* question: 'Generally speaking do you usually think of yourself as Conservative, Labour, or Liberal, or what?'

(2) The *partisan strength* question: 'How strongly [chosen party] do you generally feel—very strongly, fairly strongly, or not very strongly?'

For an analysis of turn-out, the second question is the important one. It measures the *strength of attachment* to parties. As we noted earlier, Crewe *et al.* found that strength of partisanship was the strongest influence on turn-out in British *general elections*.[26] Butler and Stokes showed that it was a similarly powerful influence on voting in *local elections*.[27] Analysis of a parallel survey for the Conservative Party by Miller, Tagg, and Britto confirms this.[28] The results of all three are shown in Table 5.3.

Butler and Stokes also presented other evidence that voters in local elections were nationally orientated. Their sample showed a 'lack of involvement in local issues'. When they asked those who had voted in the May 1963 local elections whether there were any issues that had especially concerned them, 'four out of five said no without hesitation;

Table 5.3. Turn-out rates by strength of party identification

	Strength of party identification		
	Not very strong	Fairly strong	Very strong
% who voted in 1966 general election (Miller *et al.*)	73	86	90
% who voted in all four general elections, 1966–74 (Crewe *et al.*)	54	74	84
% who voted in 1963 local government elections (Butler and Stokes)	39	54	64
% who voted in 1965 local government elections (Miller *et al.*)	39	53	65
% who voted in local government elections 1967–9 (Miller *et al.*)	41	53	63

the remainder mentioned matters that were in fact more often the concern of Westminster than of the Town Hall'.[29] However, their respondents gave those replies in the context of an interview that focused overwhelmingly on national politics, and other surveys including our 1985–6 panel have detected more interest in local issues (see Chapter 2).

What evidence there is on British local government turn-out is disparate. Each study tends to emphasize the overwhelming importance of one of the influences it has researched while neglecting the possible influence of factors that were not included in that particular research study. Taken together they highlight the importance of parties both at the individual level (in terms of *psychological identification* with parties) and at the aggregate level in terms of the nature of *party competition* (the existence of a full range of party candidatures, the closeness of the competition, the strength of party organization). They highlight the *mobilizing influences* on voting rather than the purely *personal characteristics* of the electors. And they stress the importance of *national* political factors rather than *local*. Party identification is assumed to be a psychological link to the national parties, and trends in the popularity of national parties are reflected in the overall levels of turn-out[30] and in differential turn-out.[31]

Explanatory Models of Voter Turn-Out

Studies of participation in local politics have been conducted by the Maud Committee on the Management of Local Government, by the

Redcliffe-Maud Commission and by National Opinion Polls.[32] Unfortunately their definition of participation was rather wide and did not focus on electoral turn-out. The 1975 NOP study, for example, analysed a wide range of participatory behaviour of a campaigning or pressure-group kind, but did not include local election voting in its list of participatory behaviours. Perversely, this NOP study of local government participation included a measure of parliamentary election turn-out, but not local turn-out. (Although the survey was about various forms of local participation the only question about voting was whether respondents had voted in the last parliamentary general election.) Similarly, the Maud and Redcliffe-Maud surveys focused on participatory *attitudes* and only touched briefly on actual local election voting turn-out.

It has been fashionable in recent participation studies to neglect voting and concentrate on other forms of participation.[33] But while there are valid reasons for studying participatory attitudes or non-electoral kinds of political participation, this is no substitute for an analysis of voting itself.

Before looking at detailed findings for Britain we need to set out a broad theoretical framework into which the details may fit. Complex cross-national studies of political participation by various teams have established two important propositions about mass political participation which are highly relevant to our interpretation of British studies.[34]

(1) There are several *modes* of political participation. These include voting; campaigning; community pressure; direct action; and contacting elected or appointed officials on personal matters. Although these are positively correlated—that is, individuals who engage in one form of participation tend also to engage in others—the correlations are weak, and the factors which encourage one form of participation may have little influence on others.

(2) There is a critical difference between *participatory attitudes* and *actual participation*. The difference is systematic and explicable. Some people have very participatory attitudes but are *locked out* of actual participation while others, who lack participatory attitudes are *mobilized into* actual participation by the political institutions that dominate a particular political system. Mobilization is particularly relevant to voting; lock-out is more relevant to other modes of participation.

System Effects and Individual Effects: The Interaction

Verba, Nie, and Kim's analysis centres on the interaction between the individual and the laws and institutions that characterize the political system. Everywhere, they suggest, there is a pervasive natural tendency for the individual's personal 'socio-economic resources' to encourage political participation. By socio-economic resources they mean primarily education and income. But these personal resources only directly encourage the will and motivation to participate; they affect participatory attitudes directly and participation only indirectly. Again this is particularly true for voting. Some campaign activities need wealth or education for their performance: the act of voting requires neither. Lack of wealth and education does not prevent the *act of voting* but it reduces the *personal motivation to vote*.

So in the complete absence of institutional constraints or promptings, we should expect that in all elections, everywhere, there would be a strong correlation between voting turn-out and personal socio-economic resources simply because participatory attitudes would determine actual participation. But all political systems do include institutional constraints and institutional inducements. The actual pattern of participation will therefore depend upon whether these non-personal, system factors offset the natural correlation between turn-out and socio-economic resources, or whether these system factors intensify the natural correlation.

In the USA most institutional factors operate so as to encourage even higher rates of voting turn-out by those with high socio-economic resources and a natural propensity to turn-out anyway. The critical difference between the USA and Western Europe in this respect is the absence in the former of a major working-class party to mobilize those with low socio-economic resources and weak participatory attitudes into actual voting. In Britain the strength of a major working-class party should, in the past, have provided a major stimulus to working-class voter turn-out. But as British voting becomes less class-polarized, and as the strength of identification with parties declines, the natural tendency for the educated and the comfortably-off to dominate electoral participation may become more evident.

Some studies have identified large numbers of factors related to turn-out.[35] But not all of these factors are equally important and some apparent influences on turn-out may simply reflect other, deeper influences. A recent study by Wolfinger and Rosenstone used multivariate analysis to determine the relative importance of various factors underlying American turn-out patterns. Its 'core finding' pointed to the 'transcendent importance of education'.[36] Income, occupational class, and even some age effects were small once education was taken into account, and (social status) cross-pressure effects were non-existent. Occupation affected turn-out, but it was specific job experience rather than occupational class (or status) that had a major impact—government employees, for example, were specially prone to vote. Some institutional factors were also important: restrictive registration laws in some states depressed overall national turn-out by up to 9 per cent—a good example of institutional lock-out. For Wolfinger and Rosenstone the critical 'socio-economic resource' affecting propensity to turn-out is therefore education rather than Verba, Nie, and Kim's combination of education and income.

A Two-step Model of Voter Turn-out

We have then a simple two-step model:

Step 1. Personal chracteristics produce participatory attitudes.
Step 2. Participatory attitudes combine with institutional constraints and prompting to produce actual participation.

The first step will produce a large socio-economic bias, which may then be either reduced or intensified at the second step. Within the British electorate, unlike the American, we should expect the second step to offset and reduce the natural social biases created by the first step. Great Britain has a strong party committed to working-class interests which should mobilize working-class people both psychologically through identification with the Labour Party, and organizationally through intensive canvassing of working-class housing areas for example. These effects should happen in both local and parliamentary elections.

System Characteristics of Local Government Elections

Verba and his associates, like most analysts of participation in the United States, were primarily interested in the relationship between social inequality and political inequality. Consequently the aspects of institutional constraints and mobilizations that interested them were those aspects that differentially affected *high status and low status individuals.*

Our concern here is rather different. If we are to understand turn-out in local elections we should pay some attention to those aspects of institutional constraint and mobilization that differentially affect turn-out in *national and local elections.*

Let us start with Martin Lipset's classic international study of *Political Man.*[37] He presents the two tables reproduced here as Tables 5.4 and 5.5. The first is a non-theoretic listing of observed regularities that tend to occur in all countries, at all times, and in all kinds of elections. The second table constitutes his attempt at a theoretical explanation of these observed correlations.

Table 5.4. Lipset's table of observations

Social characteristics correlated with voting turn-out

Higher turn-out	Lower turn-out
High income	Low income
High education	Low education
Occupational groups:	Occupational groups:
Businessmen	Unskilled workers
White-collar employees	Servants
Government employees	Service workers
Commercial crop farmers	Peasants, subsistence farmers
Whites	Negroes
Men	Women
Middle-aged people (35–55)	Young people (under 35)
Older people (over 55)	
Old residents in community	Newcomers in community
Workers in Western Europe	Workers in United States
Crisis situations	Normal situations
Married people	Single
Members of organizations	Isolated individuals

Lipset supports his explanations with a wealth of data and argument which we need not repeat here. For us they provide a useful structured check-list, and it is not too difficult to see how they relate to British local government. We cannot read Lipset's list of the various ways in which government policy may appear relevant to the individual without being reminded of local government's lack of autonomy. Let us run through the points on his list in Table 5.5. Local government budgets are large, local government employs (directly) far more people than central government. But its revenue, expenditure, and employment are

Table 5.5. Lipset's table of explanations

Social factors affecting rates of voting turn-out

1.   The relevance of government policies to the individual

a.   Dependence on government as one's employer
b.   Exposure to economic pressures requiring government action
c.   Exposure to government economic restrictions
d.   Possession of moral or religious values affected by government politics
e.   Availability of relevant policy alternatives
f.   General crisis situations

2.   Access to information

a.   Direct visibility of effects of government politics
b.   Occupational training and experience making for general insight
c.   Contact and communiction
d.   Amount of leisure

3.   Group pressure to vote or not vote

a.   Under-privilege and alienation (reduced turn-out)
b.   Strength of class political organisation
c.   Extent of social contacts
d.   Group norms opposing voting (reduced turn-out)

4.   Cross-pressures (which reduce turn-out)

a.   Conflicting interests
b.   Conflicting information
c.   Conflicting group pressures

Note: All factors listed increase turn-out unless there is a contrary indication.

all visibly controlled by central government. Local government is not responsible for major economic decisions such as subsidies to agriculture or industry. Its influence over moral or religious policies is slight. Contenders for local government office are not usually seen as offering dramatic policy alternatives. And local government elections cannot be held in a crisis atmosphere when central government stands such close watch over local councils.

In short, when we go through Lipset's list, we are struck by the comparative irrelevance of local government to the individual. This irrelevance is reflected in lack of access to information and lack of public visibility. In so far as information depends upon the individual receiving it there will be variations between individuals. But in so far as it depends upon the object of that information, turn-out will be depressed by the generally low visibility of local government.

A Two-level, Two-step Model of Voter Turn-out

So if we are to take into account the subordinate role of local government in British politics, as well as the distinction between personal motivation and institutional inducement towards voter turn-out, then we need a model that encompasses the two levels of politics (national and local) as well as the two steps (personal motivation and institutional constraint or mobilization). The simplest such model would look like that in the diagram.

Much more complex, interactive models might well be specified. This is intended as a relatively simple but realistic model. The arrows

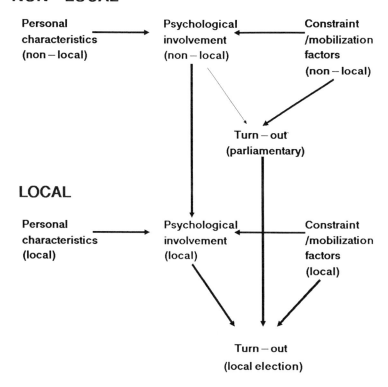

Fig. 5.1. A two-level, two-step model of voter turn-out

indicate major causal effects relevant to the explanation of local government turnout.

In the top line of the diagram psychological involvement with national politics is shown as dependent upon both personal and institutional factors. Turn-out in national elections is shown as dependent upon both involvement and institutional factors.

The lower line of the diagram deals with local variables. Psychological involvement in local politics is portrayed as dependent upon personal characteristics with a local dimension (length of residence in the locality, for example) and upon institutional factors with a local dimension (paying rates, for example). Local election turn-out is shown as dependent upon local involvement and local constraint/mobilization factors.

The two vertical lines indicate important links between national and local politics. Psychological involvement in local politics is shown as dependent upon general psychological involvement in (national) politics. And turn-out in local elections is shown as dependent upon turn-out in national elections.

As sketched out here, this is just the bare framework of a model that would seem to account for local election turn-out in terms of general findings drawn from international studies of political participation. We can now go on to measure this model against the evidence provided by our panel.

Notes

1. K. Newton, *Second City Politics* (Oxford: Oxford University Press, 1976), 15. See also T. Byrne, *Local Government in Britain* (Harmondsworth: Penguin, 1986), 317.
2. T. J. Karran and H. Bochel, *The County Council Elections in England and Wales 1985* (Dundee: University of Dundee, 1986), 141; T. Byrne, *Local Government in Britain* (Harmondsworth: Penguin, 1986), 10; C. Rallings and M. Thrasher, *The 1986 Metropolitan Borough Council Election Results* (Plymouth: Plymouth Polytechnic, 1986), p. i.
3. J. Todd and B. Butcher, *Electoral Registration in 1981* (London: Office of Population Censuses and Surveys, 1982), 10.
4. Ibid. 11.
5. See for example E. L. Hasluck, *Local Government in England* (Cambridge: Cambridge University Press, 1948), on Britain between the wars. For a discussion of abysmally low rates of contest and turn-out in Scottish cities in the nineteenth century see W. L. Miller, 'Politics in the Scottish City

1832–1982' in G. Gordon (ed.), *Perspectives of the Scottish City* (Aberdeen: Aberdeen University Press, 1985).

6. W. L. Miller, *Electoral Dynamics* (London: Macmillan, 1977).

7. I. Crewe, A. Fox, and J. Alt, 'Non-voting in British General Elections 1966–Oct. 1974' in C. Crouch (ed.), *The British Sociology Yearbook*, vol. iii: *Participation* (London: Croom Helm, 1976).

8. M. C. Dyer and A. G. Jordan, 'Who Votes in Aberdeen? Marked Electoral Registers as a Data Source', *Strathclyde Papers in Government* No. 42 (1985); A. Mughan, *Party and Participation in British Elections* (London: Pinter, 1986), 147.

9. T. Byrne, *Local Government in Britain* (Harmondsworth: Penguin, 1986), 96.

10. 'Maud' is my short title for the *Report of Committee on the Management of Local Government*, vol. iii: *The Local Government Elector* by Mary Horton (London: HMSO for Ministry of Housing and Local Government, 1967); 'Redcliffe-Maud' is my short title for *Royal Commission on Local Government in England. Research Study 9. Community Attitudes Survey* by Research Services Limited (London: HMSO Cmnd. 4040, 1969).

11. F. Bealey, J. Blondel, and W. P. McCann, *Constituency Politics: A Study of Newcastle-under-Lyme* (London: Faber, 1965); A. H. Birch *et al.*, *Small Town Politics: A Study of Political Life in Glossop* (Oxford: Oxford University Press, 1959).

12. A. H. Birch *et al.*, *Small Town Politics: A Study of Political Life in Glossop* (Oxford: Oxford University Press, 1959); W. Hampton, *Democracy and Community: A Study of Politics in Sheffield* (Oxford: Oxford University Press, 1970); F. Bealey, J. Blondel, and W. P. McCann, *Constituency Politics: A Study of Newcastle-under-Lyme* (London: Faber, 1965); L. J. Sharpe (ed.), *Voting in Cities: The 1964 Borough Elections* (London: Macmillan, 1967); J. Stanyer, 'Why Does Turnout Vary?', *New Society* 13 May 1971; J. Stanyer, *Understanding Local Government* (London: Fontana, 1976); D. Butler and D. Stokes, *Political Change in Britain* (London: Macmillan, 1974).

13. See K. Newton, 'Turnout and Marginality in Local Elections', *British Journal of Political Science* 2 (1972), 251–5, for a contrary view.

14. W. Hampton, *Democracy and Community: A Study of Politics in Sheffield* (Oxford: Oxford University Press, 1970); P. Fletcher, 'An Explanation of Variations in Turnout in Local Elections', *Political Studies* 17 (1969), 495–502.

15. For extreme examples see R. Masterson and E. Masterson, 'The Scottish Community Elections: The Second Round', *Local Government Studies* 6 (1980), 63–82.

16. J. Stanyer, *Understanding Local Government* (London: Fontana, 1976).

17. J. Stanyer, 'Why does Turnout Vary?' *New Society*, 13 May 1971.

18. S. Verba and N. H. Nie, *Participation in America: Political Democracy and Social Equality* (New York: Harper and Row, 1972).
19. P. Fletcher, 'An Explanation of Variations in Turnout in Local Elections', *Political Studies* 17 (1969), 495–502.
20. T. E. Mann, *Unsafe at Any Margin* (Washington: American Enterprise Institute, 1978).
21. J. M. Bochel and D. T. Denver, 'Canvassing, Turnout and Party Support: An Experiment', *British Journal of Political Science* 1 (1971), 257–69; J. M. Bochel and D. T. Denver, 'The Impact of the Campaign on the Results of Local Government Elections', *British Journal of Political Science* 2 (1972), 239–44; A. Bruce and G. Lee, 'Local Election Campaigns', *Political Studies* 30 (1982), 247–61; J. C. Brown, 'Local Party Efficiency as a Factor in the Outcome of British Elections', *Political Studies* 6 (1958), 174–8; T. Brown, M. J. C. Vile, and M. F. Whitemore, 'Community Studies and Decision Taking', *British Journal of Political Science* 2 (1972), 133–53; J. Gyford, *Local Politics in Britain* (London: Croom Helm, 1976, 1984); G. W. Jones, 'Wolverhampton' in L. J. Sharpe (ed.), *Voting in Cities: The 1964 Borough Elections* (London: Macmillan, 1967); A. Rees, 'West Hartlepool' in L. J. Sharpe (ed.), *Voting in Cities: The 1964 Borough Elections* (London: Macmillan, 1967); B. Pimlott, 'Does Local Party Organisation Matter?', *British Journal of Political Science* 2 (1972), 381–3; B. Pimlott, 'Local Party Organisation, Turnout and Marginality', *British Journal of Political Science* 3 (1973), 252–5.
22. This time the contrary view appears in K. Newton, 'Turnout and Marginality in Local Elections', *British Journal of Political Science* 2 (1972), 251–5.
23. K. Newton, *Second City Politics* (Oxford: Oxford University Press, 1976).
24. Ibid. 28.
25. D. Butler and D. Stokes, *Political Change in Britain* (London: Macmillan, 1974).
26. I. Crewe, A. Fox, and J. Alt, 'Non-voting in British General Elections 1966–Oct. 1974' in C. Crouch (ed.), *The British Sociology Yearbook*, vol. iii: *Participation* (London: Croom Helm, 1976).
27. D. Butler and D. Stokes, *Political Change in Britain*, (London: Macmillan, 1974), 40–4.
28. W. L. Miller, S. Tagg, and K. Britto, 'Partisanship and Party Preference in Government and Opposition: The Mid-Term Perspective', *Electoral Studies* 5 (1986).
29. D. Butler and D. Stokes, *Political Change in Britain* (London: Macmillan, 1974), 41.
30. K. Newton, *Second City Politics* (Oxford: Oxford University Press, 1976).
31. P. Fletcher, 'An Explanation of Variations in Turnout in Local Elections', *Political Studies* 17 (1969), 495–502.

32. *Report of Committee on the Management of Local Government*, vol. iii, *The Local Government Elector* by Mary Horton (London: HMSO for Ministry of Housing and Local Government, 1967); *Royal Commission on Local Government in England. Research Study 9. Community Attitudes Survey* by Research Services Limited (London: HMSO Cmnd. 4040, 1969); National Opinion Polls, 'Public Participation in Local Government', *Political Social Economic Review* 1 (1975), 17–34.

33. Examples include R. Darke and R. Walker (eds.), *Local Government and the Public* (London: Leonard Hill, 1977); D. Hill, *Participating in Local Affairs* (Harmondsworth: Penguin, 1970); D. M. Hill, *Democratic Theory and Local Government* (London: Allen and Unwin, 1974); G. Parry (ed.), *Participation in Politics* (Manchester: Manchester University Press, 1972); J. Gyford, 'Diversity, Sectionalism and Local Democracy', in *Research Volume IV of the Committee of Inquiry into the Conduct of Local Authority Business Cmnd 9800* (London: HMSO, 1986).

34. S. Verba and N. H. Nie, *Participation in America: Political Democracy and Social Equality* (New York: Harper and Row, 1972); S. Verba, N. H. Nie, and J. Kim, *Participation and Political Equality: A Seven National Comparison* (New York: Cambridge University Press, 1978); S. Barnes and M. Kaase, *Political Action: Mass Participation in Five Western Democracies* (Beverly Hills: Sage, 1979).

35. See for example the classic by L. W. Milbrath, *Political Participation* (Chicago: Rand McNally, 1965).

36. R. E. Wolfinger and S. J. Rosenstone, *Who Votes?* (New Haven: Yale University Press, 1980), 102.

37. Originally published in 1959, but recently updated: S. M. Lipset, *Political Man: The Social Bases of Politics*, updated edn. (London: Heinemann, 1983). The tables of observations and explanations appear on pp. 189–90 of the updated edition.

6 Turn-out Memories, Intentions, and Behaviour

Before we look for the patterns and motivations underlying turn-out in local elections let us first look at our panel's claims about their electoral turn-out itself.

Between the two waves of interviews we asked a total of nine questions simply about memories of turn-out or intentions to turn out. Two of these questions concerned memories of the very recent past. These were the questions put during May 1986 about voting in the local elections for the districts or for the ILEA during that same month. All these interviews were conducted within the fortnight after the elections; so if we can discount deliberate falsehoods we can take questions in May about turn-out in May as reports of actual *behaviour*. All other turn-out questions indicate (fallible) longer-term *memories* or (unreliable) future *intentions*.

Our questions about past voting asked whether respondents had or had not voted. Questions about future intentions to vote were less categorical: respondents were asked 'how likely' they were to vote. We shall find it useful to treat respondents who said they were 'certain' or 'very likely' to vote as intending voters, and the rest as intending non-voters.

To cope with these nine measures of past and future turn-out it will be helpful to use some labels: T83NOV, T83MAY, TCTY, TDIST, TLGNOV, TGENOV, TGEMAY, T86, and TILEA. Their definitions and values are set out in Table 6.1.

Trends and Differences

In aggregate, our panel's memories of the 1983 parliamentary general election did not change between November and May: 77 per cent remembered voting and only 15 per cent remembered abstaining. Nor was there any change in their intentions with regard to a future parliamentary election: in both interviews 65 per cent said they were

Table 6.1. Turn-out memories, intentions, and behaviour

	% voted	% did not	% DK/NA too young
Memories:			
of 1983 general election, remembered in Nov. 85: T83NOV	77	15	8
of 1983 general election, remembered in May 86: T83MAY	77	15	8
of last county election, remembered in Nov. 85: TCTY	54	39	7
of last district election, remembered in Nov. 85: TDIST	57	36	6

	% Certain to vote	% Very likely	% Fairly likely	% Fairly unlikely	% Very unlikely	% Certain not to
Intentions to vote:						
in a local election (in Nov. 85): TLGNOV	46	17	13	8	6	8
in a parliamentary election (in Nov. 85): TGENOV	65	15	8	3	4	6
in a parliamentary election (in May 86): TGEMAY	65	15	7	2	5	5

	% (of those living where elections occurred)		
	Voted	Did not	DK/n.a. Too young
Behaviour:			
Voted in 1986 local elections: T86	55	45	0
Voted in 1986 ILEA election: TILEA	64	36	0

Note: Only 22 respondents lived in the ILEA area, so ILEA figures are subject to large sampling errors.

'certain' to vote and another 15 per cent said they were 'very likely' to vote.

We put three questions about *local* election turn-out to all members of the panel in November. In May we asked those who lived in areas without elections whether they would have voted, given the opportunity. At the same time we asked those panel members who lived in areas which did have local government elections in May whether they had actually voted. In inner London we asked whether they had voted in the elections for the ILEA (Inner London Education Authority) as well as in the council elections.

In November 54 per cent remembered voting in the preceding county election and 57 per cent in the preceding district election. These figures are higher than the 41 per cent of the register who voted in the 1985 county elections in England, for example, but given the known inaccuracies of the electoral register, they are acceptable. Although they indicate some over-reporting (and perhaps the selection of a relatively interested and participatory sample of the electorate) the panel clearly distinguished between national and local turn-out, reporting a 23 per cent difference in turn-outs (though the difference in official turn-out rates between national and local elections is about 10 per cent more than in our sample's reports).

The third question asked in November about local election turn-out, concerned intention to vote in a future local election: 46 per cent said they 'certainly' would—which was 19 per cent less than said they would 'certainly' vote in a parliamentary general election. Once again, respondents clearly distinguished between turn-out for national and local elections.

Ignoring those areas without elections in May, 55 per cent had voted in the district elections (regional elections in Scotland) and, out of a very small sample of only 22 respondents in the ILEA area, 64 per cent had voted in the ILEA election.

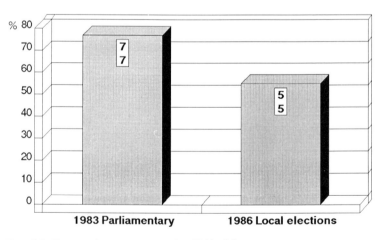

Fig. 6.1. Reported turn-out rates (*see Table 6.1*)

Table 6.2. The relationship between local turn-out intentions and behaviour

	% turn-out in local elections (May 1986)
Nov. 1985 local election voting intention:	
Certain to	70
Very likely to	54
Fairly likely to	40
Fairly unlikely to	39
Very unlikely to	32
Certain not to	19
Don't Know	28

*Amongst those who lived in areas with local elections at that time.

Intention and Behaviour Compared

> Count not his broken promises a crime
> He meant them, how he meant them!—at the time.

So goes the famous couplet about 'the politician'. We should be as sceptical about the electorate as about the politicians. How did actual turn-out in May compare with intentions in November? Moderately well: 70 per cent of those who said they 'would certainly vote' in a local election held 'tomorrow' (in November) actually voted in May, while only 19 per cent of those who said in November that they 'certainly would not vote' actually voted. Intermediate statements of voting intention went with intermediate levels of actual voting (Table 6.2).

To simplify later tables of turn-out intentions, we will find it convenient to categorize intentions into just two groups. Since a majority of those who said they were 'certain' or 'very likely' to vote actually did so, while a majority of those with less intention of voting actually did not, we shall from now on divide respondents into those who intended to vote (i.e. were 'certain' or 'very likely' to) and those who did not intend to vote (i.e. the rest). This turns all nine turn-out measures into 'vote/no vote' dichotomies.

Correlations between Turn-out Memories, Intentions, and Behaviour

How far do the nine turn-out measures correlate with each other? Is it the same people who regularly vote in local elections? Do the people who vote in local elections have a higher rate of voting in parliamentary elections also? Are turn-out intentions consistent? For that matter, are memories consistent, or do the same people report different memories of the same event at different interviews?

The simplest way to begin answering these questions is to construct a table of correlations like that in Table 6.3. Each entry can range from minus 100 through to zero to plus 100. A value of plus 100 would indicate that exactly the same people voted on each of two occasions; minus 100 would indicate that all those who voted on one occasion abstained on the other; zero would indicate that voting on one occasion provides no guide to whether people vote on the other occasion.

All the entries are positive: so those who vote (or remember voting or intend to vote) on one occasion always tend to be more likely to do so on other occasions also. But the correlations range widely from a low of 18 to a high of 67 (higher still if we include the correlations

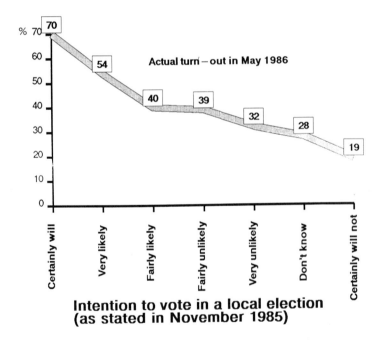

Fig. 6.2. Intention and behaviour (*see Table 6.2*)

Table 6.3. Correlations between turn-out memories, intentions, and behaviour

	Memories of general elections		Nov. memories and intentions for local elections			Local election behaviour in May		General election intentions	
	T83NOV	T83MAY	TCTY	TDIST	TLGNOV	T86	TILEA	TGENOV	TGEMAY
T83NOV	100	67	32	36	30	19	(53)	44	37
T83MAY		100	35	33	35	27	(68)	41	48
TCTY			100	62	51	28	(19)	33	33
TDIST				100	51	29	(29)	29	30
TLGNOV					100	31	(39)	56	34
T86						100	(72)	18	28
TILEA							100	(27)	(50)
TGENOV								100	44
TGEMAY									100

Notes:
1. All correlations are Pearson correlations calculated on dichotomies, multiplied by 100% for ease of reading.
2. In this and all subsequent tables we have dichotomized responses to the voting intention questions, counting those who said they were 'certain' or 'very likely' to vote as intending to vote, the rest as intending not to vote.
3. Memories and behaviours of those who were too young, could not remember, or refused to say whether they had voted have been excluded.
4. This table uses SPSSPC 'pairwise deletion'—i.e. each correlation is based only on relevant cases. Thus, for example, correlations with TILEA are based upon central London respondents only and correlations with T86 are based only upon respondents in areas with local elections in 1986.
5. Because there were only 22 central London respondents, all correlations with TILEA have been placed in brackets, since they are subject to large sampling errors.

based upon the few electors in the ILEA area—but these are subject to large sampling errors because of the small sample).

Let us try to calibrate these figures. We have already compared local election turn-out intentions in November (TLGNOV) with actual local election voting in May (T86). That relationship corresponds to the correlation of 31 in Table 6.3—so these correlation figures take a harsh view of consistency: they do not produce high values very easily.

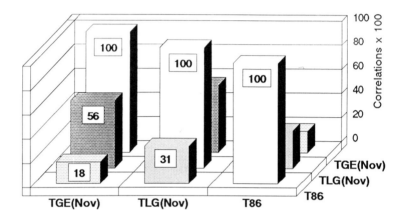

Fig. 6.3. Intentions and behaviour (correlations) (*see Table 6.3*)

In Table 6.4 we show the percentages of panel respondents who gave consistent answers (i.e. vote/vote or no vote/no vote) to each pair of turn-out questions. This table flatters the electors' consistency compared with Table 6.3. The reason why the correlations appear to understate consistency is that when the vast majority of electors remember voting, or intend to vote, as they do in parliamentary general elections, the percentages giving consistent answers to two questions cannot fail to be high since so many say 'vote' to both. Yet the correlation appears much lower because those who give inconsistent answers are almost as large in number as those who consistently give the 'no vote' reply. Despite its apparent harshness therefore, the table of correlations, Table 6.3 is the better guide to turn-out consistency, though the reader should compare both tables. (We discussed this statistical quirk in detail in Chapter 4—look back for a full discussion.)

Whichever table is used, they both distinguish those turn-outs which are more consistent from those which are less consistent. The

Table 6.4. Percentages with same turn-out memory, intention, or behaviour on pairs of occasions

	T83NOV	T83MAY	TCTY	TDIST	TLG	T86	TILEA	TGENOV	TGEMAY
T83NOV	100	91	67	71	71	61	79	84	82
T83MAY		100	68	70	72	64	84	83	85
TCTY			100	82	76	65	63	68	68
TDIST				100	77	65	65	68	68
TLG					100	66	73	80	71
T86						100	86	60	64
ILEA							100	68	77
TGENOV								100	82
TGEMAY									100

Note: These figures are correct, but misleading—see text for warning and explanation. See Ch. 4 for a full discussion of the statistical dangers when using crude continuity percentages.

highest correlation, 67, is for memories of 1983 parliamentary election turn-out as reported in November 1985 and May 1986. Since this is a factual question, only simple inaccuracy prevents the correlation attaining 100. The correlation between future parliamentary voting intentions, as reported in November and May is much lower, at 44, though we accept that changing intentions may represent real change rather than pure inaccuracy.

What about *local* election turn-out? There is a relatively high correlation of 62 between memories of county and district election turn-out, both reported at the same time, however, in November—and neither memory relating to a very recent event. Local election turn-out *intentions* in November correlated at 51 with *memories* of past county and district turn-out intentions, and at 56 with future parliamentary turn-out intentions (all of them as reported in November however). But local election turn-out *intentions* in November correlated far less well, at only 31, with actual *behaviour* in May.

Thus while local election voting intentions expressed in November formed part of a set of highly intercorrelated responses to different turn-out questions posed at that time, actual turn-out in the May local elections did *not* correlate at all well with this set.

To put it more sharply: in November it was difficult to distinguish between local and parliamentary turn-out *intentions*, but in May's local elections turn-out *behaviour* was clearly distinct both from parliamentary turn-out intentions and from the local election turn-out intentions that had been expressed in the previous November. This quite radically alters previous conclusions about turn-out in local elections: contrary to previous findings, it appears that actual local turn-out is not simply a consequence of a general propensity to turn-out in any and every kind of election.

Finally, is it the same people that turn out consistently in local elections? Turn-out in May 1986 correlated with memories of turn-out in previous local elections, but the correlations were low (28 with TCTY, 29 with TDIST). Again contrary to previous findings, it appears that there is not a consistent subgroup of local election voters who turn out regularly in local elections while others do not. Instead, at least a third of electors switch between voting and non-voting in successive local elections. Intermittent voters are about as numerous as regular voters though, just because they only intermittently vote, they only make up a minority of the vote at any particular election (Table 6.5).

A comparison with memories of parliamentary voting in 1983 shows

Table 6.5. Regular and intermittent local election turn-out

		Behaviour in May 1986 (T86)		
		% DNV	% VOTED	TOTAL
Nov. memory of previous District election (TDIST)	% DNV	25	14	39
	% VOTED	20	41	61
	TOTAL	45	55	100

	On basis of TDIST and T86		
	Regular local voters %	Regular local non-voters %	Intermittent local voters %
Amongst			
All respondents	41	25	34
1983 Conservatives	48	16	37
1983 Labour voters	44	19	37
1983 Alliance voters	45	15	41
1983 non-voters	12	62	25

that no one party enjoyed a specially high rate of regular local election turn-out; but those who abstained in the 1983 parliamentary election were very much more likely to be regular non-voters in local elections than those who voted in the 1983 election.

Why Does the Panel Study Contradict Previous Findings?

There is a simple reason why the findings from our panel contradict previous findings based upon single-wave, cross-sectional surveys. When people are asked several questions about turn-out (past, present, and future; local and national) *in the same interview* they tend to give much the same answer to all the questions. Memories are hazy, intentions are ill-formed, future elections are hypothetical. Hence a single-wave study (like the first wave of our panel, taken by itself) indicates fairly high correlations between past and future turn-out, and between local and national turn-out.

But when we are able to compare the answers to questions asked in different interviews, at widely separated points in time, it becomes evident that those who have voted in one local election are *not* the same as those who vote in the next; that those who intend to vote are *not* the same as those who do vote; and that the propensity to vote in a parliamentary election does *not* completely determine propensity to vote in a local election.

Factors Underlying Turn-out Memories, Intentions, and Behaviour

It can be difficult to distinguish the wood from the trees when we stare at such a large table of correlations such as Table 6.3. One automatic method for highlighting the general patterns implicit in a table of correlations is factor analysis. In Tables 6.6 and 6.7 we show the results of a sequence of factor analyses. Using principal components and varimax rotations (the most popular methods) we sought factor solutions based upon one, two, three, four, and then five underlying factors. This sequential approach gradually unravels the complex interconnections evident in the correlation table.

It begins with the single factor solution, which groups all the turn-out variables together, and shows that almost half their total variation can be explained by a single underlying factor: there is such a thing as a general propensity to vote or not vote.

The two-factor analysis distinguishes November memories of local turn-outs (TCTY and TDIST) and November intentions to turn out in local and parliamentary elections (TLGNOV and TGENOV) from the rest of the turn-out variables. In other words, the various answers given to different turn-out questions in the November wave of the panel survey tend to 'hang together'.

The three-factor solution, which is the one that conventional factor analysis criteria would select as optimal, distinguishes three groups of variables: first, all those that relate to *parliamentary* turn-out, whether memories or intentions; second, the three questions about *local* election turn-out which were *asked in November*, whether memories or intentions; third, local election *turn-out behaviour in May*.

Subsequent factor solutions distinguish up to five groups of turn-out variables. Significantly one group consists of T86 and TILEA— that is turn-out behaviour in May; while another consists of TGENOV and TLGNOV—that is November statements of turn-out intentions in local and parliamentary elections.

This sequence of factor analyses emphasizes two facts. First, that in November it was difficult to distinguish turn-out intentions for local and parliamentary elections. So analysis of the November interviews by

Table 6.6. Factor analyses of the turn-out variables

Number of factors	% of variation explained	Largest correlations with factors (restricted to those that correlate at over 0.60)				
		Factor 1	Factor 2	Factor 3	Factor 4	Factor 5
1	46	none				
2	60	94:TILEA 77:T83MAY 66:T86 65:T83NOV	82:TCTY 78:TDIST 76:TLGNOV 60:TGENOV			
3	72	82:T83MAY 81:T83NOV 63:TGENOV 62:TGEMAY	83:TCTY 80:TDIST 73:TLGNOV	91:T86 80:TILEA		
4	81	86:T83NOV 84:T83MAY	84:TDIST 84:TCTY	87:TGENOV 66:TLGNOV	93:T86 78:TILEA	
5	87	88:T83NOV 81:T83MAY	86:TCTY 85:TDIST	94:T86 77:TILEA	87:TGENOV 74:TLGNOV	91:TGEMAY

Notes:
1. Figures before colons are the correlations × 100 between the factors and variables indicated.
2. All these factor analyses used SPSSPC principal components analysis followed by varimax rotation. They were constrained to use the number of factors indicated.
3. The usual default settings in SPSSPC select the solution with three factors.
4. Pairwise deletion of missing values has been used because of the small subsets of the small subsets to which T86 and especially TILEA apply.
5. A large number of other factor analyses using different methods, different treatments of missing cases, and restricted sets of variables (e.g. omitting TILEA) produced results broadly in accord with the conclusions drawn from the set of analyses shown here.

Table 6.7. Interpretations of the factor analyses

Number factors	Total % of variation explained	Description of factors selected				
		Factor 1	Factor 2	Factor 3	Factor 4	Factor 5
1	46	General Factor				
2	60	1983 + LG (MAY)	NOV.			
3	72	GE	LG (NOV.)	LG (MAY)		
4	81	1983	NOV. memories	NOV. intentions	LG (MAY)	
5	87	1983	NOV. memories	LG (MAY)	NOV. intentions	MAY intentions

Key:
General factor: General turn-out factor, correlating fairly well with all the turn-out variables—minimum correlation 32, maximum 58.
1983: Memories of turn-out in 1983 general election.
LG (MAY): Turn-out behaviour May 1986 local elections.
NOV.: Local election memories, and both local and parliamentary intentions as stated in Nov.
LG (NOV.): Local election memories and intentions in Nov.
NOV. memories: Local election memories in Nov.
NOV. intentions: Both local and parliamentary intentions in Nov.
MAY intentions: Parliamentary intentions in May.

themselves leads to the conclusion that local election turn-out intentions largely reflect general (national) turn-out propensity. Second, actual local election turn-outs in May were grouped into a different factor. Or to put it another way, actual turn-out in local elections was probably motivated by different factors than those that underlay the intentions expressed in November. In an elegant, statistical way these factor analyses restate our central conclusion that previous findings based upon single-wave studies are wrong: local turn-out behaviour *does* vary over time, and the electorate is *not* divided into regular local election voters and regular local election abstainers.

We turn in the next chapter to an explicit comparison of the factors underlying (1) local election turn-out intentions expressed in November and (2) actual local election turn-out behaviour in May. We now know that they are different. We will want to know how different; and whether there is any systematic explanation of the difference.

7 Patterns of Turn-out Intentions and Behaviour

In this chapter we look at the social and attitudinal patterns of turn-out to see: first, what variables correlate highly with turn-out; and second, whether there is or is not a systematic (as distinct from random) difference between intentions and behaviour. We want to know: *who says they will vote? who does vote? and who says they will vote but fails to do so?*

Intentions and Behaviour

In Chapter 6 we saw that there was a marked difference between turn-out intentions and actual turn-out in local elections. That could suggest that we need different models to explain intentions and behaviour.

Despite the difference between intentions and behaviour it is still possible that many of the variables that influence turn-out affect both intentions and behaviour in similar ways: the differences between intentions and behaviour could be random rather than systematic. To put it another way: although the *individuals* who intended to vote differed from those who actually did vote, the *sort of people* (groups, categories, classes) who intended to vote may have been exactly the same as the sort of people who did vote.

Suppose, for example, that we could divide electors into two types, Type A and Type B. Suppose further that there are equal numbers of each type and that the first type has a 60 per cent probability of voting while the second has only a 40 per cent probability of voting. Even if these probabilities remain constant the actual people who would vote at two elections would not be the same. The statistically expected overall turn-out rate would be 50 per cent in each election, but only 26 per cent of electors would vote in both elections ($0.6 \times 0.6 \times 50\%$ + $0.4 \times 0.4 \times 50\% = 26\%$). None the less the *pattern* of turn-out, that is the higher turn-out amongst Type A electors would be the same at both elections. Thus the low correlations that we observed between intentions and behaviour in Chapter 6 *do not necessarily* imply systematic differences between intentions and behaviour—random differences would produce the same effect. On the other hand, the differences between intentions and behaviour may be systematic.

Throughout this chapter we use a very simple methodological approach: we tabulate the percentages TLGNOV (i.e. the per cent who said in November that they were 'certain' or 'very likely' to vote in a local election) and T86 (i.e. the percentage of those in areas with local elections in May 1986 who actually did vote) amongst various subgroups of electors. In the panel as a whole TLGNOV averages 64 per cent and T86 averages 55 per cent. So generally we might expect each group of electors to have a T86 figure about 9 per cent less than their TLGNOV figures while leaving the *pattern* of actual turn-out the same as the *pattern* of turn-out intentions. Any deviation from this 9 per cent drop-off between November and May would indicate a change in the pattern of turn-out, a more systematic difference between intentions and behaviour.

The model of national and local election turn-out rates which we developed in Chapter 5 was based on the concepts of *personal characteristics, psychological involvement,* and *institutional constraint or mobilization.* Each of these was subdivided into two levels: *national* and *local.* Our panel survey includes a number of questions that can serve as indicators of these concepts. They are listed below, under the three concept headings with, in brackets, a note of whether the indicator seems to have a specifically local dimension.

Concept I. Personal Characteristics

Age
Sex
Children
Employment status
Education
Religious affiliation
Class
House tenure (local)
Length of local residence (local)

Concept 2. Psychological Involvement

Interest in national politics.
Discussion of national politics.
Interest in local politics (local).
Discussion of local politics (local).
Knowledge of county name (local).
Knowledge of district name (local).
Knowledge of local councillors' names (local).
Knowledge of local councillors' parties (local).
Knowledge of which party controls county (local).
Knowledge of which party controls district (local).

Concept 3. Political Mobilization/Constraint Factors

Feel strongly on political issues.
Have strong sense of psychological identification with a party, or with an ideology, or with a social group.
Association with a trade union.
Religiosity (local?).
Concern about local issues (local).
Feel most important political issue is matter for local rather than national government (local).
Blame local councils for cash shortages (local).
View on how well county council is running things (local).
View on how well district council is running things (local).
Ever wanted to complain about local government (local).
Ever actually complained about local government (local).
Pay rates (local).
Use local news media (local).
Psychological alienation from local government elections (local).
Attitude to local government autonomy (local).
Perception of marginality of local council.

We can look at the relationship between turn-out and each of these groups of indicators in turn, before going on in the next chapter to a more formal evaluation of the two-step, two-level model itself.

Turn-out by Personal Characteristics

The most striking correlations are with age and length of residence in

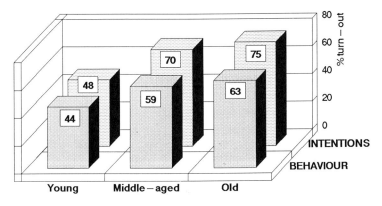

Fig. **7.1.** Turn-out by age (*see Table 7.1*)

the locality. Older people, those without children in the household, and long-term residents turn out more. So do the few with very high levels of education. Negative findings can easily be overlooked but are important none the less. Correlations between turn-out and sex, religious affiliation, employment status, class, and house tenure were low.

There were notable differences between patterns of intentions and behaviour, however. The unemployed showed a very low level of intention to turn out in November but (on a small sample, hence no

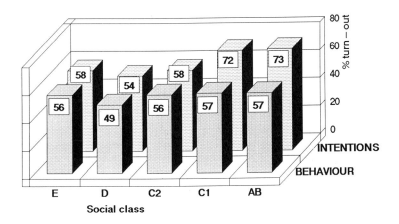

Fig. **7.2.** Turn-out by class (*see Table 7.1*)

entry in table) their actual turn-out rate in May was average. Middle-class electors (ABC1s) expressed a strong inclination to vote but when the election came they did not turn out more than working-class electors. Similarly, house-owners intended to vote (slightly) more than council tenants but, in the event, council tenants voted (slightly) more than house-owners. By contrast, one pattern that strengthened was the correlation with length of residence, because recent arrivals turned out in even smaller numbers than they had intended. But generally, patterns of behaviour were weaker versions of patterns of intentions—recognizably the same, but less sharply defined.

Verba and his associates argue very strongly that these correlations—especially those that relate to behaviour rather than intentions—are *unnaturally* weak. If only personal factors operated, they say, we should expect much more social inequality in turn-out rates. Thus low correlations with class, education, and house tenure provide indirect evidence of strong mobilizing or constraint factors. Indeed the difference we observe between patterns of intentions and behaviour adds weight to their argument. Social groups whose own personal motivations to participate in politics are weak had slightly lower than average intentions to turn out but their actual voting rates equalled or exceeded the average.

Turn-out by Psychological Involvement

Generally turn-out correlated more strongly with psychological involvement than with social characteristics. Altogether we have ten measures of interest in and knowledge about politics. All of them correlated with turn-out. Those who regularly discussed local politics, for example, expressed over twice as much as intention to turn out (89 per cent) as those who never discussed local politics (44 per cent); and although the difference was less in the event it was still substantial: 74 per cent compared to 46 per cent actual turn-out.

In November it was striking that the correlations varied little according to the level (i.e. national or local) of turn-out, interest, or discussion. Comparing patterns of local election turn-out intentions with patterns of parliamentary turn-out intentions, there was a tendency for interest and discussion of national politics to correlate slightly more with national turn-out, while interest and discussion of local politics correlated slightly more with local turn-out—but these

Table 7.1. The relationship between turn-out and personal characteristics

	Local election % turn-out	
	Intention (TLGNOV)	Behaviour (T86)
All respondents	64	55
Age:		
Young (under 35)	48	44
Middle Aged (35–54)	70	59
Old (over 55)	75	63
Sex:		
Male	67	57
Female	61	54
Children:		
Have children	58	48
Have no children	67	59
Employment:		
In full-time employment	63	52
In part-time employment	66	59
Unemployed	41	—
Not working	67	58
Education:		
Terminal age of education 16 years or less	50	50
Terminal age of education 17 years	52	37
Terminal age of education 18 years	50	46
Terminal age of education 19 years plus	72	68
Religious affiliation:		
Church of England	61	58
Church of Scotland	66	65
Nonconformist	71	—
Roman Catholic	74	62
None	63	—
Class:		
AB	73	57
C1	72	57
C2	58	56
D	54	49
E	58	56
Tenure:		
Owner	64	54
Rent from council	60	59
Resident:		
In locality for 2–5 years	55	44
In locality for 5–10 years	62	47
In locality for over 10 years	66	59

Note: All entries are based on at least 50 respondents. A dash indicates fewer than 50 respondents in a category. Since sampling variability would be high, turn-out percentages based upon such small subgroups of respondents are not shown.

variations in correlations were slight, even though they were consistent across a range of indicators. In the event, actual local election turn-out was less strongly related to expressions of interest in politics (national or local) than were turn-out intentions in November; and actual local turn-out correlated particularly weakly with discussion of national politics.

More persuasive evidence of independent local political influences comes from the pattern of correlations between turn-out and knowledge, particularly knowledge of councillors names. Knowledge of councillors names correlated more strongly with local election turn-out intentions than with parliamentary turn-out intentions, and more strongly still with actual local turn-out. The national/local distinction was less evident in correlations with other forms of local political knowledge however.

None the less, while local turn-out is strongly related to psychological involvement in local politics, it is also related to psychological involvement in national politics. We must further suspect that interest and discussion of local politics itself reflects a more general involvement with politics in all its manifestations and that local interest is not purely local.

The first two columns in Table 7.2 show that those who were interested and knowledgeable at a particular time tended to vote or to express an intention to vote *at that same time*. Unfortunately there are logical problems in interpreting that finding: although interest, discussion, knowledge, and turn-out coincide, there is no evidence here that one causes the other. It would, after all, be rather surprising if the act of voting itself failed to stimulate some interest and discussion about local politics. We may vote because a friend steers us towards the polling station on the way home from a shopping expedition, or because a persistent party canvasser arrives with a car to take us to the polling station. In such circumstances, the vote is more likely to cause our interest in local politics than to result from it. (Or consider levels of knowledge: those who had just voted in May 1986 were *in consequence* particularly likely to know the name of the councillors elected in May 1986).

This is a place where we can put our panel survey design to good use. The third column in Table 7.2 shows the relationship between actual turn-out in May 1986 and expressions of interest and knowledge *in November 1985*, six months before the vote. Naturally the patterns are weaker, but they are more meaningful. Instead of asking

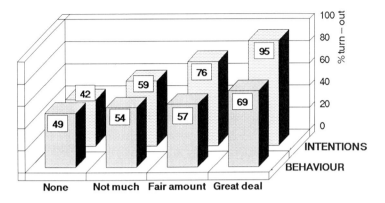

Fig. 7.3. Turn-out by interest in local politics (*see Table 7.2*)

'do people who are interested now, vote now?' we ask 'do people who were interested in local politics *six months ago*, vote now?'

As we suspected, voting itself may influence knowledge: knowledge in November was much worse than knowledge in May at predicting turn-out in May. For example, the difference in actual turn-out rates between those who had or had not known their councillor's name *six months before* the election was 13 per cent; the difference in the turn-out rates between those who did or did not know the name of their councillor *at the time of the election* was a huge 32 per cent; but many voters probably learnt the names of the candidates at the polling station—so voting caused knowledge, not the reverse, in many cases.

Levels of interest and discussion in November were as effective predictors of turn-out in May as levels of interest and discussion in May itself, however. This suggests that our measures of interest and discussion do tap something which is separate from local election participation and something which really does influence local turn-out. But although local turn-out is linked a little more strongly to prior interest and discussion of local rather than national politics, it is still evident that the difference is slight: local turn-out really does depend upon political interest, but perhaps not exclusively on local political interest.

Turn-out by National Mobilization/Constraint Factors

Reading a paper, especially something more heavyweight than a

Table 7.2. The relationship between turn-out and psychological involvement

	% Turn-out		
Tabulated by attitudes in	TLGNOV Nov.	T86 May	T86 Nov.
Interest in national politics:			
None at all	46	44	42
Not much	55	51	55
Fair amount	72	59	55
Great deal	79	62	69
Discuss national politics:			
Never	43	45	46
Rarely	56	49	51
Occasionally	68	61	57
Quite often	78	59	62
Interest in local politics:			
None at all	42	49	44
Not much	59	54	53
Fair amount	76	57	58
Great deal	95	69	81

Discuss local politics:

	Name of councillors	Party of county	Party of district
Never	44	46	43
Rarely	60	48	59
Occasionally	71	60	54
Quite often	89	74	68

Knowledgeable about:

In	County name			District name			Name of councillors			Party of councillors			Party of county			Party of district		
	Nov.	May	Nov.	Nov.	May	Nov.	Nov.	May	Nov.	Nov.	May	Nov.	Nov.	May	Nov.	Nov.	May	Nov.
	TLG	T86	T86	TLG	T86	T86	TLG	T86	T86	TLG	T86	T86	TLG	T86	T86	TLG	T86	T86
DK:	59	35	53	48	40	45	59	42	52	49	32	40	46	35*	45	43	35*	41
Correct:	69	62	58	69	59	58	74	74	65	72	63	61	71	58*	61	70	58*	59
Diff:	10	27	5	21	19	13	15	32	13	23	31	21	25	23*	16	27	23*	18

Notes:
1. In the part of the table which deals with knowledge, the percentages do not refer to the numbers of respondents who had the various items of knowledge, but to the turn-out rates amongst the knowledgeable and the ignorant. That is, they have the same meaning as all the other percentages in the table.
2. Few respondents gave wrong answers on the knowledge questions, and they have been excluded from the table.
* The entries marked with an asterisk are based upon knowledge of party control after the May election on the council that had just been elected (region in Scotland, district in England and Wales).

tabloid, seemed to encourage slightly higher turn-out, especially for parliamentary rather than local elections.

Psychologically mobilizing factors had more effect, particularly upon turn-out intentions in November. Turn-out intentions correlated with strong feelings of identification with political issues or political parties and with religiosity. Trade union connections did not encourage high levels of turn-out intentions, but a right-wing ideology or strong police sympathies did. In the event however, most of these patterns were weakened when it came to actual voting.

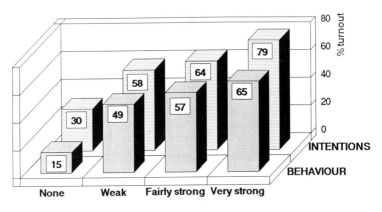

Fig. 7.4. Turn-out by strength of partisanship (*see Table 7.3*)

We had asked respondents whether they felt 'particularly sympathetic' or 'unsympathetic' to a list of twenty-three social groups. Our hypothesis was that those who had strong feelings towards social groups might be motivated to participate in politics in general, and in local elections in particular—irrespective of whether these strong feelings were friendly or unfriendly. Alas, we found no evidence that positive or negative feelings towards particular social groups (other than the police) raised local election turn-out; but electors who were sympathetic to Blacks and Asians had particularly *low* levels of actual turn-out despite their earlier good intentions about voting (Table 7.3).

Turn-out by Local Mobilization/Constraint Factors

Naturally, a survey focused on local government included a wider range of questions about *locally* orientated mobilization factors, but

Table 7.3. The relationship between turn-out and national mobilization/constraint factors

	% Turn-out		
Tabulated by attitudes in	TLGNOV NOV.	T86 MAY	T86 NOV.
Issue feelings:			
Do not feel strongly on any issue	55	50	52
Do feel strongly on some issue	70	57	58
Feeling of identification with a party:			
None	30	—	—
Not very strong	58	49	65
Fairly strong	64	57	50
Very strong	79	65	64
Trade union connection:			
Self member	63	53	n.a.
Someone else in household member	57	54	n.a.
None	66	57	n.a.
Left/Right position on self-assigned ideology scale:			
Left	59	51	n.a.
Centre	60	58	n.a.
Right	75	57	n.a.
Religiosity: attend religious services			
Weekly	77	68	n.a.
Less than monthly	63	49	n.a.
Never	55	54	n.a.
Group sympathy:			
particularly sympathetic to:			
Blacks	58	41	n.a.
Asians	66	46	n.a.
Police	76	59	n.a.
particularly unsympathetic to:			
Blacks	59	—	n.a.
Asians	56	—	n.a.
Strikers	68	58	n.a.
No one	65	58	n.a.

n.a. = question not asked in November.
— = less than 50 respondents in this category; see note to Table 7.1.

these generally had less effect on turn-out than did party identification (though religiosity has a local dimension since it involves meeting people in the locality as well as adhering to a faith).

Table 7.4. The relationship between turn-out and local mobilization/ constraint factors I: Attitude to local politics

	% Turn-out		
Tabulated by attitudes in	TLGNOV NOV.	T86 MAY	T86 NOV.
Vote on local rather than national issues in local elections:			
Local	69	58	57
Both equally	70	67	66
National	61	50	60
Feel most important issue is matter for:			
Central government	68	57	55
Both	83	—	—
Local councils	72	—	—
Blame:			
Blame government for local cash shortages	63	56	54
Blame both for local cash shortages	66	53	55
Blame councils for local cash shortages	65	56	61
County council runs things:			
Not at all well	63	47	63
Fairly well	64	57	55
Very well	67	—	—
District council runs things:			
Not at all well	62	54	58
Fairly well	64	55	56
Very well	66	65	—
Government runs things:			
Not at all well	n.a.	54	n.a.
Fairly well	n.a.	55	n.a.
Very well	n.a.	—	n.a.
Ever wanted to complain about local council:			
No	61	n.a.	59
Yes	68	n.a.	52
Pay rates:			
Pay rates in full	63	58	58
Partial rebate	74	56	55
Full rebate or no rates	63	54	52
Contacted councillor:			
Complained	76	n.a.	68
Contacted (not necessarily to complain)	73	69	68
No	60	51	52
Contacted council offices:			
Complained	77	n.a.	63
Contacted (not necessarily to complain)	66	58	54
No	56	50	52

cont.

Table 7.4. *cont.*

| | % Turn-out | | |
| | TLGNOV | T86 | T86 |
Tabulated by attitudes in	NOV.	MAY	NOV.
Use local media:			
Take evening paper: no	62	55	56
yes	68	55	53
Take local weekly: no	60	46	49
yes	66	59	58
Watch local TV news: no	60	49	54
yes	65	57	55
Listen to local radio news: no	62	55	55
yes	67	56	55

n.a. = question not asked in Nov. or May.
— = less than 50 respondents in this category: see note to Table 7.1.

Attitude to Local Politics

Those who claimed to vote on local issues in local elections or who listed specific local government issues that they claimed influenced their choice in local government elections had a slight tendency to turn out more—though that was true for parliamentary elections as much as local elections. But those who, in answer to another question, stated that their principal concern was more a matter for local government rather than national government showed only the merest trace of higher than average turn-out in local elections (but lower than average turn-out in parliamentary).

Satisfaction with the way local councils are running things has an inherently ambiguous relationship to turn-out. Those who are well satisfied may turn out in a fit of good humour, those who are dissatisfied may turn out to protest. Overall there was little correlation between turn-out and satisfaction with councils, or blaming local or national government for financial problems, or wanting to complain about local councils.

Turn-out was higher amongst those who actually *did* complain to their councillors or even had direct contact with their councillors but that is explicable as much in terms of activity/inactivity, as satisfaction/dissatisfaction—those who have enough initiative and determination to actually complain or contact their councillor also have enough to turn out and vote. There was no correlation between turn-out and satisfaction with council contacts amongst those who actually had contacted councils.

Rate-paying had no effect upon turn-out—perhaps to the surprise of those who are inclined to over-intellectualize or over-rationalize the behaviour of mass electorates. Significantly almost all respondents claimed they did pay rates until they were specifically questioned about rebates. Psychologically, local electorates are ratepayers, whether or not they actually pay rates.

Our measures of exposure to local news media show a fairly consistent tendency for slightly above-average turn-out amongst those who read local papers or listened to local news on radio or TV.

Attitude to Local Elections

We used four measures of political alienation from local elections (five in our May survey). All of them correlated more or less strongly with turn-out. All of them correlated a little more strongly with local than national turn-out intentions.

The weakest relationships were with attitudes towards the effectiveness of local government and politicians' broken promises. The strongest relationships are between turn-out and attitudes to elections being 'too complicated to understand' or involving 'so many people' that individual votes were not important. Although these last two variables correlate very well with turn-out, they are so close to an expressed intention to turn out (or not turn out) that the *span* of explanation provided by these variables is not great, whatever its *strength*. There is a danger that we are almost measuring turn-out intention twice with different forms of words.

As with the relationship between turn-out and knowledge of councillors' names, the direction of causal influence may run *from* voting rather than *towards* it. Significantly, the predictive power of these attitude scales is dramatically reduced when we use alienation attitudes in November to predict actual turn-out in May. For example, amongst those who thought, in May, that local election voting was unimportant, only 10 per cent voted; but amongst those who had been equally sceptical about elections six months beforehand, fully 28 per cent voted on the day (Table 7.5). None the less there is some evidence here that those who turn out to vote believe that local elections are not too complicated and that their votes are important.

Table 7.5. The relationship between turn-out and local mobilization/constraint factors II: Attitude to local elections

Tabulated by attitudes in	% Turn-out		
	TLGNOV NOV.	T86 MAY	T86 NOV.
The people who get in at local elections can have a big effect on the way people like me live:			
Disagree	n.a.	51	n.a.
Neither	n.a.	49	n.a.
Agree	n.a.	59	n.a.
The people you vote for say they'll do things for you but once they're in power they forget what they've said:			
Disagree	82	59	65
Neither	62	61	54
Agree	60	53	54
The way that people vote at local council elections is the main thing that decides how things are run in this area:			
Disagree	58	49	59
Neither	62	56	55
Agree	68	59	55
Local council elections are sometimes so complicated that I really don't know who to vote for:			
Disagree	78	64	63
Neither	41	—	—
Agree	47	35	45
So many other people vote in local council elections that it's not important whether I vote or not:			
Disagree	76	64	61
Neither	—	—	—
Agree	18	10	28

n.a. = question not asked in November.

Attitudes towards local government autonomy had little effect upon turn-out. Surprisingly, those who felt that MPs rather than councils should speak for their area actually had an *above* average turn-out rate in May. Those who supported the concept of elected local government rather than appointed boards did turn-out more than others—it would have been very surprising if they had not. But neither perceptions of central control nor support for more local autonomy produced higher turn-out rates (Table 7.6).

Table 7.6. The relationship between turn-out and local mobilization/ constraint factors III: Attitudes to local government autonomy

	% Turn-out		
Tabulated by attitudes in	TLGNOV NOV.	T86 MAY	T86 NOV.
Should council try to get best deal for area or should it leave this to local MP?			
Leave it to MP	64	66	56
Council action	66	51	56
Good or bad idea for central government to appoint local councillors?			
Bad idea	66	59	57
Good idea	59	44	50
How much control do you think the local councils here have over the levels of local rates and services?			
Councils more than government	66	56	59
Shared equally	69	54	51
Government more than councils	63	56	59
Should local councils be controlled more (or less) by central government?			
Less	65	54	57
Same	63	58	57
More	68	51	53

Last we had one measure of the perceived marginality of the local council: that is, whether it was likely to change party control after the next election. We had no measure that corresponds to marginality as defined by Fletcher and others who have worked with ward election results. Turn-out was substantially higher amongst those few respondents who thought a change of party control was 'very likely', but anything less by way of marginality had little effect on turn-out.

Who Voted?

By far the most impressive predictors of turn-out considered in this chapter have now been those highlighted in previous studies of electoral participation: age, psychological involvement in local (and national) politics, and a strong sense of identification with a political party. Knowledge of councillors' names and explicit support for local elections also correlated well with turn-out, but at best the span of prediction from these variables to turn-out is very short and, at worst,

Table 7.7. The relationship between turn-out and perceived marginality

Tabulated by attitudes in	% Turn-out		
	TLGNOV NOV.	T86 MAY	T86 NOV.
Perceived marginality of local council (how likely to change control at next election?)			
Not at all likely	71	n.a.	51
Not very likely	67	n.a.	65
Fairly likely	69	n.a.	55
Very likely	80	n.a.	—

— = less than 50 respondents in this category; see note to Table 7.1.

the correlation may owe a great deal to reverse causation—that is, to the act of voting increasing knowledge and increasing approval for the electoral process.

Party identification has been a key variable in studies of electoral behaviour for decades past. We have tested its influence upon turn-out in the standard way and it has passed the standard test: those with a strong sense of party identification are very likely to vote.

However, if we use our panel to apply a more stringent test this key predictor of turn-out performs relatively badly. By any test, those who do not identify at all with any party had outstandingly low rates of turn-out. But the differences between turn-out rates amongst those with strong and weak identification are not so stable. In November fully 21 per cent more strong identifiers than weak intended to turn out. In May 16 per cent more strong identifiers actually did turn out. So far so good. But if we compare actual behaviour in May with strength of party identification in November we see that the strong party identifiers of November had an actual turn-out rate in May that was 1 per cent less than amongst the weak identifiers. Part of the explanation for this paradox lies in the fact that strength of party identification was only moderately stable—as we saw in Chapter 4.

When we applied this same stringent test to the interest and discussion variables they were able to predict future turn-out patterns remarkably well. Those who had a great deal of interest in local politics in November had an intended turn-out rate 53 per cent higher than those with no interest in local politics then; and when the election came, their actual turn-out rate was still 37 per cent higher.

Party identification is sufficiently different from turn-out itself, both in concept and measurement, that we should not regard it as another way of asking the same question. (Unlike the alienation questions where affirming the value of voting and turning out to vote do seem very similar measures of closely entwined concepts.) Nor do we suggest that turn-out, by itself, causes strength of party identification. At any one time enthusiasm for a party probably is a major cause of turn-out—as previous studies have concluded. But party enthusiasm waxes and wanes so much that it is not a very reliable guide to future turn-out behaviour.

8 Testing the Two-step, Two-level Model

The tables of turn-out percentages presented in Chapter 7 only reveal the bivariate relationship between particular influences and turn-out. For an overview of our turn-out model we need a system of analysis that is at once simpler and multivariate. We now return to the model set out in Chapter 5 and work through it using multiple regression techniques which evaluate the independent impact of each causal variable after taking into account the impact of other, simultaneous causes.

First we need to put specific survey-based variables against the concepts used in that model. We use a simplified subset of the variables we discussed in Chapter 7. In Figure 8.1 we have placed several variable names under each of the concepts in our turn-out model. The precise definitions of our analytic variables are set out in Table 8.1. Each variable is a dichotomy. Reducing each variable to a dichotomy loses much of the subtlety of response contained in our respondents' original answers but allows easy calculation of correlation and regression statistics. Table 8.2 shows how each of the predictive variables in our model correlates with four measures of turn-out— TLGNOV, T86, TGENOV, and TGEMAY (these measures were defined in Chapter 6). Only those correlations which exceed 0.09 are shown and all correlations are multiplied by 100 per cent for readability.

Without going into more complex analysis, or even into the details of this table, we can draw a number of tentative conclusions simply by comparing the blocks of the table that contain lots of print with the blocks that are fairly empty.

1. Demographics

There is a (relatively) strong correlation between age and turn-out which applies to both local and national elections through it affects intentions a little more than behaviour. Class correlates with turn-out intentions but not with turn-out behaviour. Otherwise, demographics do not correlate well with turn-out.

Table 8.1. Definitions of variables

AGE:	Over 35 (versus under 35 years old)
SEX:	Female (versus male)
CHILDREN:	Have children under 16 years old in household (versus do not)
*UNEM:	Respondent currently unemployed (versus not)
EDUC:	Finished education at over 19 years old (versus finished earlier)
CLASS:	Middle-class, i.e. non-manual head of household (versus working-class)
OWN:	Owner-occupier (versus rent housing)
CTEN:	Council tenant (versus own or rent privately)
LRES:	Long term resident, i.e. over 10 years in area (versus not)
*NINV:	Composite score on interest in and discussion of national politics is high (versus low)
*LINV:	Composite score on interest in and discussion of local politics is high (versus low)
*LKNOW:	Local knowledge high (versus low)
*TGE:	'Certain' or 'very likely' to vote in next parliamentary general election (versus any other answer)
TLGNOV:	'Certain' or 'very likely' to vote in a local election (versus any other answer), asked in Nov. 1985
T86:	Voted in 1986 local elections (versus lived in area where elections were held, but did not vote)
*NISSIMP:	Respondent named at least one issue in politics that he or she felt strongly about (versus did not)
*LGISSIMP:	Respondent named at least one local issue which would be important in deciding how to vote in a local election (versus did not)
*PTYID:	'Very' or 'fairly' strong sense of partisanship (versus 'not very' strong, or 'no' party identification)
*PAPER:	Regularly reads a morning paper (versus does not)
RELIG:	Attends religious services at least once a month (versus attends less frequently or non-religious)
TU:	Someone in household is a member of a trade union (versus not)
ANTIGP:	Respondent names at least one of the 23 social groups as a group with which he or she is 'not at all sympathetic' (versus does not)
IDEOL:	Places self on left or right of ideological spectrum (versus places self in middle or does not know)
*LGSAT:	'Very well' or 'fairly well' satisfied with both county council and district council (versus not)
*LGAUT:	Composite score on support for local autonomy high (versus not)
LGMARG:	'Very likely' that a different party will win control of district council at next local elections (versus not), asked in Nov. 1985
*LVNISS:	Claim to vote on local rather than national issues in local elections (versus not)
*LMORN:	Regular reader of a local or regional morning paper including *Glasgow Herald* and *Scotsman* (versus not)
*LWEEK:	Regular reader of a local weekly paper (versus not)
*RATES:	Pay rates in full (versus get partial or full rebate, or not required to pay rates at all)

Notes:
1. * means that the variable was measured both in Nov. 1985 and in May 1986.

cont.

Notes cont.
2. LINV, NINV: Interest was scored from 1 = 'none' to 4 = 'a great deal', and discussion from 1 = 'never' to 4 = 'quite often'. These scores were added together. Then composite scores up to 4 were taken as indicating low involvement, while scores 5 up to 8 were taken as indicating high involvement.
3. LKNOW: Knowledge was based upon a composite score adding 1 if the respondent knew the county name, the district name, a councillor's name, and the councillor's party. Scores up to 2 were taken as indicating low knowledge, while scores 3 and 4 were taken as indicating high knowledge.
4. LGAUT: Attitude to central government appointing local government scored 1 = 'a very good idea, or fairly good idea', 2 = 'don't know, or neither good nor bad', 3 = 'fairly bad idea, or very bad idea'; attitude to whether local councils should be controlled by central government scored 1 = 'a lot more or a little more', 2 = 'don't know', 3 = 'a little less or a lot less'; then these two scores added together; then composite scores up to 4 taken as low support for local autonomy.

2. Psychological involvement

By contrast, all measures of psychological involvement correlate well with all measures of turn-out. Turn-out in parliamentary elections correlates more with involvement in national politics than with involvement in local politics; conversely, turn-out in local elections correlates more with psychological involvement in local politics than with involvement in national politics. Table 8.2 also shows quite strikingly that psychological involvement generally correlates far better with turn-out intentions than with actual turn-out behaviour—which suggests that mobilization factors of some kind are as important for their direct effect upon turn-out as for their indirect effect through psychological involvement. One exception is our local knowledge variable which correlates best with actual turn-out; but it was almost inevitably influenced by the act of voting and we shall not use it as a predictor of turn-out in the multivariate analyses that follow.

3. Mobilization Factors

Most of our mobilization variables fail to correlate well with turn-out, though there are some notable exceptions. Concern for national political issues correlates with turn-out intentions, whether national or local, but not with actual local turn-out. A strong sense of party identification correlates with all measures of turn-out though much more strongly with national turn-out intentions than with local. Church attendance correlates well with local turn-out intentions and behaviour but not with national turn-out intentions. Apart from this, there is little evidence of powerful links between mobilization factors and turn-out.

In particular, none of the local mobilization factors seems influential, unless we regard church attendance as more local than national.

Table 8.2. Correlations with turn-out variables

Correlation with:	TLGNOV	T86	TGENOV	TGEMAY
Demographics:				
AGE	24**	18**	24**	23**
SEX	—	—	—	—
CHILDREN	−9*	−10	—	−9
UNEM (Nov.)	−12**	—	−9*	—
UNEM (May)	—	—	—	—
EDUC	—	11	—	14**
CLASS	16**	—	12**	14**
Demographics with local relevance:				
OWN	—	—	—	—
CTEN	—	—	—	—
LRES	—	11*	—	9*
National psychological involvement:				
NINV (Nov.)	24**	10	26**	29**
NINV (May)	17**	9	19**	30**
Local psychological involvement:				
LINV (Nov.)	28**	13**	16**	21**
LINV (May)	22**	14**	15**	21**
LKNOW (Nov.)	23**	16**	25**	27**
LKNOW (May)	18**	27**	22**	27**
Political mobilization factors (national):				
NISSIMP (Nov.)	16**	—	19**	17**
NISSIMP (May)	12**	—	12**	21**
PTYID (Nov.)	16**	—	28**	21**
PTYID (May)	14**	13*	21**	27**
PAPER (Nov.)	—	—	—	12**
PAPER (May)	—	10	—	—
RELIG	20**	15*	—	—
TU	—	—	—	—
ANTIGP	—	—	—	—
IDEOL	11*	—	12**	10**
Political mobilization factors (local):				
LGISSIMP (Nov.)	11**	11*	10*	11*
LGISSIMP (May)	—	—	—	—
LGSAT (Nov.)	—	—	—	—
LGSAT (May)	—	—	—	—
LGAUT (Nov.)	—	—	10*	11*
LGAUT (May)	—	9	9*	11*
LGMARG (Nov. only)	9*	9*	—	—
LVNISS (Nov.)	11*	—	—	—

cont.

Table 8.2. *cont.*

Correlation with:	TLGNOV	T86	TGENOV	TGEMAY
LVNISS (May)	—	—	—	9*
LMORN (Nov.)	—	—	9*	—
LMORN (May)	9*	—	—	—
LWEEK (Nov.)	—	9*	—	9*
LWEEK (May)	—	12*	—	9*
RATES (Nov.)	—	—	—	—
RATES (May)	—	—	—	—

Notes:
1. Only correlations of 0.09 or greater are shown. (— *indicates correlation smaller than this*).
2. ** indicates those significant at the 0.01 level, * at 0.05.
3. Pairwise deletion of missing values is used in this and other tables; thus correlations involving actual turn-out in 1986 are based only on those who had the opportunity to turn out, i.e. who lived in areas with elections.

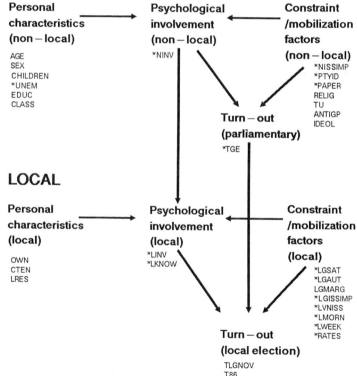

Fig. 8.1 Survey variables in the two-step, two-level model

That would be appropriate if churches operated not simply as organizations that stimulate their members to action but as local organizations that link their members to their immediate neighbours and neighbourhood. Certainly religiosity as measured here does, on the face of it, have a more local content than party identification. We have not measured depth of religious belief after all, but only the frequency of meetings with other church members in the locality.

Multivariate Analysis

We turn now to a multivariate analysis of our turn-out model. To do this we go through the model shown in our causal diagram in four stages. At each stage we use multiple regression to assess the relative influence of causative variables.

At stage 1 we use (national) personal characteristics and (national) mobilization factors to predict (national) psychological involvement.

At stage 2 our model postulates that (national) psychological involvement and (national) mobilization factors influence parliamentary turn-out intentions, but we also check for any influences from (national) personal characteristics.

At stage 3 our model postulates that national psychological involvement, local personal characteristics, and local mobilization will influence local psychological involvement but we take a more empirical approach and use all the personal characteristics and mobilization factors as predictors.

At stage 4 the model postulates that local election turn-out will depend principally upon local involvement, local mobilization factors, and a general (national) propensity to turn out but once again we use all prior predictors.

At each stage we use SPSSPC Stepwise Regression and retain only those predictor variables that satisfy its default conditions for significance. We can interpret the results as showing all the significant independent influences on the dependent variables at each stage.

Table 8.3 shows the regression weights (often called standardized regression coefficients, or path coefficients) for predicting psychological involvement with national politics. In theory these coefficients can range up to 100 (and in exceptional circumstances even above 100) but with dichotomous survey data they are unlikely ever to get anywhere near so high. The RSQ figure (often called R squared, or the squared multiple correlation) measures the proportion of the variation in the

Table 8.3. Stage 1. Influences on psychological involvement with national politics

Predictors	Dependent Variables:	
	NINV in Nov.	NINV in May
	Multiple regression weights	
Personal characteristics:		
AGE	—	—
SEX	−9	—
CHILDREN	—	—
UNEM	—	—
EDUC	10	11
CLASS	22	19
Mobilization factors:		
NISSIMP	25	28
PTYID	19	16
PAPER	—	—
RELIG	—	—
TU	10	9
ANTIGP	—	—
IDEOL	—	8
Proportion of variation explained (RSQ)	24%	23%

Notes:
1. Where predictors were measured in both Nov. and May we have used the corresponding measure to predict involvement in Nov. or May.
2. — = this variable was not selected by the stepwise regression as having a significant independent influence.

dependent variable—in this case psychological involvement, which is explained by the joint influence of all the predictor variables.

As suggested by Verba and his associates, involvement, i.e. interest and discussion, is greater in the higher social classes and more educated groups for essentially personal reasons. But it is also greater amongst those who feel there are important issues or who identify with parties or have links to trade unions. These factors mobilize people into a greater involvement with politics. Perhaps it is worth noting that the religiosity variable did not seem to increase involvement with national politics.

Strictly speaking, Verba and his associates' model suggested that mobilization factors would affect turn-out directly and not through the medium of psychological involvement. Thus for Verba, psychological involvement and mobilization factors were the two great competing influences upon turn-out. Our regressions in Table 8.4 suggest

Table 8.4. Stage 2. Influences on parliamentary turn-out intentions

Predictors	Dependent Variables: TGE in Nov. Multiple regression weights	TGE in May
Personal characteristics:		
AGE	23	16
SEX	—	—
CHILDREN	—	-8
UNEM	—	—
EDUC	—	9
CLASS	—	—
Mobilization factors:		
NISSIMP	15	13
PTYID	18	20
PAPER	—	—
RELIG	—	—
TU	—	—
ANTIGP	—	—
IDEOL	—	—
Psychological involvement:		
NINV	15	13
Proportion of variation explained (RSQ)	17%	18%

that parliamentary turn-out intention was directly influenced by psychological involvement, by two mobilization factors (issue concern and party identification), and also by age.

The third stage of our analysis is to predict psychological involvement with local politics. The regressions in Table 8.5 show that by far the most powerful predictor of psychological involvement in local politics is psychological involvement with national politics. It is generally not the case that some people are interested in local politics and others in national politics: by and large people are either interested in politics, both national and local, or they are not. Apart from that one clear finding the entries in Table 8.5 are rather mixed, but it seems our postulated local mobilization factors do not have a greater influence upon involvement with local politics than do national mobilization factors such as party identification or concern for national issues.

Finally we come to the fourth stage, in which we predict local election turn-out. What is remarkable about the results shown in Table 8.6 is that there are so few non-zero entries. Local turn-out is clearly strongly related to parliamentary turn-out, that is with a general propensity to turn out and vote. But once that factor is taken into account very little else matters.

There is a consistent (though weaker) influence from age. Local psychological involvement and religiosity seem to influence local turn-out intentions, but not actual local turn-out.

Indeed there is a striking difference between the predictability of local turn-out intentions, which is quite high, and the predictability of

Table 8.5. Stage 3. Influences on psychological involvement with local politics

Predictors	Dependent Variables: LINV in Nov. Multiple regression weights	LINV in May
Personal characteristics (national):		
AGE	—	15
SEX	—	—
CHILDREN	—	—
UNEM	—	—
EDUC	—	8
CLASS	—	—
Personal characteristics (local):		
OWN	—	—
CTEN	—	—
LRES	9	—
National psychological involvement:		
NINV	38	37
Mobilization factors (national):		
NISSIMP	—	14
PTYID	16	—
PAPER	—	—
RELIG	11	—
TU	10	—
ANTIGP	—	—
IDEOL	—	—
Mobilization factors (local):		
LGSAT	—	—
LGAUT	13	—
LGMARG	—	—
LGISSIMP	9	—
LVNISS	—	10
LMORN	—	—
LWEEK	—	—
RATES	—	—
Proportion of variation explained (RSQ)	30%	26%

Table 8.6. Stage 4. Influences on local election turn-out intentions and behaviour

Predictors	Dependent Variables:	
	TLGNOV in Nov.	T86 in May
	Multiple regression weights	
Personal characteristics (national):		
AGE	11	12
SEX	—	—
CHILDREN	−7	—
UNEM	—	—
EDUC	—	—
CLASS	8	—
Personal characteristics (local):		
OWN	—	—
CTEN	—	—
LRES	—	—
Local psychological involvement:		
LINV	12	—
Mobilization factors (national):		
NISSIMP	—	—
PTYID	—	—
PAPER	—	—
RELIG	12	—
TU	—	—
ANTIGP	—	—
IDEOL	—	—
Mobilization factors (local):		
LGSAT	—	—
LGAUT	—	—
LGMARG	—	—
LGISSIMP	—	—
LVNISS	—	—
LMORN	—	—
LWEEK	—	—
RATES	—	—
Parliamentary turn-out intentions TGE	50	30
Proportion of variation explained (RSQ)	40%	11%

local turn-out behaviour, which is much lower. Without much evidence, we might guess that this is caused by mobilization factors of a kind that are not included in our analysis—namely, the activism of local political parties.

Critical Tests

The influence of parliamentary turn-out intentions appears so overwhelming in Table 8.6 that it is worth considering some simpler multiple regressions which exclude its influence. In Table 8.7 we report three 'critical tests' of the relative influence of pairs of predictors of local turn-out. These tests show that when local and national psychological involvement are compared, both have some influence, but local involvement has much more influence than national involvement. When we compare the influence of national party identification and local involvement the result is less clear-cut: the local factor is more influential on local turn-out intentions but not on local turn-out behaviour. Finally, when we compare the influence of general propensities to vote (TGE) with the influence of local involvement the results indicate that general propensities to vote are much more influential than an interest in local politics, but they also show that in absolute terms, general propensities to turn-out are very much less influential on actual behaviour than on intentions.

Table 8.7. Critical tests of influence on turn-out intentions and behaviour

| Predictors | Dependent Variables: | |
	TLGNOV in Nov. Multiple regression weights	T86 in May
NINV	14	3
LINV	22	12
Proportion of variation explained (RSQ)	9%	2%
PTYID	10	12
LINV	26	12
Proportion of variation explained (RSQ)	9%	3%
TGE	53	26
LINV	19	8
Proportion of variation explained (RSQ)	36%	8%

Conclusion

We can summarize the results of these multivariate analyses by producing a revised diagram of the two-level, two-step model, including arrows only where the regressions have shown significant causal links. This shows Verba's two-step model working rather well at

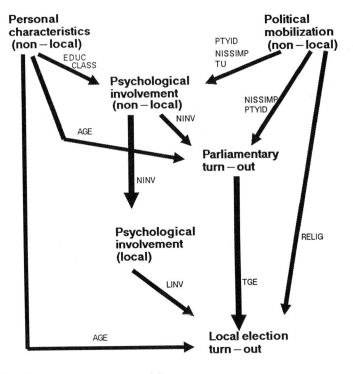

Fig. 8.2. Revised turn-out model

the national level: personal characteristics and mobilization factors combine to influence psychological involvement; psychological involvement and mobilization factors then combine to influence turn-out intentions.

But there is scant evidence of Verba's model working very strongly at the local level: psychological involvement with local politics seems to derive from psychological involvement with national politics; local turn-out derives from national turn-out intentions; psychological involvement with local politics and local mobilization factors do not exert strong and independent influences upon local turn-out.

Our regressions and critical test analyses suggest that local factors do have a small independent influence upon local turn-out intentions; but actual local turn-out is remarkably unpredictable, unstructured, unpatterned. We can predict who will declare an intention to vote, but not who will actually do so.

9 Does Turn-out Matter? Party, Group, and Attitude Bias amongst Local Election Voters

Does it matter who votes? If some social classes have higher turn-out rates than others surely that will add political inequalities to social and economic inequalities. Paradoxically, but perhaps only superficially, the problem is to some extent its own solution. Where class polarization in politics is weak, working-class parties do not exist to mobilize working-class electors into voting. But by definition politics in these places is not about class and so the under-representation of working-class people in voter turn-out does not matter as much as it would elsewhere.

Wolfinger and Rosenstone found that differential turn-out in America biased the vote 4 per cent in favour of the Republicans. But there was no bias in terms of liberal versus conservative ideology—none, for example, on social welfare policy. So despite the enormous *socio-economic bias* that exists in American turn-out they concluded that the *political bias* was relatively small: 'as long as attitudes on issues are so weakly related to social class and race, the poor and minorities will find enough allies to avoid political weakness in proportion to their own voting rates'.[1]

This is a comforting conclusion, but raises the deeper question of whether socio-economic turn-out biases affect the whole structure of political competition. It is difficult for the Democrats to articulate strong support for the poor as long as the poor stay away from the polling stations; and they will stay away as long as there is no major party committed to mobilizing their vote. So there may be a vicious circle linking social and political bias; and the degree of political bias may be obscured by its sheer magnitude and extent. If political bias affects the *nature* of political competition it may have *too large* an effect to be detectable by studying only the *outcome* of political competition.

Verba and Nie's study of community voting in America reached a less complacent conclusion than Wolfinger and Rosenstone.[2] By comparing the political priorities of elected officials with those of their electorates in sixty-four communities in different parts of the USA they found a close agreement between officials and electorates where participation was high, less agreement where it was low, and least agreement where participation was moderate. At intermediate levels of participation the activists were numerous enough to influence the elected officials, but not numerous enough to be representative of the whole electorate. Happily for our present concerns, this perverse effect of medium participation levels did not apply to voting turn-out, but only to other forms of political participation in which activists could convey more clearly articulated demands. For voting, but not for other forms of participation, there was a simple linear relationship: a higher level of turn-out produced a greater concurrence of public and official attitudes.

At one time writers on British local government elections—like writers on American national and local elections—tried to make a virtue out of necessity by arguing that 'moderate participation levels are helpful in maintaining a balance between consensus and cleavage in society', or that élites had internalized democratic values more fully than the masses, or even that high electoral turn-outs might be destabilizing.[3]

It is certainly true that a very high turn-out may be a symptom of crisis and cleavage, though not necessarily the cause. But it is difficult to make a virtue of turn-outs as low as 30 or 40 per cent. It is a poor guarantee of stability, for example, when election results can be overturned so easily by differential turn-out rather than attitude change. Low turn-out is not necessarily a threat to the political system and it need not represent massive alienation, but it is not much of a defence either.

In particular, low turn-out in British local elections invites British cental government to play the part of disruptive revolutionaries and manipulate, override, or destroy the system of elected local councils whenever they prove inconvenient to central administrators. Any evidence of bias produced by low turn-out reduces the legitimacy of local councils and encourages central government interference still more.

Turn-out Bias in British Local Government Elections

To say that age influences turn-out rates is also to say that turn-out is biased in terms of age. These are just two different ways of looking at

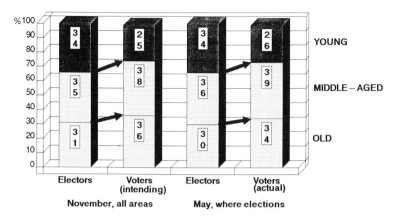

Fig. 9.1. Age bias (*see Table 9.1*)

the same phenomenon. As we have seen, turn-out correlates fairly well with age: so voters over-represent middle-aged and older electors. At the 1986 local elections the voters included 8 per cent too many middle-aged and older electors and 8 per cent too few young electors.

Class correlated with local election turn-out intentions in November 1985 but not with actual local election turn-out in May 1986. The class profile of intending voters was biased 6 per cent towards the

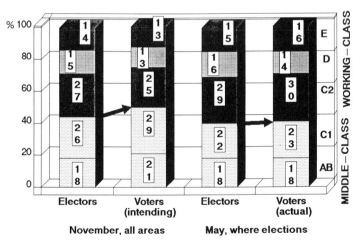

Fig. 9.2. Class bias (*see Table 9.1*)

middle class in November but the bias disappeared at the May election. (Note that the areas with elections were themselves somewhat less middle-class than the nation as a whole; so it is important to make the proper comparisons.) Similarly there was a very slight bias towards owner-occupiers amongst turn-out intenders in November but a slightly larger bias towards council tenants amongst actual voters in May, even when we take account of the fact that the areas with elections had more council tenants (Table 9.1).

Table 9.1. Turn-out bias and social characteristics

AGE PROFILES

	All areas			Areas with elections (May)		
	All respondents	Intending voters (Nov.)	Bias	All respondents	Actual voters	Bias
Age:						
% young	34.1	25.4	−9	33.9	26.3	−8
% middle-aged	34.9	38.3	+3	36.5	39.4	+3
% old	31.0	36.3	+5	29.6	34.2	+5
	100%	100%		100%	100%	

CLASS PROFILES

	All areas			Areas with elections (May)		
	All respondents	Intending voters (Nov.)	Bias	All respondents	Actual voters	Bias
Class:						
% AB*	18.0	20.6	+3	17.7	18.2	+1
% C1	25.5	28.8	+3	22.2	22.7	+1
% C2	26.9	24.5	−2	29.3	29.8	+1
% D	15.4	13.2	−2	15.5	13.8	−2
% E	14.2	13.0	−1	15.4	15.5	−1
	100%	100%		100%	100%	

TENURE PROFILES

	All areas			Areas with elections (May)		
	All respondents	Intending Voters (Nov.)	Bias	All respondents	Actual voters	Bias
Tenure:						
% owner	73.2	73.2	0	68.2	67.0	−1
% council	19.2	18.2	−1	23.4	25.0	+2
% other	7.6	8.6	+1	8.4	8.0	0
	100%	100%		100%	100%	

* AB = upper-middle; C1 = lower-middle; C2 = upper-working; D = lower-working; E = dependants.

These findings about class and tenure hint at the possibility that the relationship between partisanship and turn-out changed between November and May—and that proves to be so. In November 1985 Conservative party identifiers declared a much stronger intention to vote than Labour party identifiers. (Alliance identifiers had an intermediate level of turn-out intentions, and those with no party identification expressed little inclination to vote.) But in the event, at the election in May 1986, the proportion of (November) Labour identifiers who voted was *higher* than the proportions of Conservative and Alliance identifiers who voted. Thus between November and May something happened to mobilize Labour identifiers into voting and thereby eliminate the anticipated partisan bias (Table 9.2).

It could be that this was the normal action of the British political system in which *party mobilization on the left* (through canvassing on council estates and other party activities) offsets the natural tendency of *higher status individuals* to turn out more. But in the period

Table 9.2. Turn-out bias and party support

PARTY IDENTIFICATION PROFILES

	All areas			Areas with Elections (May)		
	(Party identifiers in Nov.)			(Party identifiers in May)		
	All respondents	Intending voters (Nov.)	Bias	All respondents	Actual voters	Bias
Party identification:						
% Con.	32.8	38.0	+5	26.3	27.7	+1
% Lab.	34.6	32.0	−3	44.1	45.8	+2
% All.	17.9	20.0	+2	18.2	17.2	−1
% other/none	14.7	10.0	−5	11.4	9.3	−2
	100%	100%		100%	100%	

NATIONAL PARTY PREFERENCE PROFILES

	All areas			Areas with Elections (May)		
	(Preferences in Nov.)			(Preferences in May)		
	All respondents	Intending voters (Nov.)	Bias	All respondents	Actual voters	Bias
Party preference:						
% Con.	29.9	34.2	+4	25.7	25.0	−1
% Lab.	33.7	30.1	−4	39.8	41.2	+1
% All.	17.7	18.5	+1	19.5	19.9	0
% other/none	18.7	17.2	−1	15.0	13.9	−1
	100%	100%		100%	100%	

November 1985 to May 1986 there may also have been a period effect on mobilization. It was a bad six months for the Conservative Party in national politics. Two senior Cabinet Ministers resigned. The *Guardian's* running average of the last five national opinion polls taken before the end of each month gave Labour a 1 per cent lead over the Conservatives in November and none at all in December, but 5 per cent in January 1986 which widened to 7 per cent by May.

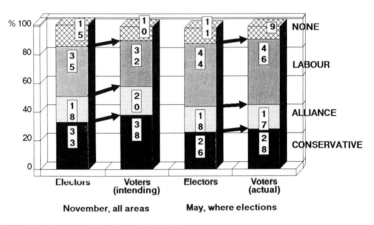

Fig. 9.3. Partisan bias (*see Table 9.2*)

Our panel reflected this trend with a general move away from the Conservatives and a decline in morale amongst those who remained: in November there were 24 per cent with a very or fairly strong Conservative identification and 26 per cent with a very or fairly strong Labour identification, but by May the Conservative figure had only edged up from 24 to 25 per cent while the Labour figure had increased from 26 to 30 per cent.

Amongst those who had in November expressed an intention to vote, 74 per cent of the Labour identifiers (i.e. 74 per cent of those who had identified with Labour *in November*) actually did go on to vote when the election came in May, but only 61 per cent of (November's) Conservative identifiers and 57 per cent of (November's) Alliance identifiers did so.

The net result of these discrepancies between intentions and behaviour was that while those who intended to vote in November were 5 per cent more Conservative and 3 per cent less Labour than the

Table 9.3. Changes in partisanship and morale, November 1985–May 1986

	Nov. 1985	May 1986	Change
% with Conservative identification			
very strongly held	8.8	8.5	−0.3
fairly strongly held	15.2	16.5	+1.3
not very strongly held	8.8	6.9	−1.9
don't know or n.a.	0	0	0
% with Labour identification			
very strongly held	11.0	12.6	+1.6
fairly strongly held	14.9	17.3	+2.4
not very strongly held	8.3	8.2	−0.1
don't know or n.a.	0.4	0	−0.4
% with Alliance identification (including Liberal or SDP)			
very strongly held	2.8	3.6	+0.8
fairly strongly held	9.6	9.8	+0.2
not very strongly held	5.5	5.0	−0.5
don't know or n.a.	0	0	0
% with other party identification	1.5	1.6	+0.1
% with no party identification	7.1	4.9	−2.2
% of 'don't know'	3.8	3.1	−0.7
% refused	2.4	1.9	−0.5
	100%	100%	100%

public as a whole, those who actually did vote in May were only one per cent more Conservative and 2 per cent more Labour than the public at large (in areas with elections). Thus in the event, the partisan bias caused by differential turn-out was negligible, though the partisan bias in turn-out intentions had been fairly substantial!

Finally let us look for ideological bias. We asked: 'In politics people often talk about *left* and *right*. Where would you put yourself on this (eleven-point) scale?' Then: 'Some people say we should have *tax cuts* even if that means we have to cut government and council services. Others say we should have *more services* even if that means more taxes. Where would you put yourself on this (eleven-point) scale?' With both questions a large number of people located themselves at the exact centre point of our eleven-point scales; so the simplest way to view the results is to divide each into three—the first into a left/centre/right scale, and the second into a more/same/less taxes-and-services scale (Table 9.4).

Table 9.4. Turn-out bias and ideology

	All Areas			Areas with Elections (May)		
	All respondents	Intending voters (Nov.)	Bias	All respondents	Actual voters	Bias
Left or right?						
% left	21.7	20.0	−2	20.6	18.8	−2
% centre	36.9	34.9	−2	37.8	39.9	+2
% right	33.3	39.1	+6	32.4	33.4	+1
% DK	7.7	5.8	−2	8.6	7.2	−1
	100%	100%		100%	100%	
	All Areas			Areas with Elections (May)		
	All respondents	Intending voters (Nov.)	Bias	All respondents	Actual voters	Bias
More or less tax:						
% more	45.7	46.1	0	46.3	48.8	+3
% same	28.1	27.3	−1	27.8	27.8	0
% cut	18.8	19.3	+1	17.2	15.3	−2
% DK	6.5	5.8	−1	7.3	6.2	−1
	100%	100%		100%	100%	

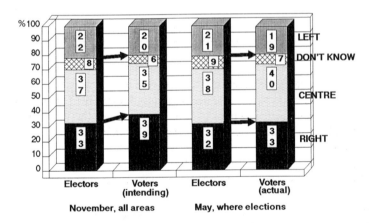

Fig. 9.4. Ideological bias (*see Table 9.4*)

As might be expected from our analysis of partisan bias the ideological bias changed from turn-out intentions in November 1985 to actual turn-out in May 1986. In November, those who intended to vote were 6 per cent more right-wing than the general public but by

May the actual voters were only one per cent more right-wing than the general public (in areas with elections). And the trend, at least, was the same with respect to the taxes-and-services scale: in November those who intended to vote were closely representative of the general public but by May the actual voters were 3 per cent biased in favour of more taxes.

Central government was especially worried about irresponsible non-ratepayers perverting the political process by voting themselves local services at someone else's expense. Ignoring for the moment the point that this possibility exists in any democracy, national or local, we can look for evidence of political hyperactivity amongst non-ratepayers leading to biased turn-out.

Alas for this simple but seductive rational-choice theory, there is no evidence to support it. There was virtually no bias either towards or against ratepayers in the subset of electors who intended to vote in November or who, when given the chance, actually did vote in May (Table 9.5).

Table 9.5. Turn-out bias and ratepaying

	All Areas			Areas with Elections (May)		
	All respondents	Intending voters (Nov.)	Bias	All respondents	Actual voters	Bias
Pay rates?						
% full	78	77	−1	77	78	+1
% some	11	12	+1	12	11	−1
% no	11	11	0	11	11	0
	100%	100%		100%	100%	

Conclusion

So does turn-out matter? Did the unrepresentativeness of those who turned out to vote lead to a serious misrepresentation of the general public? There was a clear, substantial, and stable under-representation of the young and over-representation of the middle-aged and old. But apart from that, the bias caused by differential turn-out was small. Moreover it was unstable. The apparent bias towards the middle class, the Conservative Party, and right-wing ideological attitudes that was visible in turn-out intentions in November disappeared at the actual election in May.

Perhaps we should include turn-out intention with psychological involvement and distinguish sharply between turn-out intention and turn-out behaviour, rather than between psychological involvement and turn-out questions. Mobilization factors can clearly intervene even at a very late stage in the causal chain, between turn-out intentions and turn-out behaviour.

Notes

1. R. E. Wolfinger and S. J. Rosenstone, *Who Votes?* (New Haven: Yale University Press, 1980), 111.
2. S. Verba and N. H. Nie, *Participation in America: Political Democracy and Social Equality* (New York: Harper and Row, 1972).
3. See L. W. Milbrath, *Political Participation* (Chicago: Rand McNally, 1965), on the United States. On British local government see W. H. Morris-Jones, 'In Defence of Apathy', *Political Studies* 2 (1954); or J. A. Griffiths, *From Policy to Administration* (London: Allen and Unwin, 1976).

Part III

Voter Choice in Local Elections

10 What Influences Choice? A Two-level Model

Until quite recently, doubts about the existence of effective local government policy autonomy have been accompanied by the certainty that local government elections are a judgement on central rather than local government.

National and Local Trends

A *Times* editorial described local elections as a 'kind of large but primitive public opinion poll on the popularity of the [Central] Government of the day'.[1] Newton described them as 'a sort of annual General Election' and added that the term 'local election . . . is something of a misnomer for there is very little that is local about them and they tell us practically nothing about the preferences and attitudes of citizens to purely local issues and events'.[2] Gyford notes that this traditional view of British local government elections has been prevalent since local government elections were introduced in the early nineteenth century and it is still probably the dominant view.[3] A recent issue of the *Economist* notes, 'academic evidence suggests that local factors have little influence on local elections'.[4] Fletcher noted the 'close conformity of local election behaviour to national political trends'.[5] Gregory, Johnson, NOP, Schofield, and Gyford have all pointed to what Schofield called the 'nationalisation of local politics'.[6]

Because there was a snap general election in 1979, local and central government elections took place simultaneously in much of England and Wales. Waller tabulates and compares the voting figures constituency by constituency.[7] In the boroughs especially the fit between party shares of the local and national votes is very close. Indeed the BBC and ITN used this close fit in order to construct 1979 base-line voting figures for the new parliamentary constituencies introduced in 1983.[8]

Alexander notes that 'because of the mid-term unpopularity of (central) governments, local elections invariably show major swings against the party in power nationally'.[9] He quotes the pro-Labour swing in 1973, the pro-Conservative swing in 1977, and emphasizes particularly the pro-Labour swing in the 1981 local elections 'at a time when the party was in considerably internal disarray'. In his view that confirms the 1981 local elections as a reaction against central government rather than as evidence of a successful Labour campaign on local issues. Similarly, Byrne claims that throughout the period 1965–79 local elections just prior to central government elections clearly forecast the parliamentary result.[10] Following Newton,[11] he charts the year-by-year swings in post-war local elections in Birmingham against the swings in national opinion polls. Judged visually, the fit is extremely close.

Events of the early 1980s confirm Byrne in his view that there is a close relationship between national and local trends. He points to a surge of SDP/Liberal Alliance support in the 1981 local elections which reflected the Alliance's entry into central government politics. The next year, the 'Falklands factor' was as apparent in the local government elections as in national opinion polls. Many of the trends and divergencies in local election results (Scotland and the north versus the south, for example) foreshadowed similar divergencies in the parliamentary general election and could thus be described as nationally orientated in terms of politics even if local in their geographical impact.

These studies can easily be over-interpreted however. Gregory, for example, presents a table which gives the percentage Labour vote in annual local elections in Reading 1945–67 and the party's Gallup poll rating in April and May of the corresponding years.[12] He draws attention to the tendency for the two series to vary together and calculates a statistically significant correlation of 0.63. But statistically significant only means that it is unlikely that the correlation is zero. And a correlation of 0.63 means that less than 40 per cent (0.63 × 0.63 × 100%) of the variation in Reading votes can be explained by variation in Gallup poll ratings. Correlations between variables based on aggregates are frequently high, unlike correlations based on survey data. The reasons for this are simple and technical. Thus a correlation of 0.63, which would be very impressive if derived from survey data on individuals, is not so impressive when derived from aggregate borough results.

Moreover the existence of a nation-wide trend does not preclude local variations around the average trend. The question of local versus national influences is not necessarily an either/or question; it can be both/and. National trends only explain a proportion of the variation in actual results.

Green used a more sophisticated statistical technique but unfortunately he, like Gregory and Newton, restricted his analysis to a small area—this time Sheffield and Leeds.[13] Using principal component analysis on the ward election results from 1951 to 1966 he concluded that 73 per cent of the variation in party support could be attributed to national factors, 6 per cent to city-wide factors, and 21 per cent to more local factors. However it should be noted that Green's 'national factor' was simply what Sheffield and Leeds had in common, which may or may not have been truly 'national'.

Butler and Stokes, in their series of national election surveys, asked about local election voting in 1963 and 1969. Their findings have been interpreted as supporting the 'nationalized' view of local government elections. They wrote:

One of the clearest evidences for the generalised nature of partisan dispositions in Britain comes from local government elections. In 1963 those who went to the polls in local elections that were fought on a party basis voted to an overwhelming degree in line with their expressed party self-image (party identification) . . . well over 90 per cent of our respondents stayed with their generalised tie to the national parties, though local elections might be thought to be fought on entirely special local issues. This dominant role of a more general partisan tie is entirely consistent with the evidence our sample gave of their lack of involvement in local issues. When we asked those who voted in the May 1963 elections whether there were any issues that had especially concerned them, four out of five said 'no' without hesitation; the remainder mentioned matters that were in fact more often the concern of Westminster than of the Town Hall.[14]

Perhaps the one caveat that should be mentioned is that Butler and Stokes's measure of party identification relates to generalized party attachment, not necessarily to specifically national party attachment, and it might have reflected local government influences to some degree. Our own question, which we put to the 1985–6 local election panel was different: it specifically asked respondents to think in terms of national politics when describing their sense of party identification.

The Impact of Rates

Newton prepared a short report for the Layfield Committee on 'the impact of rates on local elections'.[15] In his view 'the evidence, though not extensive, clearly indicates that rate changes have had a negligible effect on local (election) results'.

Only three studies had used any quantity of reliable statistical data to examine the relationship between rate changes and local election results. Hinckley had compared Coventry's variation from the average rate change and the average electoral swing over the period 1949–64.[16] He found no significant correlation. Newton himself had repeated the exercise for Birmingham over the period 1949–71 and again found no significant correlation.[17] Alt had analysed forty-four county boroughs over the years 1958–68 and found no correlation between competitiveness (i.e. marginality) and rate levels: 'if rate increases are a sensitive issue one might have expected to find lower rates in the consistently more competitive boroughs but this does not appear to be the case'.[18]

Case-studies suggested that rates had seldom been a major debating point in local politics.[19] Sample surveys had shown that few electors knew much about their local rate levels, or mentioned rates as an important local election issue, or contacted their local council members about any matter connected with rates, though councillors themselves were unwilling to discount the effects of rate increases on their own or their party's electoral prospects.[20]

However Newton concluded his report to the Layfield Committee by warning that local government was moving into a new era. In the decades prior to his report, rate increases had been small and had been matched or exceeded by increases in real income. He warned that large rate increases might produce an electoral response.

Local Influences

Newton may simply have missed or disregarded some of the contrary evidence. Gregory had noted that in 1957 an unusually sharp rise in the rates in Labour-controlled Reading coincided with a 3 per cent drop in Labour's share of the local vote, at a time when national Gallup polls were showing a 3 per cent rise and when Labour was gaining many seats in other local elections.[21] Budge et al. had shown that, in Glasgow, rates were the one issue on which electors claimed (and had!) accurate knowledge of the issue positions of their ward councillors.[22] Rees and Hampton had detected some local factors at work in local elections.[23]

But in any case, as Newton himself warned, his report to the

Layfield Committee was written when national and local political conditions were changing. Since then Brown *et al.*, Redcliffe-Maud and Wood, Ferry, Waller, and Bristow amongst others, have pointed to the effects of *local issues*.[24] Moreover, the influence of *local organization* and *local campaigning* on turn-out, which we discussed earlier, is relevant to party choice in so far as turn-out effects operate differentially to the advantage of one party or another. *Local influences* need not be synonymous with *local issues*. They include much more.

Increasing political volatility in opinion polls and by-elections had been noticed in the late 1960s. By 1974 increased political volatility was also evident in general elections, and the SSRC's sequence of election surveys showed a dramatic fall in the number of electors willing to describe themselves as strongly committed to a political party. Class divisions also declined sharply in the 1970s as middle- and working-class people became much less distinct in their voting choices. In short, people became less committed, less constrained, and more volatile in their voting behaviour. Thus the potential for a split between national political choices and local election voting increased.

The Rates Revolt of the 1970s

At the same time Britain entered an era of hyperinflation and rates no longer increased by small amounts. So rates increases became more visible and more likely to provoke controversy. Writers on local government frequently noted the relatively high visibility and unpopularity of rates compared with other taxes.[25]

Newton quoted his own survey of Birmingham councillors to suggest that even though there was no evidence of public reaction against rates increases in the 1950s and 1960s, councillors *felt* that rates rises could adversely affect them.[26] Gregory entitled his paper the 'rule of anticipated reactions' because he too, found that 'local issues and local controversies exerted very little influence on the municipal election results in Reading since the war' but local councillors 'overestimate their own salience in the eyes of the electorate' and 'try to anticipate popular reactions'.[27] Bruce and Lee now dispute Gregory's conclusions but their own 1978 data show that only half the councillors in Manchester, Salford, and Stockport thought that national factors alone determined the outcome of their local elections, though these councillors attributed more impact to *local candidates* than to *local issues*.[28]

Cowan found indirect evidence that councillors believe that rate decisions influence election results: in 1978 average rates increases in the 44 authorities with elections that year was less than half average rates increases in the 252 authorities with no elections that year.[29] Ferry did a longitudinal analysis of county and borough rates from 1950 to 1974: 'in each election year we see a reduced rate of increase, followed in the succeeding year by a steeper one, which restores the rate call to its longer-term trend'.[30]

Some evidence suggests these councillors were right to fear the possibility of reactions against unusually visible rates increases. Nugent, and King and Nugent discuss the so-called 'ratepayers' revolts' of the mid 1970s in Tyne and Wear, and in Wakefield.[31] Like Grant[32] and Dowse and Hughes,[33] King and Nugent find that 'sporadic interventionists', new to politics, go swiftly from initial enthusiasm and euphoria to disillusion and apathy. The ratepayers' organizations that flourished in 1975, when ratepayers faced dramatic increases, had lost most of their support by 1978. As direct influences on local politics they were 'relatively ineffective' and to maintain their existence they slowly transformed into environmental pressure groups concerned with pavements, speed limits, the quality of local life (and the value of houses!) rather than rates. However Nugent claimed that they did have a significant effect upon the 'general climate of political opinion'. Local politicians became more cost-conscious, grandiose building plans were abandoned, and national government increased its grants to local authorities in order to keep rates down. Politically, ratepayers' groups operated through demonstrations, petitions, and well-publicized questionnaires to major-party candidates, as well as by fielding candidates of their own. Consequently the influence of these ratepayer groups is difficult to measure and certainly goes far beyond the election of Ratepayers Association candidates.

The potential for a rates revolt was also shown when the Labour-controlled Coventry City Council held an 'advisory' referendum in which it asked voters whether they preferred higher rates or reduced services. In the summer of 1981 the Secretary of State for the Environment introduced a bill to require local authorities to hold a referendum before exceeding central government's spending guidelines. In the event the bill was dropped but while it was under consideration, Coventry held a voluntary referendum. On a 25 per cent turn-out the voters opposed further increases in the rates by a margin of seven to one.[34] Questions about public expenditure are notoriously sensitive to question wording, however. A more detailed set of questions put by MORI (Market and Opinion International) to a sample of Coventry electors in the week before the referendum showed that although there was broad support for general expenditure cuts there was massive opposition to cuts in education and social services, which together totalled 79 per cent of Coventry's budget.[35] So it would be wrong to assume that the low-rates, low-expenditure reflex would always prove reliable.

In an analysis of the London borough elections of 1978, Ferry finds that 'rates do seem to have influenced the results of those elections, at least in recent years'.[36] For the eighteen Labour councils especially there was a close correlation between that year's rate change and the number of seats won or lost. Wandsworth, Hammersmith, and Hillingdon increased rates sharply and lost seats heavily. Brent, Waltham Forest, and Newham held their rates steady and actually increased Labour's share of seats. Two years later the Wolverhampton result in the 1980 metropolitan district elections was regarded as something of a test-case. In Wolverhampton Labour raised the domestic rate by 56 per cent yet actually gained two seats. However that gain in seats reflected some accidental factors in particular wards and the overall swing in Wolverhampton votes since 1979 was 4 per cent against Labour in contrast to substantial pro-Labour swings in nearby Coventry, Sandwell, and Walsall.[37]

Bristow presents a more comprehensive analysis of the relationship between rates increases and election outcomes at the 1980 elections.[38] As part of its public expenditure reduction programme, central government refused to increase Rate Support Grant in line with inflation; so most local authorities had to raise rates or cut services. On average they raised rates by 22 per cent. Labour councils averaged a rates rise of 23 per cent and Conservative councils 21 per cent; so there was very little correlation between party control and rates rises.[39] In its analysis of these results the *Economist* claimed that 'it is hard to detect much difference between results in areas run by high-spending Labour councils from those in Tory ones; though there does appear to have been a lower (pro-Labour) swing in some extreme cases of profligacy (e.g. Newcastle, with the highest rate poundage in the country). And just a hint of a lower swing to Labour in richer (high ratepaying) wards, while the poorer wards voted Labour for public services.'[40] Bristow reanalyses these results in terms of rates *increases* rather than rates *levels* but comes to the same conclusion. Indeed, because the swing to Labour was stronger in already Labour areas (which increased rates somewhat more) the slight correlation between pro-Labour swings and rates increases was positive ($r = +0.17$). However Labour did suffer an adverse swing in Liverpool and Wolverhampton in both of which rates had increased by over 50 per cent.

Bristow also analyses the Wolverhampton result in some detail, using ward level votes and census data, plus a sample survey of 249 voters in the Oxley ward. Labour increased its support in the poorer, working-class wards and lost support in the more affluent, middle-class wards. The Oxley ward vote split 43 per cent Conservative, 30 per cent Labour, and 22 per cent ratepayer. Obviously the results of the sample survey represent Oxley rather than Wolverhampton as a whole, still less the nation as a whole. However they do show a striking awareness of the local rates issue.

When asked what was the most important issue in the election, three-quarters cited the rates increase—92 per cent of ratepayer voters and 87 per cent of Conservative voters cited the rates issue, though only 40 per cent of Labour voters did so. By comparison, Bruce and Lee found that only 14 per cent of respondents to their survey of Manchester, Salford, and Stockport in 1978 listed rates as an important issue.[41] Knowledge of the size of the rates increase was also high in Wolverhampton, however. When asked whether it was closest to a 10, 25, 50, or a 100 per cent rise, 89 per cent of Conservatives, 86 per cent of ratepayers, and even 70 per cent of Labour voters picked the correct answer. Overall 84 per cent of those who cited rates as the most important issue were also able to specify the correct size of the increase.

Bristow concludes that 'it could not be maintained that the electors were unaware of the issue before them'. 'The Wolverhampton evidence confirms the importance to local politics of local campaigns on issues directly relevant to the locality.' He attributes the swing against Labour in Wolverhampton, which ran against the national trend, to the 'salience of the peculiarly high rate increase [which] benefited the Conservative party at a time when it was suffering setbacks elsewhere'.

Adverse swings, however, do not automatically penalize a party under our first-past-the-post system.[42] The Conservatives not only enjoyed a favourable swing, they won 48 per cent of the Wolverhampton vote as against Labour's 41 per cent. But the Labour Party still took a majority of the seats on the council. In part at least this was because the pro-Conservative swing was accompanied by a class polarization of the vote: the Conservatives piled up extra votes in their already safe middle-class strongholds and did not win extra seats.

Wherever an issue polarizes classes or other residential groupings, it is likely to have a large effect on individuals but a small effect upon the number of seats won. Moreover, although this does not apply to a marginal borough like Wolverhampton, even a large effect upon council seats may not affect party control of the council because some areas are so socially homogeneous that Labour is unlikely ever to win them (if homogeneously middle-class) or lose them (if homogeneously working-class). One party on the council has an effectively permanent majority.[43]

However parties may be sensitive to variations in the size of their majority. Certainly individual councillors are unlikely to welcome losing their seats, whether or not the party majority on the council survives.

In 1982 an outstanding feature of local election results in Scotland was the so-called 'Lothian effect'.[44] Turn-out increased in Lothian, whereas it decreased in Scotland as a whole. Secondly, the SDP/Liberal Alliance recorded an above-average share of the vote in Lothian, and the Conservatives recorded a below-average decline. So Labour suffered a setback in Lothian while making advances elsewhere. Lothian had imposed a large rates increase, but perhaps more important it had engaged in a highly publicized fight with the Secretary of State for Scotland about levels of expenditure and rates.[45] Unlike Labour in Wolverhampton, Labour in Lothian lost control of the region as a result of the 1982 election.

National Opinion Polls have reported a number of special local election surveys.[46] In the 1982 London Boroughs survey they asked: 'why will you vote for (chosen party)?' Most respondents gave fairly general answers like 'they've got the best policies'. Only 3 per cent of all voters (7 per cent of Conservatives, however) spontaneously mentioned 'keeping the rates down'. But when asked about the 'important issues in deciding your vote', local issues were much more prominent: 56 per cent mentioned only local issues. 27 per cent mentioned both local and national, while 13 per cent mentioned national issues exclusively. The most frequently mentioned single issue was rates, quoted by 35 per cent of all voters. These findings flagrantly contradict the findings of Butler and Stokes on local issue salience which were quoted earlier. The difference probably reflects both methodological differences and a change in the political context since the 1960s.

In 1984, NOP put local government questions to a nation-wide sample. Rates were 'not at the front of many people's minds' in the sense that, when asked for 'any particular complaints' about the local council, half said they had none, and only 6 per cent spontaneously mentioned rates (though 10 per cent did so in Labour-controlled areas).[47] However, when asked 'how concerned are you about the level of rates in your areas?' 50 per cent said 'very concerned'—46 per cent in Conservative-controlled areas and 57 per cent in Labour-controlled areas. When asked whether 'over the last four years do you think the increase in local rates has been reasonable or unreasonable?' 12 per cent did not know, while the rest divided right down the middle—44 per cent opted for 'reasonable' and 44 per cent for 'unreasonable'. There was little difference between Conservative and Labour partisans, but a large difference between those who lived in Labour and Conservative-controlled areas—34 per cent said 'reasonable' in Labour-controlled areas, while 50 per cent said 'reasonable' in Conservative-controlled areas.

By a narrow majority of 47 per cent to 43 per cent, respondents rejected the idea that central government should stay out of local financial affairs; and by a much larger majority of 58 per cent to 34 per cent they approved statutory rate-capping. On both these questions there was a huge difference of opinion (presumably motivated by party identification) between Labour and Conservative partisans. By 2 to 1, Conservatives approved central government intervention, while by a similar 2 to 1 margin, Labour partisans rejected central government intervention. Alliance supporters were equally divided between support and opposition.

Rates were the most prominent local issue in the 1970s. But local issues include more than rates, and local influences on voting include more than local issues—local candidates, local party organization and campaigning, local scandals are all likely to have an impact on the result without being 'issues' in the strict sense. Bruce and Lee's survey in Manchester, Salford, and Stockport asked respondents what would be the major issues in their minds when they decided how to vote in the 1978 local election. The top four items mentioned by respondents were (in order): partisan loyalty, housing, rates, education. The local candidate, the performance of national government, inflation, and law and order tied for fifth place. Only a tenth of respondents failed to name some concern. For their sample, important items were clearly not restricted to national politics, and local concerns were not restricted to the rates.

National Trends and Local Variations

Once again a comparison with studies of American congressional voting is illuminating. In the last decade or so, American academics have begun intensive, survey-based studies of congressional (as opposed to presidential) voting. An excellent summary of the relevant literature is given by Gary Jacobson.[48] There is a paradox to congressional voting patterns that may be of some relevance to our understanding of British local government elections. Just as the traditional assumption about British local government elections has been that they reflect central government popularity, so in the United States the traditional assumption about congressional elections was that they reflected the personal and party popularity of the incumbent President. Just as the Westminster governing party loses ground at mid-term local elections, so the President's party typically loses ground at mid-term congressional elections. Tufte showed that voting in congressional elections was strongly and systematically related to simple measures of the economy and presidential popularity.[49]

Unfortunately, direct survey studies of congressional voting show that the voters in congressional elections focus very strongly on local concerns rather than national, on the local Congressman and his challenger rather than on the President. And they split their tickets to an increasing degree; so that individuals and even districts do not vote the same way for both President and Congressman.

Here is the paradox: direct survey evidence shows that voters in congressional elections vote largely on their knowledge and evalution of the particular pair of candidates in the locality yet in aggregate their votes appear to follow clear and easily predictable national trends. Jacobson solves the puzzle by arguing that potentially strong challengers are so influenced by their belief in national trends that they are reluctant to fight congressional elections for the President's party when the President is unpopular. This 'party-morale' or 'candidate-morale' effect then affects the congressional election outcome.

It is highly unlikely that British voters in a local government election are anywhere near as locally orientated as American voters in a congressional election, despite the fact that British local government is a local institution and the American Congress is a national institution! However, the American paradox does make it clear that national uniformities and trends in the aggregate of local election results may conceal a substantial degree of locally orientated motivations. Party morale, if not challenger morale, may well vary with the popularity of central government and, given the known effect of canvassing and campaigning in low turn-out elections, may have a substantial effect on outcomes. What we cannot do, is infer motivations from aggregate patterns and trends. And if we do not understand motivations we cannot understand the true constraints and dynamics of local election voting.

Simultaneous local and central government elections in 1979 provide some evidence of split-ticket voting in Britain. While split-ticket voting seems to have been limited in urban areas, in the more rural areas it was substantial, both between local and central voting and between local candidates on the same party ticket: 'it was not unusual for a candidate to poll over twice the vote of a ward running mate'.[50] There was an almost invariable tendency for Liberals to poll better in local contests than in the parliamentary election. In Liverpool the Liberals won 28 per cent of the local government vote but only 14 per cent of the central government vote. While Liverpool was an extreme case, in many other places the Liberal vote was significantly higher in the local election than in the parliamentary. Cox and Laver present an intensive analysis of the difference between local and national results in Liverpool.[51]

Jones and Stewart describe as a fallacy the notion that local government elections are solely determined by the popularity of national government.[52] They accept that national government popularity has a 'dominant effect upon local elections' but maintain that local factors have additional effects, overlaid on the national trends. Many analyses of local elections, in their view, detect only national factors simply because they only look for national factors. 'Forms of explanation (that stress) north–south divides or the level of unemployment' or the 'Falklands factor' are valid and do reveal genuine national influences but they suppress, by averaging out, the variety of local effects that are also operating: 'Because analysis is directed at finding uniformities, local variation goes unrecorded. But since the mid-1970s local factors increasingly influence the results.' Nationally orientated media commentators only recognize this development when complaining about 'unevenness' in the results. Jones and Stewart ask why Tameside swung to Labour against the tide in 1978, why the Liberals consistently do better in local than in national contests, why Labour made gains at the 1982 elections in Wolverhampton, Barnsley, Oldham, and Strathclyde, but lost ground at the same time in nearby areas like Walsall, Bradford, Leeds, Rochdale, and Lothian. 'The salutary lesson is that local elections can matter and that the actions of a local authority can affect the election even when a Falklands factor is at work.'

However, Jones and Stewart rightly warn against substituting one nationally orientated explanation for another: it is clearly not the case that the public everywhere simply reacted against left-wing or right-wing policies. Some left-wing councils did much better than others in the elections either because the electorate reacted to non-policy characteristics like style, presentation, or personality, or because different electorates wished to make different policy choices. Thus Jones and Stewart document the variations in electoral response without presenting any data on the electors' motivations.[53] Similarly Laver attributes the Liberals' local government strength in Liverpool to their representation of a particular social group—the residents in ageing, poor-quality, private housing, rather than to specific policy reactions.[54]

Conclusion

The literature suggests:

(1) There is a lot of variation round and about the overall national trend which reflects different local influences in different localities. The national trend in the aggregate of local govern-ment election results only emerges when these local variations are suppressed by a process of 'averaging out'.

(2) As the American congressional studies show, a national trend in the aggregate can be consistent with almost exclusively local orientations amongst the voters—however paradoxical that sounds on first hearing.

(3) The so-called national trend may be in part a public response to what is perceived to be happening in local government up and down the land. In the early 1980s Ken Livingstone (leader of the London GLC) was probably much better known than most

shadow cabinet members—both inside London and outside London. Similarly those who could not name the deputy leader of the Labour Party (Hattersley) may well have been able to name the deputy leader of Liverpool Council (Hatton—widely portrayed in the media as a leading Militant and left-wing extremist.)

(4) Rates rises are only likely to be salient when they are unusually high—that is higher than in the past or higher than in other places. Moreover local government voters' reactions to rates increases are likely to be affected by media debates and may be a response to rates increases in places other than their own locality, or to increases in the rates levied by a different level of local government in the same locality. One local authority's image may be affected by another local authority's performance.

(5) Although voters will generally choose a cut in services rather than a rise in rates, when they are confronted with specific cuts in the big-spending services then they tend to favour the maintenance of those services.

(6) But it would be totally wrong to equate local variations in local government election results with reactions to rates policy or even with reactions to local government policy outputs generally. Variations in style and presentation, variations in local media coverage, variations in the personal qualities of candidates or the campaigning efficiency of organizations can all affect the result. Scandals and corruption amongst councillors, especially if they become public just prior to an election may have a large but non-policy-based impact, for example.

A Model of Local Election Choice

Before we go on to look at the evidence in our survey it will be helpful to sketch out a model which gives an overview of the factors influencing voters' choices in local elections.

The literature suggests that local election choice will to a large extent reflect underlying partisanship or current reactions to the (central) government of the day.[55]

But overlaid on these national influences and trends will be other, local influences—some reflecting local policy outputs, some reflecting local policy debates, some reflecting the influence of local personalities, local scandals, local organization.[56] As Britain has emerged from the period of hyperinflation the visibility and impact of rates rises are likely to be less significant now than a decade ago.

The structure of this model is shown in the diagram: party identification is influenced by both long- and short-term national influences; national voting preferences reflect both party identification and short-term reactions; local voting choices reflect national influences from party identification, national voting intention, and short-term reactions to (central) government; but local voting choices also reflect local influences.

Although this model has a relatively simple form, it would be extremely difficult to test it by incorporating specific measures of local influences. We should need measures of the policy outputs of each particular local authority, measures of the visibility and popularity of thousands of local politicians, and measures of media coverage (primarily local media coverage) of the special issues in each particular locality. Our panel survey cannot provide these requirements.

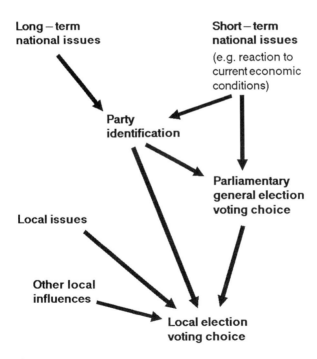

Fig. 10.1. A model of local election voting choice

Fortunately we can test the model in a much easier way by looking at the influence of the national factors in the model. If, for example, local electors vote entirely in accordance with their national party identification then we hardly need any measures of local factors which might influence local voting choice since there would be no scope for them to exert influence. By quantifying the extent of national influence on local election choice, we do at least set limits to the possible influence of local factors.

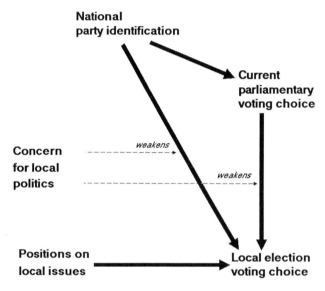

Fig. 10.2. A revised model of local election choice

When we looked at turn-out patterns in local elections we used a number of survey-based measures of local interest and concern to predict turn-out rates. We can incorporate similar measures into our analysis of local voting choice. However, they enter the model in a more complex fashion, as interactive rather than *additive* influences. We do not suppose that local concerns will influence voters towards or against particular parties throughout the nation. Instead, we postulate that those voters with more local concerns will be more willing to cast local election votes which are *out of line with their national party identification* and out of line with their national voting preference.

So the effect of a concern for local politics could not be represented in the model by an arrow pointing towards voting choice. Instead it could be represented by an arrow pointing at other arrows, since it affects *relationships not variables*. Diagrammatically, therefore, our revised model of local voting choice has the structure shown in Figure 10.2: the greater the concern for local politics, the weaker the influence of national factors on local election choices.

Notes

1. Leading Article, *The Times*, 5 May 1980.
2. K. Newton, *Second City Politics* (Oxford: Oxford University Press, 1976), 16.
3. J. Gyford, *Local Politics in Britain* (London: Croom Helm, 1976), 128.
4. 'Local Government', *Economist*, 16 Mar. 1985, 38–40.
5. P. Fletcher, 'The Results Analysed' in L. J. Sharpe (ed.), *Voting in Cities: the 1964 Borough Elections* (London: Macmillan, 1967).
6. R. Gregory, 'Local Elections and the Rule of Anticipated Reactions', *Political Studies* 17 (1969), 31–47; R. W. Johnson, 'The Nationalisation of English Rural Politics. Norfolk Southwest 1945–70', *Parliamentary Affairs* 26 (1972), 8–55; NOP, 'GLC Elections', *National Opinion Polls Bulletin* April 1973; M. I. Schofield, 'The Nationalisation of Local Politics', *New Society*, 28 Apr. 1977; J. Gyford, 'Political Parties and Central Local Relations' in G. Jones (ed.), *New Approaches to the Study of Central–Local Government Relationships* (Farnborough: Gower Press, 1980).
7. R. Waller, 'The 1979 Local and General Elections in England and Wales: Is There a Local/National Differential?', *Political Studies* 28 (1980), 443–50.
8. *BBC/ITN Guide to the New Parliamentary Constituencies* (Chichester: Parliamentary Research Services, 1983).
9. A. Alexander, *The Politics of Local Government in the United Kingdom* (London: Longmans, 1982).
10. T. Byrne, *Local Government in Britain* (Harmondsworth: Penguin, 1983).
11. K. Newton, *Second City Politics* (Oxford: Oxford University Press, 1976).
12. R. Gregory, 'Local Elections and the Rule of Anticipated Reactions', *Political Studies* 17 (1969), 31–47.
13. G. Green, 'National City and Ward Components of Local Voting', *Policy and Politics* 1 (1972), 45–54.
14. D. Butler and D. Stokes, *Political Change in Britain* (London: Macmillan, 1974), 40–1.
15. K. Newton, 'The Impact of Rates on Local Elections' in *Local Government Finance: Report of the Committee of Inquiry, Cmnd. 6453*, Appendix 6, (London: HMSO, 1976), 98–101.
16. D. Hinckley, 'Factors Influencing Local Government Elections' in P.

Spencer (ed.), *The Political Structure of Local Government in Coventry* (Coventry: Institute for Operational Research, 1966).

17. K. Newton, *Second City Politics* (Oxford: Oxford University Press, 1976).

18. J. Alt, 'Some Social and Political Correlates of County Borough Expenditures', *British Journal of Political Science* 1 (1971), 54.

19. F. Bealey, J. Blondel, and W. P. McCann, *Constituency Politics: A Study of Newcastle-under-Lyme* (London: Faber, 1965); A. H. Birch *et al.*, *Small Town Politics: A Study of Political Life in Glossop* (Oxford: Oxford University Press, 1959); J. G. Bulpitt, *Party Politics in English Local Government* (London: Longmans, 1967); J. Dearlove, *The Politics of Policy in Local Government* (Cambridge: Cambridge University Press, 1973); W. Hampton, *Democracy and Community: A Study of Politics in Sheffield* (Oxford: Oxford University Press, 1970); G. W. Jones, *Borough Politics: A Study of the Wolverhampton Borough Council 1888–1964* (London: Macmillan, 1969); L. J. Sharpe, *A Metropolis Votes* (London: London School of Economics, 1962); L. J. Sharpe (ed.), *Voting in Cities: the 1964 Borough Elections* (London: Macmillan, 1967).

20. F. Bealey, J. Blondel, and W. P. McCann, *Constituency Politics: A Study of Newcastle-under-Lyme* (London: Faber, 1965); W. Hampton, *Democracy and Community: A Study of Politics in Sheffield* (Oxford: Oxford University Press, 1970); *Report of Committee on the Management of Local Government. Vol. 3: The Local Government Elector* by Mary Horton (London: HMSO for Ministry of Housing and Local Government, 1967).

21. R. Gregory, 'Local Elections and the Rule of Anticipated Reactions', *Political Studies* 17 (1969), 45.

22. I. Budge, J. A. Brand, M. Margolis, and A. L. M. Smith, *Political Stratification and Democracy* (London: Macmillan, 1972).

23. A. Rees, 'West Hartlepool' in L. J. Sharpe (ed.), *Voting in Cities: the 1964 Borough Elections* (London: Macmillan, 1967); W. Hampton, *Democracy and Community: A Study of Politics in Sheffield* (Oxford: Oxford University Press, 1970).

24. T. Brown, M. J. C. Vile, and M. F. Whitemore, 'Community Studies and Decision Taking', *British Journal of Political Science* 2 (1972), 133–53; Lord Redcliffe-Maud and B. Wood, *English Local Government Reformed* (Oxford: Oxford University Press, 1974); J. Ferry, 'Rates and Elections', *Centre for Environmental Studies Review* 5 (1979), 5–7; R. Waller, 'The 1979 Local and General Elections in England and Wales: Is There a Local/National Differential?', *Political Studies* 28 (1980), 443–50; S. L. Bristow, 'Rates and Votes: The 1980 District Council Elections', *Policy and Politics* 10 (1982), 163–80.

25. See for example, J. Stanyer, *Understanding Local Government* (London: Fontana, 1976); P. G. Richards, *The Reformed Local Government System* (London: Allen and Unwin, 1980); B. Keith-Lucas and P. G. Richards,

A History of Local Government in the Twentieth Century (London: Allen and Unwin, 1978).

26. K. Newton, 'The Impact of Rates on Local Elections' in *Local Government Finance: Report of the Committee of Inquiry, Cmnd 6453*, Appendix 6, (London: HMSO, 1976), 98–101.

27. R. Gregory, 'Local Elections and the Rule of Anticipated Reactions', *Political Studies* 17 (1969), 31–47.

28. A. Bruce and G. Lee, 'Local Election Campaigns', *Political Studies* 30 (1982), 247–61.

29. M. Cowan, 'The Old Election-year Phobia: But do the Rates Matter?', *Municipal Journal*, June 1978, 562.

30. J. Ferry, 'Politics and the Rates', *Centre for Environmental Studies Review* 4 (1978), 57.

31. See R. King and N. Nugent, 'Ratepayers Associations in Newcastle and Wakefield' in J. Garrard, D. Jary, M. Goldsmith, and A. Oldfield (eds.), *The Middle Class in Politics* (Farnborough: Saxon House, 1978); and N. Nugent, 'The Ratepayers' in R. King and N. Nugent (eds.), *Respectable Rebels: Middle-class Campaigns in Britain in the 1970s* (London: Hodder and Stoughton, 1979). For another, generally less useful study of local government elections in the mid 1970s, see D. M. Clarke, *Battle for the Counties* (Newcastle upon Tyne: Redrose, 1977).

32. W. Grant, *Independent Local Politics in England and Wales* (London: Saxon House, 1978).

33. R. E. Dowse and J. A. Hughes, 'Sporadic Interventionists', *Political Studies* 25 (1977), 84–92.

34. A. Alexander, *The Politics of Local Government in the United Kingdom* (London: Longmans, 1982).

35. C. Game, 'Budget-making by Opinion Poll: Must Services Always Suffer?', *Local Government Studies* 8 (1982), 11–18.

36. J. Ferry, 'Rates and Elections', *Centre for Environmental Studies Review* 5 (1979), 5–7.

37. C. Game, 'Local Elections', *Local Government Studies* 7 (1981), 63–8.

38. S. L. Bristow, 'Rates and Votes: The 1980 District Council Elections', *Policy and Politics* 10 (1982), 163–80.

39. Ibid. 164.

40. 'Swing Low', *Economist*, 10 May 1980, 44.

41. A. Bruce and G. Lee, 'Local Election Campaigns', *Political Studies* 30 (1982), 247–61.

42. V. Bogdanor, 'Why the Local Election System Makes Us Appear More Divided', *The Times*, 19 May 1980; V. Bogdanor, 'It's Time to End Town Hall Caucus Rule', *Guardian*, 17 Nov. 1980.

43. See J. G. Bulpitt, *Party Politics in English Local Government* (London: Longmans, 1967), for a development of this argument.

44. J. M. Bochel and D. T. Denver, *Scottish Regional Elections 1982* (Dundee: University of Dundee, 1982).

45. A. Midwinter, M. Keating, and P. Taylor, 'Excessive and Unreasonable: The Politics of the Scottish Hit List', *Political Studies* 31 (1983), 394–417.

46. NOP, 'GLC Elections' *National Opinion Polls Bulletin*, Apr. 1973; NOP, 'London Borough Elections', *Political Social Economic Review* 37 (1982), 5–10; NOP, 'Local Government', *Political Social Economic Review* 47 (1984), 7–12.

47. NOP, 'Local Government', *Political Social Economic Review* 47 (1984), 8.

48. G. C. Jacobson, *The Politics of Congressional Elections* (Boston: Little Brown, 1983).

49. E. R. Tufte, *Political Control of the Economy* (Princeton: Princeton University Press, 1978).

50. R. Waller, 'The 1979 Local and General Elections in England and Wales': Is There a Local/National Differential?', *Political Studies* 28 (1980), 443–50.

51. W. H. Cox and M. Laver, 'Local and National Voting in Britain', *Parliamentary Affairs* 32 (1979), 383–93.

52. G. Jones and J. Stewart, *The Case for Local Government* (London: Allen and Unwin, 1983).

53. Ibid. See also G. Jones, 'Varieties of Local Politics', *Local Government Studies*, Apr. 1975; G. Jones and J. Stewart, 'The Local Factor in a Local Election', *Local Government Chronicle*, 18 June, 1982.

54. M. Laver, 'Are the Liverpool Liberals Really Different? A Path Analytic Interpretation of Local Voting in Liverpool 1973–82', *British Journal of Political Science* 14 (1984), 243–8.

55. On the first point see the references already made to D. Butler and D. Stokes, *Political Change in Britain* (London: Macmillan, 1974); and on the second, see the references made to T. Byrne, *Local Government in Britain* (Harmondsworth: Penguin, 1983).

56. See the references made earlier to G. Jones and J. Stewart, *The Case for Local Government* (London: Allen and Unwin, 1983).

11 National and Local Influences on Choice in Local Elections

The principal question we seek to answer in this chapter is whether local voting choice simply reflects national (i.e. parliamentary) voting choice. If national party identification or general election voting preferences perfectly predict local preferences then there is no sense in which local elections can be local. On the other hand, if these indicators of national electoral choice do not completely predict local choice then there is at least the possibility that local influences affect local choice: *either* some of our local issue variables may help to predict local voting choice, *or* local voting choice may be so unpredictable that we are led to speculate on the influence of local personalities and local party organizations, or local issues peculiar to specific localities.

A Format for Analysis

The model of local electoral choice which we developed at the end of Chapter 10 can be investigated by regression methods similar to those we used in our study of turn-out patterns.

Care is needed, however, in defining the partisan and voting choice variables for these regression analyses. For turn-out analyses we used a single-dimensional measure of whether people voted or not. But choice is more multidimensional: even if we simplify the analysis by neglecting the possibilities of voting for Independents, Scottish and Welsh Nationalists, and the multitude of 'other' candidates we are still left with a three-way choice between Conservative, Labour, and Alliance. Logically, we need *two variables* to describe a *three-way choice*.

We need only two, because in a three-way choice situation knowledge of whether or not a person voted Conservative, plus a knowledge of whether or not they voted Labour, automatically guarantees that we can deduce whether or not they voted Alliance (if they did vote Conservative or Labour they *could not possibly* have voted Alliance; if they voted neither Conservative or Labour then in a three-way choice situation they *must necessarily* have voted Alliance). The presence of Independent, Nationalist, and other candidates makes things a little less logically tidy but is not sufficiently troublesome to warrant a more complex analysis. We could use voting for any two of the three parties as our measures of three-way choice. Instead, we use one measure of the choice between the old class-based parties and a second measure of support for the third party challenge to the old two-party system. This approach is logically equivalent to working with two single-party voting measures but the results are easier to interpret.

First we define a *Labour versus Conservative* choice, LABCON, scoring respondents who choose Labour as plus 1, those who choose Conservative as minus 1, and all others as zero. Second we define an *Alliance versus the rest* choice, ALLIANCE, scoring respondents who choose the Liberal/SDP Alliance as plus 1, and all others as zero. This scoring system for LABCON and ALLIANCE can be applied to party identification, to voting preferences in hypothetical national or local elections held 'tomorrow', and to actual voting choice in real elections.

Our format of analysis consists of three stages. At each stage we predict local election voting choices. At the first stage we use seven ideological, issue, or social variables to predict local choice. At the second, we use these seven predictors plus the respondent's sense of party identification. At the third, we predict local voting choice from a combination of the original seven predictors, plus party identification plus current national party preference.

The seven predictors we use at the first stage of the analysis include two measures of general ideological position, LEFT/RIGHT and LIBERTARIAN, and one measure of social class position, WCLASS, all three of which can be considered essentially national influences. We also include a measure of attitudes towards local rates, POLLTAX, and local financial responsibility, GBLAME, which have a clearly local orientation. The remaining two predictors have both local and national overtones: house tenure, CTENURE, and attitudes towards tax versus service cuts, TAXCUT. Precise definitions of these variables are given in Table 11.1.

Local election preferences in November were simple enough to measure, even if they were hypothetical. Respondents were asked who they would vote for in a local council election (held 'tomorrow'); if they were undecided or refused they were asked for which party they were *most inclined* to vote. Answers to these two questions were combined to give a single local election preference in November.

Table 11.1. Definitions of the predictors of local voting choice

LEFT/RIGHT: Coded + 1 if respondent located him/herself on the right of our 11 point right/left scale; coded − 1 if on the left; coded zero if the respondent chose the exact centre point (many did!).

LIBERTARIAN: This is based upon the question pioneered by Inglehart in his studies of post-materialism. Respondents were asked to pick two priorities from: (1) maintaining order; (2) giving people more say; (3) fighting rising prices; (4) freedom of speech. Those who picked options 2 and 4 were coded + 1 (i.e. libertarians); those who picked options 1 and 3 were coded − 1 (i.e. authoritarians); the rest were coded zero.

WCLASS: Coded + 1 if in class C2D (i.e. head of household in (or retired from) manual occupation—working-class); coded zero if in class ABC1 (i.e. head of household in non-manual occupation—middle-class); those in class E, pure state dependants, excluded.

POLLTAX: Coded + 1 if respondent favours the newly proposed residents' tax (also called 'community charge' or 'poll tax') and zero if respondent favours retention of existing system of local rates.

GBLAME: Coded + 1 if respondent blames central government for local financial difficulties; coded zero if he or she blames local councils; those with other views excluded. (Note: this variable was measured twice, in Nov. and May. In regressions the appropriate version is used when predicting local electoral choice in Nov. and May.)

CTENURE: Coded + 1 if respondent lives in a council house; coded zero if in owner-occupied household; others excluded.

TAXCUT: Coded + 1 if respondent located him/herself on the 'cut taxes and services' side of our 11 point tax versus services scale; coded − 1 if on the 'more taxes and services' side; coded zero if the respondent chose the exact centre point (many did!).

In May the situation was more complex. In many parts of the country there were local elections, but in other parts there were not. In central London there were two simultaneous local elections—for the ILEA as well as local councils. Since we have few respondents from inner London, we neglect the ILEA elections. Throughout Britain, we take the local council vote of those who voted and the local election preference of those who did not vote—whether they lived in areas with elections or not. For each person, this gives a single measure of local election choice in May, but we shall sometimes distinguish three kinds of respondents:

(1) the *voters* who actually did vote;
(2) the *abstainers* who had had the opportunity to vote but somehow did not actually manage to do so; and

Table 11.2. Local election preferences (or votes) in November and May

	Con.	Lab.	All.	Ind.	Other	Would not vote	Undecided/ refused	
% of all respondents in:								
November	29	32	21	3	2	4	10	100%
May	28	36	21	3	2	2	7	100%
% of respondents in May who:								
voted	27	46	20	1	2	0	5	100%
abstained	23	41	18	1	1	5	11	100%
lived in areas without elections	33	26	25	7	3	2	6	100%

Note: Because of rounding, figures may not sum to exactly 100% in each row.

(3) those who lived in areas with *no elections* and could not have voted even if they had had the inclination and energy to do so.

Table 11.2 shows local election voting preferences (or votes) in November and May, and also shows how party choice varied between voters, abstainers, and those who lived in areas with no elections.

Between November and May our panel reflected the trends shown in other opinion polls and swung towards Labour. In addition there was a 5 per cent reduction in the number who declared that they 'would not vote' or would not state a party preference.

Our distinction between voters, abstainers, and those in non-election areas shows very marked differences in party preferences for local elections in May. We need to emphasize that most of the abstainers were willing to give a preference: only 5 per cent of them firmly declared that they would not vote, and only 11 per cent were undecided or refused to reveal their party choice. That compares with 5 per cent of voters who would not reveal for whom they had voted. Thus the abstainers had, overall, 11 per cent less party preferences of any kind than the voters, but that is a relatively small difference between voters and abstainers and it is the only difference between them—Conservative, Labour, and Alliance preferences were all lower amongst abstainers, but relative support for the parties was much the same amongst voters and abstainers.

Patterns of Local Voting Choice: A Multivariate Analysis

However there was a very large difference between the local election preferences of voters and abstainers on the one hand and those in non-election areas on the other. Quite simply elections were held in areas where Labour was relatively strong and the Conservatives and Independents relatively weak.

Excluding all those who for one reason or another had no party preference in local elections we can look at how preferences in May varied between voters, abstainers, and those in non-election areas; and also at how they correlated with our predictor variables (Table 11.3).

There are no strong connections between any of our predictors and Alliance voting, though modest patterns show that the Alliance had more support in the centre of the left/right scale; at the libertarian end

Table 11.3. Local election choice of all those with preferences (or votes) in May

	% choosing: Con.	Lab.	All.	Ind./other	
All respondents	31	40	23	6	100%
Voter types:					
Voters	29	48	21	3	100%
Abstainers	27	48	22	3	100%
Those in non-election areas	35	28	27	11	100%
Nationally orientated predictors:					
LEFT:					
Left	6	68	20	6	100%
Centre	24	41	27	7	100%
Right	55	20	21	4	100%
LIBERTARIAN:					
Libertarian	8	52	26	14	100%
Mixed	33	39	24	5	100%
Authoritarian	36	39	20	5	100%
WCLASS:					
Working class	19	53	22	6	100%
Middle class	43	24	27	6	100%
Locally orientated predictors:					
POLLTAX:					
Favour poll tax	41	29	26	5	100%
Favour rates	20	49	24	7	100%
GBLAME:					
Blame central government	16	55	23	6	100%
Blame local councils	54	19	23	4	100%
Ambiguous national/local predictors:					
CTENURE:					
Council tenant	11	70	16	3	100%
House-owner	36	33	25	6	100%
TAXCUT:					
Cut taxes and services	41	35	20	4	100%
Neither	32	38	23	7	100%
More taxes and services	26	44	24	6	100%

Note: Because of rounding, figures may not sum to exactly 100% in each row.

of the libertarian/authoritarian scale; amongst the middle class; amongst owner-occupiers; and amongst those who wanted to increase taxes and services.

Much stronger patterns show that Labour had most support and the Conservatives had least at the left end of the left/right scale; at the libertarian end of the libertarian/authoritarian scale; in the working class; amongst those who favoured rates rather than a poll tax; amongst those who blamed central government for local financial difficulties; amongst council tenants; and amongst those who wanted taxes and services increased.

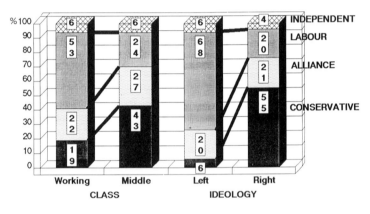

Fig. 11.1. Class, ideology, and local preferences (*see Table 11.3*)

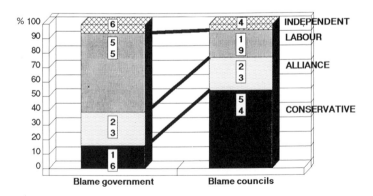

Fig. 11.2. Blame and local preferences (*see Table 11.3*)

All of this is very plausible, but we need to ask *why* local election choice shows such strong patterns on these variables. Take GBLAME for example. We must suspect that those who voted Labour in the May local elections blamed the (Conservative) central government for their council's financial problems *because they were already Labour identifiers*. If so their attribution of blame *reflected party choice rather than causing it*. And if so, an analysis that controls for the effect of party identification would show no *extra* relationship between GBLAME and local election choice.

In Table 11.4 we present the results of a number of multiple regression analyses. The first column shows the relative influence of each of the seven predictors *once account is taken of the others*. The second column shows their influence once account is also taken of *party identification*; and the third column shows their influence once account is taken both of national party identification and *current national (i.e. parliamentary) party preference*.

Table 11.4. Multiple regressions predicting local election choice (all respondents)

	Dependent variables measuring local election choice:					
	LABCON (local preference)			ALLIANCE (local preference)		
Predictors:						
LEFT	31 (29)	—	—	—	—	—
LIBERTARIAN	—	—	—	—	—	—
WCLASS	21 (22)	—	—	—	—	—
POLLTAX	—	—	—	—	—	—
GBLAME	26 (20)	—	—	—	—	—
CTENURE	—	—	—	—	—	—
TAXCUT	—	—	—	— (− 10)	—	—
LABCON IDENT	n.u.	78 (78)	36 (28)	n.u.	—	—
ALLIANCE IDENT	n.u.	—	—	n.u.	65 (62)	25 (21)
LABCON GE PREF	n.u.	n.u.	51 (59)	n.u.	n.u.	—
ALLIANCE GE PREF	n.u.	n.u.	—	n.u.	n.u.	54 (57)
RSQ (% of variation explained)	36 (29)	74 (71)	78 (78)	1 (2)	42 (39)	55 (55)

Notes:
1. Entries in main body of table are standardized multiple regression coefficients (also known as 'beta weights' or 'path coefficients').
2. — = weak effects with coefficients less than + or − 10.
3. 'n.u.' indicates predictors 'not used' in a particular regression.
4. Figures in brackets are for November, those outside are for May.
5. RSQ is the squared multiple correlation.
6. Regressions based upon all panel respondents, in all areas, using SPSSPC Regression with 'pairwise deletion' of missing values.

The first column suggests that in both November and May three predictors had an important influence on local election choice—left/right ideology, blaming the government for local financial difficulties, and class. But once we introduce party identification none of these variables had an important independent influence on local choice. Introducing current national preferences shows they are even more influential than party identification though party identification retains some independent influence. Of course these findings do not mean that class, issues, and ideology are unimportant in politics, but they appear to influence local election choices only indirectly. Our seven predictors influence general national attitudes towards political choice, and then local election choice reflects national choice.

Perhaps our very limited range of predictors simply fails to tap all the local issues that are influential? Undoubtedly that is true to some extent. But the RSQ (squared multiple correlations) line in the table shows that our measures of national political choice explain four-fifths of the variation in local election choices between Labour and Conservative and over half the variation in local support for the Alliance. The unexplained variation is partly explicable by local influences we have not measured explicitly and is partly just inexplicable (i.e. due to random chance). We cannot be sure how much of this statistically unexplained variation is potentially explicable by a variety of local political influences. But we do know that the extent of this unexplained variation in local choice is limited. Local influences may have a considerable effect upon support for the Alliance in local elections but not a great deal of influence on the choice between Labour and Conservative.

Local election voting choices were slightly more predictable in May than in November. At election time there was a little more coherence between issues and ideology on the one hand and voting choice on the other (the RSQ for predicting LABCON from our seven basic predictors rose from 29 per cent in November to 36 per cent in May) and the balance of influence on local election choices also shifted slightly from current parliamentary preferences to party identification, though not enough to make party identification the dominant influence. However the overall predictability of local choice from national choice (of one kind or another) remained virtually unchanged.

Even though national choice dominates local choice throughout the electorate as a whole there may be subsets of the electorate who are more responsive to local politics and less constrained by their national political choice. To find out if this is so we can rerun the regression analyses on subsets of the panel. Some indication that this might be a useful strategy is given by the variations in the number of respondents whose choice in local elections was 'independent or other'. Support for this category of candidate was noticeably higher in the areas without elections in May, and also amongst those respondents who had weak party identifications, who claimed to vote more on local rather than national issues, or who claimed to vote for the candidate rather than the party in local elections (Table 11.5).

Table 11.5. Variations in support for independents and others

	% of those with preferences who prefer independent or other in May:
Amongst those who:	
Voted	3
Abstained	3
Lived in areas without elections	11
Had very strong party identification	6
Had fairly strong party identification	4
Had not very strong party identification	9
Had no party identification	12
Vote on local issues in local elections	9
Vote on national issues in local elections	1
Vote for candidate in local elections	12
Vote for party in local elections	3

Regression analyses show that it was generally in these same subgroups that local election voting choice between the major parties was least predictable. Regressions using party identification and parliamentary preference could explain 87 per cent of the variation in LABCON choices at local elections amongst those with a very strong sense of party identification, but only 72 per cent amongst those with 'not very strong' identifications, and a mere 31 per cent amongst those with no party identification. Similarly the regressions predicting LABCON explained 92 per cent amongst those who voted on the basis of national issues, but only 71 per cent amongst those who voted on local issues; 89 per cent amongst those who voted for the party, but only 53 per cent amongst those who voted for the candidate (Table 11.6).

Table 11.6. Multiple regressions predicting local election choice in selected subgroups of panel respondents (in May)

	Dependent variable: LABCON local election choice										
	Type of respondent V+A+NE	V+A	V	Strength of pty ident. V	F	NV	N	Basis of vote NI	LI	C	P
RSQ using 7 basic predictors	36	34	42	58	35	27	14	43	33	29	39
RSQ using these 7 + pty. ident.	73	74	77	86	79	62	14	84	68	49	85
RSQ using these 7 + pty. ident. + parl. pref.	78	76	77	87	82	72	31	92	71	53	89

	Dependent variable: ALLIANCE local election choice										
	Type of respondent V+A+NE	V+A	V	Strength of pty ident. V	F	NV	N	Basis of vote NI	LI	C	P
RSQ using 7 basic predictors	1	3	4	2	4	8	22	6	1	5	4
RSQ using these 7 + pty. ident.	42	48	50	70	45	32	22	56	29	21	61
RSQ using these 7 + pty. ident. + parl. pref.	55	56	55	81	60	41	33	80	40	33	80

Notes:
1. Type of respondent: V = voters, A = abstainers, NE = no election.
Strength of pty. ident.: V = very, F = fairly, NV = not very, N = none.
Basis of vote: NI = national issues, LI = local issues, C = candidate, P = party.
2. Pty. ident.: this is either the LABCON or ALLIANCE coding of party identification choice, whichever is appropriate to the regression.
3. Parl. pref.: this is either the LABCON or ALLIANCE coding of current parliamentary general election preference, whichever is appropriate to the regression.

None the less, it was party identification and parliamentary preference which generally explained nearly everything that the regressions could explain: the seven issue, ideological, and class measures seldom added much to the explanation centred on national party choice. We can underline that finding by looking at the relationship between the predictability of local election choices between Labour and Conservative and the strength of party identification. It was much easier to predict local election choice from our seven issue, class, and ideology predictors amongst strong party identifiers than amongst weak party identifiers (RSQ of 58 per cent and 14 per cent respectively). Weak party identifiers did not make specially coherent issue-based local election choices, at least in terms of the issues included in regression analysis. It was the strong party identifiers who showed the greatest coherence between issue attitudes and local election choices. So the contrast revealed by our regression analyses is not between some groups whose local choices reflected national choices and other groups whose local choices reflected any of the issues or social patterns measured by our set of seven basic predictors. The contrast is between some groups whose local choices reflect national choices and other groups whose local choices deviate in statistically inexplicable ways from their national choices. These latter groups may perhaps be responding to very local issues, personalities, and campaigns in some coherent way or their deviations from their national choice may be largely random. Statistically we cannot tell. However the fact that these deviations from national choice are so large in precisely those groups that claim to be voting 'on issues' or 'for the candidate in local elections' does suggest that there are non-random factors at work. The voters in question seem conscious of deviating from nationally determined party preferences.

Finally, the regressions predicting LABCON choice reveal another intriguing pattern. Overall, current parliamentary preference seems to have more weight than party identification in determining local election choice. However, the dominance of parliamentary preference compared to party identification is less marked amongst strong identifiers (which is only to be expected) and party identification even has more weight than parliamentary preference amongst those who vote on local issues, those who vote for the candidate, and those who actually lived in areas where elections took place. What this shows is that for those relatively few people whose current parliamentary preference deviated from their party identification, their deviant parliamentary choice was generally to pull their local election choice in the same deviant direction; but it was not very effective in doing so amongst strong identifiers and still less effective amongst those with a self-declared local orientation to local elections and amongst those who actually participated in a local election.

How Many People have the Same Party Preferences for National and Local Elections?

To a considerable extent these relatively ambitious multiple regression analyses have come to a negative conclusion and cleared the way for a simpler but more detailed study of the relationship between national and local choice. If we restrict our analysis to all those who had a local election preference in May (91 per cent of the entire panel) and tabulate their local choice against their party identification and their current parliamentary preference we can see how many deviate from their national choice and in what ways.

Overall, 80 per cent had local choices for Conservative, Labour, or Alliance that were exactly in accord with their party identification—and 83 per cent in accord with their current parliamentary preference; 9 per cent had a local choice that contradicted their national choice; 4 per cent had a local preference for 'Independent or other' despite having a national preference for Conservative, Labour, or the Alliance; 7 per cent did not identify with any of the Conservative, Labour, or Alliance parties nationally, and 4 per cent did not have a parliamentary preference.

The percentage whose local choice matched their parliamentary preference rose to 95 per cent amongst those who 'voted on national issues' and dropped to 66 per cent amongst those who 'voted for the candidate' in local elections. Conversely the numbers whose local choice contradicted their national choice rose to 18 per cent amongst those who voted 'for the candidate'. At the same time, a further 11 per cent of those who voted 'for the candidate' deviated from their parliamentary preference to support an Independent or other in local elections (Table 11.7).

If we further restrict the table to include only those who *actually voted* in May, we are effectively restricting it to areas where Independent candidates are less frequent and less successful. So we should expect rather smaller defections to Independent candidates and more voting in accord with national preferences. Surprisingly, that is *not* what Table 11.8 shows.

The reduced number of defections to Independents is balanced by increased percentages whose local vote flagrantly contradicts their national preference. So amongst those who 'vote for the candidate', 27 per cent voted Conservative, Labour, or Alliance in the local elections despite identifying with another (of the three) nationally, and an enormous 38 per cent voted for one of the three locally despite expressing a parliamentary preference for one of the others. By the time we have reduced our panel to those who actually voted and who vote 'for the candidate', we are down to small numbers of respondents and the statistical margin for sampling error is large. None the less the

Table 11.7. Percentage with local *preferences* in accord with national preferences (May)

	% of all respondents with local preferences			
	In accord with national preference	Contradicting national preference	Con./Lab./All. nationally but. Ind. or other locally	Did not have Con./Lab./All. preference nationally
All respondents	83 (80)	9 (9)	4 (4)	4 (7)
Voter types:				
Voters	84 (84)	12 (9)	1 (1)	2 (6)
Abstainers	86 (83)	8 (8)	2 (2)	3 (7)
No elections	82 (74)	6 (10)	8 (8)	5 (7)
Party identification:				
Very strong	90 (90)	4 (4)	4 (4)	3 (3)
Fairly strong	86 (85)	8 (11)	3 (3)	3 (1)
Not very strong	74 (76)	14 (15)	7 (8)	5 (1)
Vote on:				
Local issues	76 (75)	13 (11)	7 (7)	5 (7)
National issues	95 (87)	3 (8)	0 (1)	2 (4)
Vote for:				
Candidate	66 (63)	18 (18)	11 (11)	6 (8)
Party	92 (88)	4 (5)	1 (1)	4 (6)

Notes:
1. Except for rounding, figures add to 100% in each row.
2. Figures in brackets relate local preference to party identification; figures not in brackets relate local preference to parliamentary prefrence.
3. Table based upon all respondents with local preferences in May, whether or not they actually voted.

Table 11.8. Percentage with local *votes* in accord with national preferences (May)

	% of all local election voters with local votes			
	In accord with national preference	Contradicting national preference	Con./Lab./All. nationally but Ind. or other locally	Did not have Con./Lab./All. preference nationally
All voters in May	84 (84)	12 (9)	1 (1)	2 (6)
Party identification:				
Very strong	89 (91)	9 (6)	0 (0)	2 (4)
Fairly strong	87 (87)	9 (10)	2 (2)	4 (2)
Not very strong	76 (81)	17 (16)	1 (2)	6 (2)
Vote on:				
Local issues	75 (79)	20 (14)	1 (2)	4 (2)
National issues	93 (89)	3 (7)	1 (1)	3 (3)
Vote for:				
Candidate	55 (62)	38 (27)	3 (4)	4 (6)
Party	91 (91)	4 (4)	0 (0)	4 (5)

Note: Figures in brackets relate local vote to party identification; figures not in brackets relate local vote to parliamentary preference.

evidence is strong that those categories of voters that might be attracted to an Independent candidate may, in the absence of such candidates, make an independent (with a small 'i' now) choice between the available candidates, a choice that owes relatively little to their national preferences.

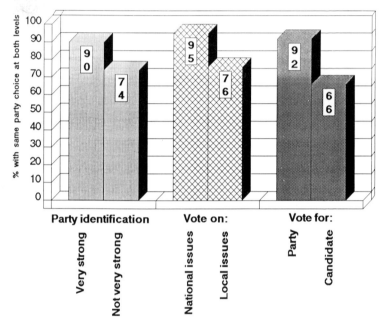

Fig. 11.3. Local and national preferences (*see Table 11.7*)

How Do Local and National Choices Differ?

Very, very few respondents identified with Labour or Conservative nationally and preferred the opposite locally. Discrepancies between party identification and local election choice consisted of respondents without party identifications; respondents who deviated from their party identification to support an Independent locally; and respondents who deviated from Conservative and Labour identifications to support the Alliance locally (or, much less frequently, vice versa) (Table 11.9).

Even within those subgroups of the electorate where the differences between national and local choice were relatively large, the numbers

Table 11.9. Local *preference* by national choice (May)

	% National Choice				
	Con.	Lab.	All.	Ind./other/ none/DK	Total
% Local election choice:					
Con.	29 (28)	1 (1)	1 (1)	1 (1)	31 (31)
Lab.	1 (0)	35 (36)	2 (1)	1 (3)	39 (40)
All.	2 (3)	2 (4)	20 (16)	1 (2)	24 (23)
Ind./other	1 (1)	1 (1)	2 (2)	2 (1)	6 (6)
Total	32 (33)	39 (41)	25 (19)	4 (7)	100%

Note: Figures in brackets relate local election choice to national party identification; figures not in brackets relate local election choice to parliamentary preference.

who chose Labour or Conservative nationally and the opposite in local elections were very small. For example, fully a third of all those who claim to vote for the candidate rather than the party in local elections had a local choice which was not a reflection of national support for Conservative, Labour, or Alliance but only 3 or 4 per cent supported Conservative or Labour nationally and the other locally (Table 11.10).

Indeed the maximum amount of Conservative/Labour cross-support found in any of our subgroup analyses (Table 11.11) is only 6

Table 11.10. Local choice by national choice amongst subgroups (May)

	% National Choice				
	Con.	Lab.	All.	Ind./other/ none/DK	Total
Local preference amongst all those who claim to vote on local issues:					
Con.	27 (29)	1 (1)	1 (1)	1 (1)	30 (32)
Lab.	1 (1)	30 (33)	4 (1)	1 (3)	36 (37)
All.	2 (4)	3 (4)	18 (13)	1 (2)	24 (23)
Ind./other	2 (2)	2 (2)	3 (3)	2 (2)	9 (9)
Total	32 (36)	36 (39)	26 (18)	5 (8)	100%
Local preference amongst all those who claim to vote for the candidate rather than the party:					
Con.	23 (23)	2 (2)	0 (1)	2 (2)	27 (28)
Lab.	2 (1)	21 (25)	6 (1)	0 (4)	29 (31)
All.	3 (6)	4 (7)	23 (15)	2 (2)	32 (30)
Ind./other	3 (4)	2 (2)	6 (4)	2 (1)	13 (11)
Total	31 (34)	29 (36)	35 (21)	6 (9)	100%

Note: Figures in brackets relate local election choice to national party identification; figures not in brackets relate local election choice to parliamentary preference.

Table 11.11. Cross-support by Conservative and Labour partisans (May)

	% who chose Lab. or Con. nationally but the other locally:
Amongst:	
All with a local preference	2 (1)
Voters	3 (2)
Abstainers	3 (2)
Those in non-election areas	0 (1)
All who vote on local issues	2 (2)
All who vote on national issues	1 (1)
All who vote for candidate	4 (3)
All who vote for party	0 (1)
Actual voters who vote on local issues	4 (4)
Actual voters who vote on national issues	0 (0)
Actual voters who vote for the candidate	6 (5)
Actual voters who vote for the party	2 (1)

Note: Figures in brackets relate local choice to national party identification; figures not in brackets relate local choice to parliamentary preference.

per cent, and that was found in such a small subsample—actual voters in May who also claimed to vote for the candidate—that according to conventional statistical tests it was not (statistically) significantly different from zero.

So our detailed analyses of the types of switching between national and local choice suggests:

(1) There is little or no switching from a Labour or Conservative national choice to the opposite local choice.

(2) Switching between parties involves the Alliance, and the Alliance gains more than it loses in local elections from the willingness of people to desert their national political choice.

(3) In addition some respondents do not have a national party preference and others defect from it to Independents and others in local elections.

Comparing the locally orientated (56 per cent of all respondents) to the nationally orientated (28 per cent of all respondents), divided according to whether they claim to vote on local or national issues in local elections, the locally orientated are:

(4) More likely to switch to the Alliance, Independents, and others

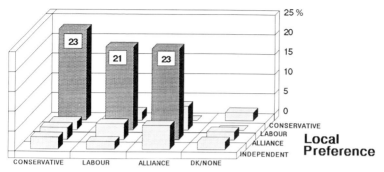

Fig. 11.4 Local and national preferences amongst those who vote for the candidate (*see Table 11.10*)

in local elections—12 per cent of the locally orientated but only 5 per cent of the nationally orientated combined a Conservative or Labour party identification with a preference for the Alliance, Independents, or others in local elections (Table 11.10).

Comparing those who claim to 'vote for the candidate' in local elections (39 per cent of all respondents) with those who claim to 'vote for the party' (58 per cent of all respondents), the candidate-orientated are also:

(5) More likely to switch to the Alliance, Independents, and others in local elections—19 per cent of the candidate-orientated but only 3 per cent of the party-orientated combined a Conservative or Labour party identification with a preference for the Alliance, Independents, or others in local elections (Table 11.10).

Conclusion

While *some* people do not follow their national political choice when considering how to vote in local elections, *most* people (about four-fifths) do; and those who do not usually have no national preferences to follow or they deviate from a Labour or Conservative choice in national elections to an Alliance or Independent choice in local elections.

Amongst those who claim to vote on local issues or, still more, amongst those who claim to vote for the candidate rather than the party in local elections, the differences between national and local voting choices are much greater. But even these people seldom combine a Labour choice at one level with a Conservative choice at the other. Instead they combine support for Alliance and Independent candidates at local level with a Labour or Conservative choice for parliament.

When US President Truman (a Democrat) was asked whether he voted 'for the party or for the man' he replied that he always voted 'for the best candidate—who is, of course, the Democrat'. British local government voters who vote for the candidate rather than the party do not follow Truman's example exactly: they do not always agree that the 'best candidate is the Democrat' but they do seem to agree with him that the 'worst candidate is the Republican'!

Part IV
Variations through Space and Time

12 Regional Differences, I: Differences of Opinion under Metropolitan, Shire, Scottish, Labour, Conservative, Sympathetic, and Unsympathetic Councils

How much do attitudes towards local government vary from one place to another? Obviously, with a relatively small sample of respondents, it would be misleading to attempt a very fine breakdown of attitudes in specific localities—all we should discover would be random variations caused by sampling errors in small subsamples. Moreover, it would not add much to a theoretical understanding of local elections merely to show that attitudes in Manchester did or did not differ from those in Newcastle.

However, we can usefully divide our panel into two or three spatial subgroups in a number of different ways. First we shall look at the differences between those who live:

(1) in London (the old GLC) and the former *metropolitan* counties of England;
(2) in the non-metropolitan or *shire* counties of England and Wales;
(3) in *Scotland*.

Although Scots make up only 9 per cent of our weighted panel, they were over-sampled; so that over a quarter of the actual interviews were conducted in Scotland. Thus we have a basis for comparisons between Scotland and elsewhere, one which is particularly interesting both because the system of local government is very different in Scotland and because the political climate is so different there. Conversely, although we might like to distinguish between the London GLC area and other metropolitan (i.e. big city) counties the sample is too small to permit us to do so reliably.

A second distinction that can usefully be made is between those who lived in areas with:

(1) *Labour*-dominated councils;
(2) *Conservative*-dominated councils.

Once again, in order to avoid small subsamples we have classified areas according to which party had most seats on the council prior to May 1986, irrespective of whether it had an overall majority, and we have excluded those interesting but unusual areas where some other party had most seats on the council. Analyses were carried out classifying areas by the leading party on the old county council and on the district council. Since they showed very much the same patterns we shall present findings only for areas classified by the partisanship of the district council.

Lastly we can distinguish between respondents who lived in an area where:

(1) their own party was the leading party on the council (a politically *sympathetic* council);

(2) their own party was not the leading party (a politically *unsympathetic* council).

We use respondents' party identifications in May 1986 and the party composition in the district council immediately prior to May 1986 in order to make this distinction between respondents who were in (partisan) sympathy with their local council and those who were not.

These three ways of contrasting different areas are not regional divisions in a conventional sense but they do distinguish areas where we might expect attitudes to differ. Scotland has a different system of local government from England and Wales and is responsible to a different Cabinet Minister. Traditionally, and increasingly during the 1980s, the Secretary of State for Scotland exercised a much tighter control of local government than his counterparts south of the border. He pioneered restrictive legislation to keep down local government expenditure and pioneered the introduction of a community charge (or 'poll tax') to replace domestic rates. At the same time, he did so as a minister of the 'British' government and had little popular support within Scotland itself. Increasingly during the 1980s, he was seen as an agent of an 'alien' government, imposed upon Scotland without a popular mandate.

Within England, the London GLC and the old metropolitan (big city) county councils were the chief targets of central government attacks on allegedly high-spending local councils. They were finally abolished by central government in 1985 with effect from 1986. They were the main public battleground between local and central government.

Our other classifications—according to the partisanship of the local council—are designed to detect any evidence that members of the public reacted differently to Labour or Conservative councils, or simply to councils of another political complexion than their own.

The Metropolitan Counties, the Shire Counties, and Scotland

As we shall see, the differences between these three areas—metropolitan counties, shire counties, and Scotland—are more numerous and striking than the differences between areas of different partisanship. Usually a difference emerges between the metropolitan counties and the rest, or between Scotland and the rest, and only very exceptionally between the shires and the rest.

In terms of knowledge, contact, and interest, London and the metropolitan counties show the least local orientation and Scotland the most (Table 12.1). Despite central government's sustained campaign against them the metropolitan counties were the least well-known to the public—only 55 per cent in metropolitan areas knew the name of their county council. Councillors' names were relatively unknown in metropolitan areas (35 per cent) but much better known in Scotland (62 per cent). This was reflected in contacts with local government. Residents of metropolitan areas were the least likely to have contacted a council office. The opposite applied in Scotland. Similarly, the level

Table 12.1. Knowledge, contact, and interest by region (May 1986)

	GLC/Metros	Shires	Scotland
% who know:			
County name	55	67	71
District name	80	81	77
Councillor's name	35	42	62
Councillor's party	69	78	82
% who have contacted:			
Councillor	21	29	30
Council offices	65	61	43
% with great deal or fair amount of interest in:			
national politics	64	55	49
local politics	44	31	39
% who vote for candidate rather than party in local elections	22	41	41

of interest in national politics was 20 per cent higher than the level of
interest in local politics in metropolitan areas but only 10 per cent
higher in Scotland; and twice as many Scots as metropolitan residents
claimed to vote 'for the candidate rather than the party in local
elections'. Elected local government was clearly much closer to Scots

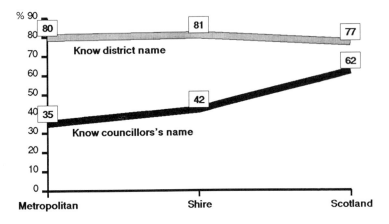

Fig. 12.1. Knowledge by region (*see Table 12.1*)

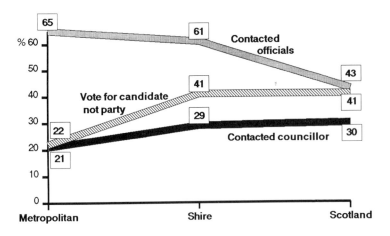

Fig. 12.2. Contacts by region (*see Table 12.1*)

than to metropolitan residents, while for those who lived in the shires it was closer than in the metropolitan areas but less so than in Scotland.

Scots were outstandingly dissatisfied with central government (Table 12.2) but a little more satisfied than others with their local councils. However, in all regions, central government aroused far more dissatisfaction than local government.

Central government's campaigns against high-spending local government were most successful in the metropolitan areas and least so in Scotland. Fewer Scots saw their local councils as having control of local affairs and more Scots wanted greater autonomy for local government. Only half as many Scots as English approved the new proposals for a flat-rate poll tax to replace the property-based local 'rates'.

The one question that united Scots and metropolitan residents in contrast to the shires was about the organization of local elections and in particular the role of parties in local elections. Shire residents were about average in their perceptions of the growing role played by parties but they were especially opposed to it (Table 12.3).

In terms of party identification the Labour party was relatively (not absolutely though!) weak in the shires, rather stronger in the metropolitan areas, and very strong indeed in Scotland. We hardly needed a special survey to find that out. What is surprising is that the

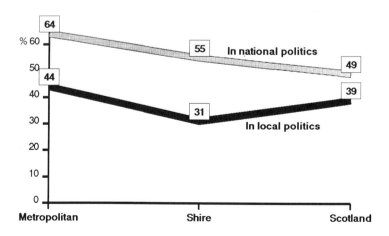

Fig. 12.3. Interest by region (*see Table 12.1*)

Table 12.2. Satisfaction, blame, and local autonomy by region (May 1986)

	GLC/Metros	Shires	Scotland
Satisfaction (% very or fairly satisfied) with:			
County council	78	84	83
District council	71	82	82
Central government	48	48	31
% who blame councils rather than government for local financial difficulties	43	36	28
% who perceive councils rather than government as having more control of local affairs	58	56	35
% who want less central control of local government	35	38	47
% who prefer poll tax to rates	61	57	33

Table 12.3. Attitudes to parties in local elections by region (May 1986)

	GLC/Metros	Shires	Scotland
% who perceive growing role of parties	71	69	68
% who prefer non-party system	52	65	49

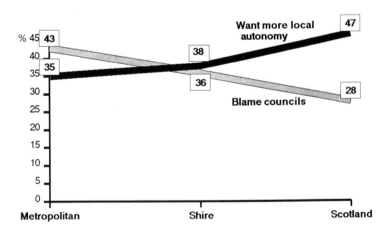

Fig. 12.4. Blame and autonomy by region (*see Table 12.2*)

survey shows that *this regional pattern of partisanship was not matched by similar variations in attitudes*. In the panel, the Scots were the *least* likely to describe themselves as being 'on the left', and they were the *least* likely to favour increases in taxes and services.

Another revealing pattern of attitudes occurred in the responses to Inglehart's 'post-materialism' question. This asked people to prioritize four possible aims of government—two 'materialist' aims (maintaining order; fighting rising prices) and two 'post-materialist' aims (giving people more say; freedom of speech). There was very little difference between the overall levels of support for the materialist aims in different regions though within the overall total Scots gave much less priority to maintaining order and much more priority to fighting rising prices. Scots were also more religious than the English. So the Scots tendency to blame central government for local financial difficulties, to want less central government control, and to oppose the poll tax did not reflect some conventional measures of leftism—self-described leftism, support for increased spending, post-materialism, or lack of religiosity. On the other hand, Scots antagonism to central government and support for their local councils did reflect Scots patterns of party identification, social class, house tenure, employment, and rate-paying. There was a gritty, materialist, and perhaps even tribal flavour to Scots support for their local councils. They were not by nature self-conscious big-spending leftists (Table 12.4).

Labour and Conservative Councils

Because British parties are based upon social class the populations living in areas where Labour was the leading party on the council were very different, socially, from the populations in Conservative-dominated areas. So patterns of attitudes reflected the different social backgrounds of the populations: Labour and Conservative councils were judged by very different juries.

None the less it is worth looking to see whether Labour councils were any less popular than Conservative councils with their own electorates. Central government claimed that they were, and tried hard to make sure that the claim was justified by frequent public attacks on Labour-controlled metropolitan councils especially—eventually abolishing them in 1986.

Labour *county* councils were 8 per cent less popular with their own electorates than were the Conservative county councils; and Labour

Table 12.4. Leftism by region (May 1986)

	GLC/Metros	Shires	Scotland
% on:			
Left	23	25	17
Centre	41	38	48
Right	35	37	34
% for:			
More taxes and services	53	49	34
Same as now	28	30	40
Less taxes and services	17	21	25
% priority for:			
Maintaining order	48	42	35
Fighting rising prices	15	15	28
% who:			
Never attend church	45	46	31
Are employed full-time	48	48	37
Live in council housing	19	16	43
Are middle-class (ABC1)	45	46	26
Pay rates in full (no rebate)	80	80	64
% of party identification:			
Conservative	33	39	19
Labour	46	38	58

Table 12.5. Satisfaction with Conservative and Labour councils (May 1986)

	Amongst respondents living in			
	Con. county	Lab. county	Con. district	Lab. district
% very or fairly satisfied with:				
County council	87	79	n.r.	n.r.
District council	n.r.	n.r.	82	71
Central government	50	43	52	41
% blame government for local financial difficulties	66	59	61	62
% want less central control of local councils	43	36	35	40
% support poll-tax to replace rates	54	57	58	55

Note: n.r. = not relevant.

Table 12.6. Sympathetic and unsympathetic councils (May 1986)

	Amongst respondents who lived under			
	Sympathetic county council	Unsympathetic county council	Sympathetic district council	Unsympathetic district council
% very or fairly satisfied with:				
County council	85	79	n.r.	n.r.
District council	n.r.	n.r.	84	71
% blame councils for local financial difficulties	27	45	34	44
% perceive councils as having more control than government	39	48	40	49
% want more central control	13	12	13	13
% know councillor's name	43	42	48	38
% have contacted councillor	30	25	31	23
% have contacted council office	60	64	57	68
% 'great deal' or 'fair' amount of interest in:				
National politics	55	61	57	60
Local politics	38	36	42	33
% support poll tax rather than rates	52	60	50	63
% prefer non-party system of local govt.	48	64	44	64

Note: n.r. = not relevant.

district councils were 11 per cent less popular with their own electorates than Conservative district councils. However, *central government* was also less popular in Labour areas, and by about the same amount (7 per cent in Labour counties, 11 per cent in Labour districts). So perhaps those who lived in Labour areas simply took a less charitable view of government in general.

On the crunch question, whether central or local government was to blame for local councils' financial difficulties, a large majority in all areas blamed central government. There is some evidence that Labour county councils were blamed a little more than Conservative county councils but no evidence of a similar effect in the districts (Table 12.5). In Labour counties, but not in Labour districts, fewer people opposed central government controls over local councils.

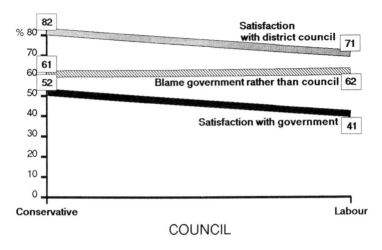

Fig. 12.5. Satisfaction under Labour and Conservative councils (*see Table 12.5*)

Sympathetic and Unsympathetic Councils

People who lived under politically unsympathetic councils were: less satisfied with them; more inclined to blame the council for financial difficulties; more inclined to think the councils had real power; and (slightly) more in favour of central control. They were less likely to know their councillor's names, less likely to contact their councillors, and more likely to contact council offices. They claimed to be more interested than other people in *national* politics, but less interested in *local* politics. They gave more support to the idea of a poll tax. Most striking of all, they were very strongly opposed to parties playing a role in local government. In short, they were somewhat alienated from elected local government.

Paradoxically this experience did not make them violently opposed to big spending. Indeed, those who lived under unsympathetic district councils were more (*not less!*) in favour of high taxation and public expenditure. There is a simple explanation for this paradox however: most Alliance supporters lived under unsympathetic local councils. Thus fully 38 per cent of those with an unsympathetic district council (and only 2 per cent of those with a sympathetic district council) were Alliance supporters. Alliance supporters were not uniformly opposed to higher levels of taxation and services than were permitted under a right-wing Conservative government (Table 12.6).

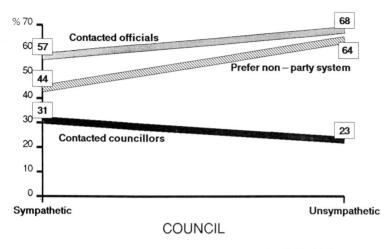

Fig. 12.6. Sympathetic and unsympathetic councils (*see Table 12.6*)

13 Regional Differences, II: Differences in Attitude Structure under Metropolitan, Shire, Scottish, Labour, Conservative, Sympathetic, and Unsympathetic Councils

So far we have looked only at variations in attitudes and characteristics of the population across different areas. We have asked: 'do attitudes towards local government vary from one place to another?' Now we turn to the rather more complex question of whether *relationships*, rather than simply attitudes, vary from place to place. For example, we can ask: 'does the *relationship between attitudes to local government and party identification* vary from one place to another?' Or: 'does the *relationship between turn-out and age* vary from place to place?' Or again: 'does the *relationship between local election voting and national party identification* vary from place to place?'

Varying Relationships: An Analytic Strategy

To discover whether relationships vary requires a very careful inspection of multi-way tabulations. A simple, effective, and automatic way of doing this is provided by a statistical procedure known as *hierarchical loglinear analysis with backwards elimination*. For brevity we shall call this just 'loglinear analysis'. To use this technique we supply a set of variables which we suspect might be locked in a complex pattern of interactive relationships. The computer programme—we use the SPSSPC PLUS Loglinear Programme here—then starts by assuming the most complex pattern of interaction possible. (This is often called the 'saturated model' because it is saturated with the maximum possible complexity.) Thereafter it successively attempts to simplify. It aims to explain the patterns in the multi-way cross-tabulation *reasonably well* on the basis of a *relatively simple structure* of interactions.

Let us take a concrete example. Suppose we supply the programme with data on our respondents': (1) attribution of blame for councils' financial difficulties; (2) party identification; and (3) region of residence. Then the programme will inspect the three-way cross-tabulation of *blame BY partisanship BY region*. It will start with the assumption that a relationship between blame and partisanship exists and that this relationship varies from region to region. Then it will successively discard notions of complex interactions, and even of the existence of relationships, to see if the pattern in the three-way cross-tabulation can be approximated by a model based upon a simple structure of relationships and interactions.

We tested nine relationships with this technique, to see whether each relationship existed in the country as a whole, and whether it varied in different parts of the country. The relationships tested were:

(1) Satisfaction with district councils BY partisanship.
(2) Satisfaction with central government BY partisanship.
(3) Blame for financial problems BY partisanship.
(4) Support for more central control BY partisanship.
(5) Turn-out (May 1986) BY partisanship.
(6) Turn-out BY strength of partisanship.
(7) Turn-out BY age.
(8) Turn-out BY interest in local politics.
(9) Local election vote (May 1986) BY (national) partisanship.

We used loglinear analysis to see whether these relationships varied between metropolitan, shire, and Scottish areas; and again to see whether they varied between Labour and Conservative areas.

The loglinear test technique is quite stringent. Specifically it tests for statistical significance at the 5 per cent level, *i.e.* we had to be sure that an observed variation between areas had less than a 5 per cent probability of occurring by chance before we accepted that the variation really occurred in the electorate (as distinct from occurring in our small sample). Our sample is fairly small to begin with, particularly small when used to analyse turn-out in May 1986 (because some councils did not hold elections), and very small when used to analyse actual voting choice (because even amongst those who were able to vote, many did not do so). Consequently we probably *underestimate* the amount of variation in relationships by taking a stringent criterion of statistical significance.

It is also important to understand that by using measures of *actual* turn-out and voting choice at the May 1986 election for analyses 5 to 9 we are restricting these analyses to (i) election *time* and (ii) those *places* which had elections then. As we shall see in Chapter 15 that double restriction has important implications: actual electoral behaviour follows different patterns from electoral intentions.

Metropolitan, Shire, and Scottish Areas

Applying this technique leads to the results set out in Table 13.1. Since loglinear analysis has only recently become a popular technique amongst practising social scientists we shall go through the table in detail.

Look at the last column. Each pair of variables linked by an asterisk means that there is a statistically significant relationship between them. Conversely if a pair of variables do *not* appear linked by an asterisk there is *not* a statistically significant relationship between them.

The first five loglinear analyses all show that partisanship varied between areas which is something we already know very well. So we can ignore the P*R terms in each model as being true but obvious.

The first analysis shows, in addition, that satisfaction with district councils also varied by region—hence the SDC*R term. But that was all: there was no significant relationship between satisfaction with the district council (SDC) and partisanship (P)—hence no SDC*P term.

The second analysis shows that satisfaction with the government varied with partisanship, and also with region. Similarly blame for financial difficulties varied with partisanship and region (analysis 3). Turn-out varied by region, by stength of partisanship, and by age (analyses 6 and 7); but turn-out did *not* vary with direction of partisanship, or with interest in local politics (analyses 5 and 8). Voting choice in the 1986 local elections varied with partisanship and with region (analysis 9).

Only one of the nine analyses in the table shows a *relationship varying across regions*. That is the fourth analysis. The term C*P*R shows that the *relationship* (C*P) between the respondent's partisanship and his/her support for more central control varied significantly across regions. What does that mean? What does it look like in simple cross-tabulation terms rather than in terms of loglinear models? Table 13.2 provides the answers.

Labour identifiers opposed central control of local government irrespective of where they lived, but Alliance attitudes to central control varied somewhat, and Conservative attitudes depended greatly

Table 13.1. Relationships in regions

Relationship	Variables used in loglinear analysis	Final simplified model calculated by loglinear analysis
1	Satisfaction with district council (SDC) Partisanship (P) Region (R) i.e. metro/shire/Scotland	SDC*R P*R
2	Satisfaction with government (SG) Partisanship (P) Region (R)	SG*P SG*R P*R
3	Blame (B) Partisanship (P) Region (R)	B*P B*R P*R
4	Support central control (C) Partisanship (P) Region (R)	C*P*R
5	Turn-out (T) Partisanship (P) Region (R)	T*R P*R
6	Turn-out (T) Strength of partisanship (SP) Region (R)	T*SP T*R
7	Turn-out (T) Age (A) Region (R)	T*A T*R
8	Turn-out (T) Interest in local politics (LI) Region (R)	T*R LI*R
9	Vote Choice (V) Partisanship (P) Region (R)	V*P V*R

Notes:
1. In the third column, an asterisk indicates that there is a statistically significant relationship between the variables linked by the asterisk. Only relationship 4 shows an interactive relationship i.e. one where the relationship between C and P itself varies across regions.
2. Partisanship is the party identification of the respondent, not the party composition of the council where the respondent lived.
3. For the regional analyses presented in this table, we used an unweighted analysis, to take advantage of the over-sampling in Scotland. A weighted analysis would have down-weighted Scots respondents from a quarter to a tenth of the sample and failed to detect significant Scots/English differences, purely because of the apparent (but not actual) lack of Scots in the sample.

on where they lived. Compare Labour and Conservative attitudes in the metropolitan areas and in Scotland: Labour identifiers favoured more local autonomy by a margin of 40 to 14 in English metropolitan areas, and by a very similar margin of 43 to 11 in Scotland; but while

Table 13.2. Attitudes to central control by partisanship and region

Respondent's Party Identification	GLC/Metros			Shires			Scotland		
	Con.	Lab.	All.	Con.	Lab.	All.	Con.	Lab.	All.
% wanting:									
More central control	28	14	20	18	13	16	4	11	6
Same as now	72	47	60	74	51	53	77	46	78
Less central control	0	40	20	9	36	31	19	43	17
Balance (% more − % less)	+28	−26	0	+9	−23	−15	−15	−32	−11

metropolitan Conservatives favoured more central control by a margin of 28 to zero, *Scots Conservatives favoured more local autonomy* by a margin of 19 to 4. No doubt Scots Conservatives felt that a London government was a long way off geographically even if it was close in ideology and partisanship. Consequently there was a large measure of cross-party agreement on the need for more local autonomy in Scotland but a

Table 13.3. Relationships in Labour and Conservative areas

Relationship	Variables used in loglinear analysis	Final simplified model calculated by loglinear analysis	
		In full sample	Amongst Lab. and Con. identifiers
1	Satisfaction with district council (SDC) Partisanship (P) Lab./Con. council (LC)	SDC*P*LC	SDC*P*LC
2	Satisfaction with government (SG) Partisanship (P) Lab./Con. council (LC)	SG*P P*LC	SG*P P*LC
3	Blame (B) Partisanship (P) Lab./Con. council (LC)	B*P P*LC	B*P P*LC
4	Support central control (C) Partisanship (P) Lab./Con. council (LC)	C*P C*LC P*LC	C*P*LC
5	Turn-out (T) Partisanship (P) Lab./Con. council (LC)	T P LC	T P*LC
6	Turn-out (T) Strength of partisanship (SP) Lab./Con. council (LC)	T*SP LC	T SP LC
7	Turn-out (T) Age (A) Lab./Con. council (LC)	T*A LC	T*A A*LC
8	Turn-out (T) Interest in local politics (LI) Lab./Con. council (LC)	T LI LC	T LI LC
9	Vote Choice (V) Partisanship (P) Lab./Con. council (LC)	V*P LC	V*P P*LC

Notes:
1. In the third and fourth columns, an asterisk indicates that there is a statistically significant relationship between the variables linked by the asterisk.
2. Partisanship is the party identification of the respondent, not the party composition of the council where the respondent lived.

sharp party polarization of attitudes towards local autonomy in London and the metropolitan areas of England.

Conservative and Labour Areas

We can repeat these same nine loglinear analyses but now distinguishing between areas with Conservative and Labour councils instead of distinguishing between metropolitan, shire, and Scottish areas (Table 13.3). The results show once again that only one relationship varied significantly between areas. That was the relationship between satisfaction with the district council and partisanship (analysis 1). And once again, having used loglinear analysis to point us in the right direction, we can examine this statistically significant variation in detail by means of a simple tabulation (Table 13.4).

Neither Labour nor Alliance identifiers distinguished much between Labour and Conservative councils—on balance Labour identifiers tended to be critical of both, and Alliance identifiers even more so. Conservative identifiers however, were much more partisan in their assessment of their local council. By 19 per cent to 6 per cent *Conservative identifiers in Conservative areas* thought the local council ran things 'very well' but by a margin of 38 per cent to 14 per cent *Conservative identifiers in Labour areas* thought the local council ran things 'not at all well'. So while Conservatives took a very partisan attitude to their local council, Labour identifiers were almost (not quite!) equally critical of Labour and Conservative councils.

It might be argued that this pattern is consistent with the superimposition of two effects: first, a partisan effect, making

Table 13.4. Satisfaction with the district council by partisanship in Conservative and Labour areas

Respondent's party identification	Conservative council			Labour council		
	Con.	Lab.	All.	Con.	Lab.	All.
% who feel the district council runs things:						
Very well	19	11	5	14	17	7
Fairly well	75	64	62	49	61	60
Not at all well	6	24	33	38	22	33
Balance (% very − % not at all)	+13	−13	−28	−24	−5	−26

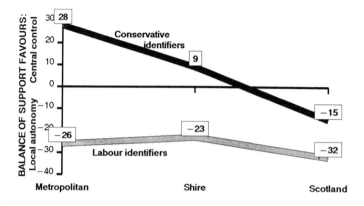

Fig. 13.1. Autonomy by partisanship in regions (*see Table 13.2*)

identifiers specially critical of the opposite party's councils; second, a 'nature of the times' effect, reflecting the success of central government and the mass media in attacking alleged extremists and spendthrift Labour councils. Amongst Labour identifiers the two effects would cancel; amongst Conservatives they would cumulate. Alas, this explanation is not consistent with the evidence that Alliance identifiers were equally critical of Labour and Conservative councils.

So we are left with the alternative conclusion that Conservative central government's strong attacks on Labour local councils only had an effect amongst Conservative identifiers.

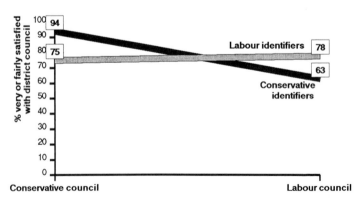

Fig. 13.2. Satisfaction by partisanship and party control (*see Table 13.2*)

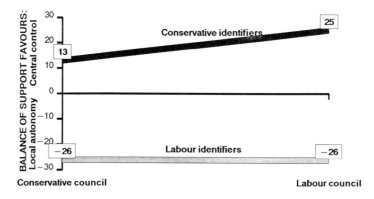

Fig. 13.3. Autonomy by partisanship and party control (*see Table 13.5*)

One other relationship came close to showing a statistically significant variation between Labour and Conservative areas: namely the relationship between support for more central control and partisanship (analysis 4). Indeed, if Alliance identifiers were excluded, the variation between areas did achieve statistical significance. The full tabulation is shown in Table 13.5.

Both Conservative and Alliance identifiers were clearly more in favour of central controls on local government in Labour areas than they were in Conservative areas. The evidence on Labour identifiers is less clear. In Labour areas, more Labour identifiers wanted increased central control but more Labour identifiers also wanted less central control, leaving the net balance unchanged. So, on balance, Labour identifiers' attitudes towards central control did not depend upon the partisanship of the local council, while both Conservative and Alliance

Table 13.5. Attitudes to central control by partisanship in Conservative and Labour areas

Respondent's party identification	Conservative council			Labour council		
	Con.	Lab.	All.	Con.	Lab.	All.
% who want:						
More central control	17	4	10	29	17	23
Same as now	79	66	59	68	41	56
Less central control	4	30	31	4	43	21
Balance (% more − % less)	+13	−26	−21	+25	−26	+2

Table 13.6. Turn-out by partisanship in Conservative and Labour areas

Respondent's party identification	Conservative council			Labour council		
	Con.	Lab.	All.	Con.	Lab.	All.
Turn-out intention (Nov.)	78	55	61	77	65	72
Actual turn-out* (May)	57	50	46	59	61	54

* in areas with elections

identifiers did favour central control to a greater extent in Labour areas than they did in Conservative areas.

None the less, the only categories of respondents who favoured more rather than less central control by a substantial margin were Conservative identifiers living under Labour councils, and (what is almost but not quite the same thing) Conservative identifiers living in London or the old metropolitan counties.

Both Noelle-Neuman's 'spiral of silence' theory[1] and the various 'contagion' theories of area partisanship[2] suggest that those who are in the political minority in a particular area may be specially prone towards political demoralization and defection.

If local minority status demoralizes partisans sufficiently to lower their political participation but not sufficiently to make them switch to the locally dominant party, then we would expect that the relationship between partisanship and turn-out would differ between areas with Labour and Conservative councils. Our loglinear analysis of the fifth relationship found no statistically significant variation in this relationship however. Table 13.6 shows that there was some tendency for Labour partisans to be more willing to turn out to vote when they lived under Labour councils: but Conservative partisans were less, not more, willing to turn out when they lived under Conservative councils. Indeed there was a general tendency towards higher turn-out by all kinds of partisans under Labour councils and no evidence that local political minorities were cowed into abstention by the local political climate.

Notes

1. E. Noelle-Neuman, 'The Spiral of Silence: A Theory of Public Opinion', *Journal of Communication* 24 (1974), 43–51.
2. See, for example, W. L. Miller, 'Social Class and Party Choice in England: A New Analysis', *British Journal of Political Science* 8 (1978), 257–84.

14 The Impact of an Election Atmosphere, I On Attitudes

Analysts of parliamentary elections have frequently pointed to the rising temperature of politics as a general election approaches. One measure of the significance of local elections would be a change in public attitudes and feeling about politics at the time of a local election.

Fieldwork for the first wave of interviews with our panel began on 23 November 1985 and ran until December—so every interview took place within about a month of Christmas Day. Midway between the county council elections of May 1985 and the district council elections of May 1986, and at the height of pre-Christmas preparations, concern for local politics should have been relatively low. If local elections do have a significant impact upon the political consciousness of the electorate it should be evident in the contrasts between our panel's responses in November 1985 and their responses in May 1986.

Some areas did not have local elections in 1986, however. Throughout Scotland there were elections for the regional councils, throughout London for the borough councils (and, in central London, for ILEA also), and throughout the metropolitan areas for the district councils. However in non-metropolitan areas some district councils were up for election, while others were not.

May 1986 was local *election time for everyone in Britain*, in so far as local election campaigning and local election news were transmitted through the mass media. Election reports and debates about council spending appeared in the national press and on national television. So, whatever area people lived in, their exposure to national news media meant that May 1986 was local election time. None the less May 1986 was specially important for those who lived in areas where elections were actually taking place.

If local elections do have an impact upon political consciousness, we might expect them to have *some impact* upon people in all areas in May, but *most impact* upon people in areas with elections. Thus, we can begin our analysis by looking at trends between November 1985 and May 1986: (1) *in our whole panel*; (2) amongst those who *lived in election areas*; and (3) amongst those who *lived in areas without elections* in May 1986.

Trends between November and Local Election Time

What impact upon mass attitudes would we expect if local elections were of great significance? For a start, we should expect an election atmosphere to raise levels of *interest* and *knowledge*. Since even local elections involve party contests we should expect an increase in *partisanship* and a greater acceptance of the *need for a party system* in local government to structure choice and make elections meaningful. A specifically local election might turn attention to *local issues* and also reinforce *support for local government* as an institution.

All these expectations, however, flow from the assumption that local elections are significant events in local politics. If they are insignificant then we should expect no measurable impact from an election atmosphere. If they are politically significant, but only as yet another battle in the ongoing *national* political struggle, then we might expect an increase in partisanship but not in concern for local politics.

What happened? Knowledge of county and district names increased substantially. And where elections occurred, the increase in knowledge of councillors' names was quite dramatic—though probably short-lived. At this very basic level of knowledge local elections had a clear impact (Table 14.1). But interest in local politics did not increase—interest in national politics did. Thus, once we are past the basic technicalities related to voting, such as knowing the names of councils and councillors, it seems that local elections had little impact on political interest; and what impact they did have suggests they were more significant as part of a national political struggle than a local one.

This view is confirmed by the trends in measures of national versus local orientation. Paradoxically, *the advent of a local election made people think more in terms of national politics*. We asked if there was 'any issue in politics, national or local, that you feel strongly about?' and then went on to ask whether the named issue, whatever it was, was a 'problem mainly for local councils or mainly for central government to deal with'. Between November and May there was a small shift towards a further emphasis on national government responsibility for the issues that concerned the electorate (Table 14.2). Moreover, this shift was most pronounced precisely in those areas which *did* have elections!

Table 14.1. Election impact on interest and knowledge

	% impact* amongst respondents:		
	total	in election areas	in areas without elections
Great deal or fair amount of interest:			
in national politics	+3	+4	+2
in local politics	0	0	−2
Often or occasionally discuss:			
national politics	+2	0	+5
local politics	0	0	+1
% who know:			
county name	+9	+9	+9
district name	+7	+7	+8
name of councillor	n.a.**	+17	n.a.
party of councillor	n.a.	+8	n.a.

*Impact indicates % in May 1986 minus % in Nov. 1985.
**n.a. indicates not asked in May except where elections.

Elsewhere in the interviews we asked respondents whether they voted more on local issues or on national issues in local elections. Although more claimed to vote on local issues than on national, the emphasis on local issues declined as local election time approached and *declined most in areas where elections were held*!

When we asked directly whether there were any local issues that influenced their local voting choice we did find an increase of 7 per cent who could name some local issue in May. Alas, the named issues

Table 14.2. Election impact on national/local issue orientation

	% impact amongst respondents:		
	total	in election areas	in areas without elections
Issue of importance a matter for central government rather than councils	+3	+6	−2
In local elections, respondent claims to vote more on local than on national issues	−3	−4	−2

failed to support the idea that local issues might gain in importance at local election time, for there was a decline in the numbers who mentioned rates and by far the largest increase was in those who named unemployment. No doubt unemployment is visible locally, but employment policy is primarily the responsibility of central rather than local government. So these electors were speaking essentially about the *local consequences of national government policies.*

The strength of party identification increased, though not dramatically. The numbers without any party identification declined by 3 per cent and party identification became a little stronger (Table 14.3) as well as a little more widespread. The numbers who said they would vote for the party rather than the candidate increased—when considering both national elections and local elections. Finally there was a slight increase in support for the idea of a party-based system of local government, especially in areas with elections.

Local elections, with their focus on local councils, did nothing to increase public perceptions of council autonomy. Especially in election areas, *perceptions* of local autonomy actually declined, though *support* for it increased quite sharply (Table 14.4). On both indicators local government seemed to be winning the argument against central government.

Satisfaction with the performance of local councils remained almost

Table 14.3. Election impact on attitudes to parties

	% impact amongst respondents:		
	total	in election areas	in areas without elections
Vote for party rather than candidate:			
in national elections	+4	+2	+8
in local elections	+2	+2	0
Strength of party identification (very or fairly strong)	+5	+2	+7
Prefer party to non-party system for local government	+2	+5	0

Note: There was also a 3% decline in those without any party identification.

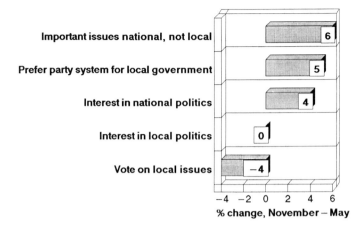

Fig. 14.1. Changes in local/national orientation (*see Tables 14.1–14.3*)

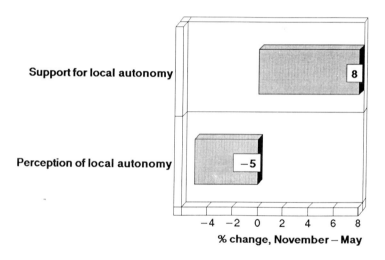

Fig. 14.2. Changes in views on local autonomy (*see Table 14.4*)

unchanged though there was a slight increase in the tendency to blame central government for local financial difficulties, and a rather larger swing away from support for tax cuts (Table 14.5). Again, on all three indicators, local government was winning the argument against central government.

Table 14.4. Election impact on attitudes towards local autonomy

	% impact amongst respondents:		
	total	in election areas	in areas without elections
Perceive central government as having more influence than local councils	+1	+5	−5
Want less rather than more central control	+4	+8	+2

Table 14.5. Election impact on attitudes to policy and performance

	% impact amongst respondents:		
	total	in election areas	in non-election areas
Blame central government rather than councils for financial difficulties	+2	+2	+1
Very or fairly satisfied with:			
county council	0	+2	−3
district council	+1	+1	0
Want cuts in taxes and services rather than increases (first two points on a four-point scale question)	−7	−8	−4

Conclusion

Overall therefore, local elections did have a small but coherent impact upon public attitudes. They raised the political temperature a little. But people did not focus on the internal politics of particular localities: instead, they became a little more partisan, and they focused on the relationship between local and central government. They became a little more aware of the restrictions placed upon local government; they became more favourable to local autonomy; and they became more favourable towards higher levels of taxes and services—a policy position that was generally supported by local governments and opposed by central government.

15 The Impact of an Election Atmosphere, II On Attitude Structure

In the last chapter, we confined our attention to trends in *levels*— trends in the level of interest, or in the level of party identification, or in the level of support for local autonomy. But we might expect that the approach of an election would lead to changes also in the *structure* or *pattern* of attitudes. Indeed earlier chapters provided some clues that suggest there were systematic changes in the structure of attitudes as the election approached.

Heightened public debate and political campaigning might be expected to increase the consistency, the correlation, the *coherence* of attitudes. In Chapter 11 we saw that social and attitudinal predictors of voting intentions were a little more effective at election time than they had been six months earlier (Table 11.4). So there was a slightly closer match between policy attitudes and party choice at local election time.

Less expected were the changes in turn-out patterns revealed in Chapter 8. There we saw that the correlations between the power of social and attitudinal variables to predict local election turn-out *decreased* as the election approached, though their ability to predict general election turn-out did not decrease (Tables 8.2 and 8.5). However we concluded that the critical distinction was between turn-out *intentions* and turn-out *behaviour*, rather than between local and national turn-out. The advent of an election and the efforts of the parties mobilized those social groups with weak motivations to turn out; so that those groups with specially strong voting intentions six months prior to the election did not, in the event, turn out much more strongly than those groups with relatively weak motivations.

Changing Relationships: An Analytic Strategy

However, in those chapters, the impact (if any) of an election atmosphere was peripheral to our principal analytic concerns and we did not analyse it in any systematic way. We can do so now, by developing the loglinear modelling technique we introduced in

Chapter 13. Some technical changes are necessary: first, we change our *unit of analysis* from the *individual respondent* to the *individual interview*—that is, we count the November and May interviews with the same person as two separate interviews; second, we introduce *time* as an additional variable.

Consider, for example, the relationship between turn-out and age in our sample of 745 respondents. We analyse this relationship by finding the best loglinear model, which relates the four variables:

(1) Local election turnout (intention or actual)
(2) Age
(3) Time (election time or non-election, i.e. May 1986 or November 1985)
(4) Place (place with an election in May 1986, or place without)

in our sample of 1,490 (= 2 × 745 interviews).

If the fitted model includes the term *turn-out*age* it means that turn-out is related to age but that the relationship is essentially the same at election and non-election times, and the relationship is also the same in election and non-election areas.

If the fitted model includes the term *turn-out*age*time* it means that the relationship between turn-out and age changed as the election approached.

If the fitted model includes the term *turn-out*age*place* it means that the relationship between turn-out and age differed between the more urban areas that had elections and the less urban areas that did not.

Finally, if the best-fitting loglinear model includes the full four-way interaction term *turn-out*age*place*time* it means that the relationship between turn-out and age differed between election and non-election areas; and that this difference was not constant, but changed as the election approached: so there were divergent or convergent trends (rather than parallel trends) in election and non-election areas.

Trends in Turn-out Patterns

In order to carry out such complex analyses on our modest-sized data set we simplified variables into the dichotomies or trichotomies shown in Table 15.1. We tested seven models to discover whether there were trends in the relationships between turn-out and age, partisanship, political interest, and political knowledge. Table 15.2 shows the seven loglinear models tested.

Table 15.1. Variables used in the loglinear turn-out analyses

Name	Values	Definitions
TLE	1	Turn-out in Local Elections. In November: 'certain or very likely' to vote in a local election. In May where no election: 'certain or very likely to have voted' if there had been an election. In May where there was an election: actually voted.
	0	Otherwise
AGE	1	Young: under 35
	2	Middle-aged: 35–55
	3	Old: over 55
DIRPID	1	Party identification: Conservative
	2	Party identification: Labour
	3	Party identification: Alliance
STRPID	1	Very or fairly strong party identification
	0	Not very strong or no party identification
NINT	1	Great deal or fair amount of interest in national politics
	0	Otherwise
LINT	1	Great deal or fair amount of interest in local politics
	0	Otherwise
KCTY	1	Know county name
	0	Otherwise
KDIST	1	Know district name
	0	Otherwise

Explicitly or implicitly all of the fitted loglinear models include a term: *turn-out*place*time* which suggests that turn-out differed between election and non-election areas and that this difference changed as the election approached. This term in fact merely reflects the replacement of *intentions* by *behaviour* in the areas which had elections. Turn-out intentions in non-election areas increased between November and election time because they were still hypothetical statements of what the respondent would do if there were an election, and the nation-wide election atmosphere led to a small increase in enthusiasm for voting. However in the areas with elections, we are necessarily comparing intentions in November with actual behaviour at election time. Many of those who felt, in November, that they were 'certain or very likely' to vote did not actually do so in May. Thus in these areas our measure of turn-out showed a substantial decline. The loglinear term: *turn-out*place*time* merely reflects these divergent trends in election and

Table 15.2. The impact of elections on turn-out relationships

Relationship number	Variable used in the loglinear analysis in addition to local election turn-out (TLE), PLACE, and TIME	Final simplified model calculated by loglinear analysis
1	Age: AGE	TLE*AGE*PLACE TLE*TIME*PLACE
2	Direction of party identification: DIRPID	TLE*DIRPID*TIME TLE*PLACE*TIME DIRPID*PLACE
3	Strength of party identification: STRPID	TLE*PLACE*TIME STRPID*TIME TLE*STRPID
4	Interest in national politics: NINT	TLE*NINT*PLACE*TIME
5	Interest in local politics: LINT	TLE*LINT*PLACE*TIME
6	Know county name: KCTY	TLE*PLACE*TIME TLE*KCTY KCTY*PLACE KCTY*TIME
7	Know district name: KDIST	TLE*PLACE*TIME TLE*KDIST KDIST*PLACE KDIST*TIME

non-election areas. It confirms the statistical significance of our earlier findings, but adds nothing new.

The most interesting terms in the loglinear analyses are those that involve turn-out and one of the seven tested social or attitudinal predictors of turn-out. The important question is whether these terms also involve *place* and/or *time* as well as turn-out and its social or attitudinal predictor. If they do not, then the turn-out pattern applies to election and non-election *times*, and to election and non-election *areas*.

In the first model, the term: *turn-out*age*place* suggests that the relationship between turn-out and age differed significantly between election and non-election areas but did not change significantly with the approach of an election (because there is no **time* element in this term). A simple tabulation of turn-out by age, place, and time shows what this means (Table 15.3).

Quite clearly the old had higher turn-out rates than the young—on average, by 28 per cent. This was true in November and at election time; and there was no statistically significant trend (a 27 per cent

Table 15.3. Variations but no trends in the turn-out by age relationship

	% turn-out rates amongst:			Difference between % turn-out rates amongst old and young
	Young	Middle-aged	Old	
In all 1490 interviews	45	67	73	28
In all areas:				
November	48	70	75	27
May	41	63	71	30
In non-election areas:				
November	36	68	71	35
May	39	71	82	43
				(Average 39)
In areas with May elections:				
November	55	71	78	23
May	43	60	64	21
				(Average 22)

difference in November rose to 30 per cent in May). Within non-election areas the age differential was much greater than in election areas (hence the term *turn-out*age*place*), running at 39 per cent in the non-election areas and only 22 per cent in the election areas. As the election approached the age differential increased slightly in non-election areas but decreased slightly in election areas, though, according to our loglinear analysis, these divergent trends were too small to be statistically significant.

In the second model, the term *turn-out*partisanship*time* suggests that there were partisan differences in turn-out but that these partisan differences changed as the election approached. Table 15.4 shows that Conservative partisans had the highest rates of turn-out, and Labour partisans had the lowest, but the partisan differential was much higher in November than at election time. However, the fact that this narrowing of the partisan bias occurred in non-election as well as in election areas, suggests that mechanical factors such as canvassing were less important as mobilizing factors than the psychological influence of the election atmosphere. So, while the partisan turn-out bias in election areas was eliminated altogether, it was at least sharply reduced even in non-election areas at election time.

In our third loglinear model the term: *turn-out*strength of identification* did not differ significantly between election and non-election areas; nor did it vary over time. The turn-out rates shown in Table 15.5 indicate that strong identifiers had turn-out rates about 17 per cent

Table 15.4. Trends in the turn-out by partisanship relationship

| | % turn-out amongst those who identify with: | | Difference |
	Con.	Lab.	
In all 1490 interviews	69	58	11
In all areas:			
November	74	59	15
May	64	58	6
In non-election areas:			
November	67	47	20
May	69	61	8
In areas with May elections:			
November	80	64	16
May	58	57	1

Note: Sharp-eyed readers may suspect a printing error here. How can a difference of 16% in election areas and 20% in non-election areas combine to give a difference of 15% in all areas? The figures are correct however. This quirk results from the fact that the elections occurred in more Labour areas than Conservative.

Table 15.5. Neither trend nor variation in the turn-out by strength of partisanship relationship

| | % turn-out amongst: | | Difference |
	Weak identifiers	Strong identifiers	
In all 1490 interviews	50	67	17
In all areas:			
November	54	70	16
May	45	64	19
In non-election areas:			
November	46	66	20
May	45	72	27
In areas with May elections:			
November	60	72	12
May	45	60	15

higher than weak identifiers, and there was only the slightest indication of a widening gap between strong and weak identifiers at election time. Somewhat surprisingly, the table does appear to show rather larger turn-out differentials in the non-election areas than in election areas, though this difference was not statistically significant according to the loglinear analysis.

The fourth and fifth analyses suggest that the relationship between turn-out and political interest differed between election and non-election time. (See Table 15.6.) Overall, those with high interest in local politics had a turn-out rate 20 per cent higher than those with low political interest. However, this turn-out differential declined sharply between November and election time, from 25 per cent to 15 per cent. But amongst those who lived in non-election areas the turn-out differential (between the turn-out intentions of those with high and low interest) rose slightly from 27 per cent to 30 per cent, while amongst those who lived in election areas this differential dropped very sharply from 22 per cent to a mere 7 per cent. These divergent trends were so very sharply divergent that they passed even the stringent loglinear test for statistical significance and so we get a full four-way interactive model: *turn-out*interest*place*time*.

This is the clearest example of a range of evidence suggesting that:

(1) The election time atmosphere had a small effect, raising the political temperature and increasing the good intentions of the good intenders even in areas which themselves did not have a local election in May 1986.

(2) But where elections actually took place, good intentions failed while other powerful mechanisms (probably party campaigning)

Table 15.6. Trends and variations in the relationship between turn-out and political interest

	Turn-out amongst those whose interest in local politics is:		Difference between turn-out rates of those with high and low interest
	Low	High	
In all 1490 interviews	54	74	20
In all areas:			
November	55	80	25
May	53	68	15
In non-election areas:			
November	49	76	27
May	54	84	30
			(Change +3)
In areas with May elections:			
November	59	81	22
May	53	60	7
			(Change −15)

came into play to encourage even the uninterested to cast their vote.

Finally our sixth and seventh models both suggest that the essential relationship between knowledge and turn-out did not vary either between areas or across time. Knowledge itself increased sharply at election time (hence the *knowledge*time* terms), but its relationship to actual or intended turn-out did not. (Hence the terms *turn-out*knowledge* without a time element.) An inspection of tables of turn-out rates confirms this: in election and non-election areas, and at both election and non-election times turn-out rates were approximately 12 per cent higher amongst those who knew their county name than amongst those who did not.

Trends in Patterns of Party Choice

We can apply the same system of loglinear analysis to the question whether *local election vote preference patterns* changed as the election approached. We looked at five patterns—the relationship between local election vote preferences and (1) class, (2) attitudes to tax and service cuts, (3) blame for local financial difficulties, (4) national party identification, and (5) parliamentary general election vote preferences.

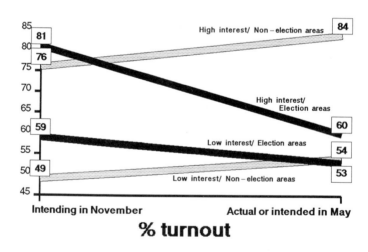

Fig. 15.1. Trends in the relationship between political interest and turn-out (*see Table 15.6*)

Table 15.7 summarizes the results of our loglinear analysis. Amongst other things they show that there were significant social class differences between the election and non-election areas, and there was a significant change in attitudes towards tax and service cuts as the election approached. But for our present purposes the interesting terms are those that involve local election vote preferences.

In all our loglinear models the term *preference*place* appears explicitly or implicitly. That simply tells us that party support in the less urban areas without elections differed consistently from party support in the more urban, more working-class areas which did have local elections in May 1986. While true, we hardly needed a loglinear analysis to tell us that. So it is the remaining terms which constitute the important findings.

Our first loglinear analysis contains the term *preference*class* which suggests that the influence of class did not vary across either space or time. A tabulation of local voting preferences by class, place, and time confirms this: the middle class were approximately 25 per cent more Conservative, 7 per cent more Alliance, and 31 per cent less Labour in their local voting intentions than were the working class in both election and non-election areas and at both election and non-election times.

Similarly, the second loglinear analysis contains the term *preference* taxcut* which suggests that the relationship between local voting preferences and attitudes to tax and service cuts did not vary across

Table 15.7. The impact of elections on voting preference patterns

Pattern number	Variable used in the loglinear analysis in addition to local election preference (LPREF), PLACE, and TIME	Final simplified model calculated by loglinear analysis
1	Social class: CLASS	LPREF*CLASS LPREF*PLACE CLASS*PLACE
2	Support for tax and service cuts: TAXCUT	LPREF*TAXCUT LPREF*PLACE TAXCUT*TIME
3	Blame central government for local financial difficulties: BLAME	LPREF*BLAME*PLACE
4	Direction of party identification: DIRPID	LPREF*DIRPID LPREF*PLACE
5	Party choice for a parliamentary general election: GEPREF	LPREF*GEPREF*PLACE*TIME

either space or time. Tabulating percentages shows that those who preferred cuts in tax and spending were approximately 12 per cent more Conservative, 8 per cent less Alliance, and 5 per cent less Labour than those who wanted increased spending, irrespective of time or place.

However, our third loglinear analysis contains the term *preference* blame*place* which suggests that the relationship between vote preferences and allocating blame for local financial difficulties differed between election and non-election areas, but not between election and non-election times. Overall, those who blamed the councils were 37 per cent more Conservative than those who blamed central government. There was little overall trend: the figure was 35 per cent in November and 38 per cent in May. However, in the non-election areas the vote preference differential was rather less than this (about 30 per cent), while in election areas the differential was rather more (about 41 per cent). The areas also differed more in November than they did at the time of the May election, but these convergent trends were not judged statistically significant by the loglinear analysis (Table 15.8).

The fourth loglinear analysis contains the term *preference*direction of partisanship* suggesting that the relationship between local preferences and national partisanship did not vary significantly across space or time. In sharp contrast to this, the fifth loglinear analysis comprises

Table 15.8. Variations without trends in the relationship between local preferences and blame for local financial difficulties

| | Amongst those who blame: | | Difference |
	Central govt. %Con.	Local council %Con.	
In all 1490 interviews	18	55	37
In all areas:			
November	18	53	35
May	18	56	38
In non-election areas:			
November	28	53	25
May	26	60	34
In areas with May elections:			
November	13	53	40
May	13	54	41

Note: Entries show Conservative share of Conservative plus Labour plus Alliance preferences.

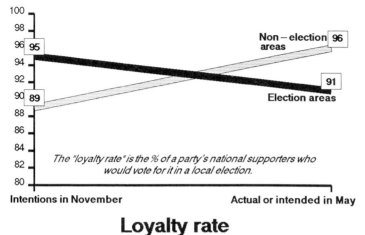

Fig. 15.2. Trends in loyalty rates (*see Table 15.10*)

only the term *local preference*general election preference*place*time* which suggests that the relationship between local preferences and national voting intentions did vary across both space and time.

These loglinear analyses are based upon a complete matrix of relationships between Conservative, Labour, and Alliance choices at national and local level. However, the tabulations of loyalty rates in Tables 15.9 and 15.10 confirm the loglinear conclusions. If we calculate a 'loyalty rate' for each party—that is, the percentage of its identifiers who give it their local vote preference—we notice that the loyalty rates (in terms of identifiers) did not change between November and election time, and were only slightly higher in the election areas than in the non-election areas. But if we calculate a second 'loyalty rate', taking the percentage of a party's current national election supporters who give it their local vote preference, then we notice that loyalty rates (in terms of national and local vote preferences) did indeed change between November and election time.

In non-election areas the fit between national and local preferences went *up* by 7 per cent at local election time, while in areas with local elections this fit went *down* by 4 per cent. This suggests that the *election-time atmosphere* made those in non-election areas a little more

Table 15.9. Stability in the relationship between local preferences and national party identification

| | Local vote % loyalty rates amongst those with: | | Average |
	Con. id.	Lab. id.	
In all 1490 interviews	90	90	90
In all areas:			
November	90	91	90
May	90	89	90
In non-election areas:			
November	89	86	88
May	89	84	87
In areas with May elections:			
November	91	93	92
May	91	91	91

Note: Loyalty rate is the % of a party's identifiers that would vote for it in a local election. Based on those with Conservative, Labour, and Alliance identifications and local election preferences.

Table 15.10. Trends and variations in the relationship between local and national vote preferences

| | Local vote % loyalty rates amongst those with: | | Average |
	Con. natl. pref.	Lab. natl. pref.	
In all 1490 interviews	93	93	93
In all areas:			
November	93	93	93
May	92	93	93
In non-election areas:			
November	91	87	89
May	96	96	96 (Change +7)
In areas with May elections:			
November	95	95	95
May	90	91	91 (Change −4)

Note: Loyalty rate is the % of a party's current national support that would vote for it in a local election. Based on those with Conservative, Labour, and Alliance national and local election preferences.

consistent in their party preferences, while at the same time, the *actual occurrence of an election*, with real councils and real candidates—'warts and all'—encouraged those in election areas to distinguish their local vote preference from their national election preference.

One qualification to this finding must be stated however. We have reached it by restricting attention to those with Conservative, Labour, or Alliance preferences for both national and local elections. In Chapter 11 we found that in the areas without elections in 1986 the social and political environment was such that relatively large numbers of respondents did not have a national or local preference for any of these parties. Despite this, our conclusions about the impact of an election on trends in patterns of relationship between national and local preferences is probably still correct as a general statement, and it is, of course, certainly correct for those with Conservative, Labour, or Alliance preferences.

Conclusion

Our analyses of trends in the patterns of turn-out and party choice in local elections have indicated that local elections have an impact both in the areas in which they occur and in the rest of the country.

Patterns of turn-out intentions strengthened at election time in areas that did not actually have elections but they became weaker in areas that actually did have an election. Similarly the fit between national and local party preferences increased at local election time in areas that did not actually have elections but it declined in areas that actually had elections.

We have discovered the difference between the psychological effects of an election atmosphere without an election, and the behavioural effects of an actual election with real candidates and real party organizations locked in battle.

16 How Voters Resolved the Contradictions between their Policy Attitudes and their Party Choices

We can look at changing attitude structures in another way: how far did those with inconsistent policy attitudes and party preferences in November 1985 change their attitudes or party preferences so as to make them more consistent by the time of the election in May 1986?

Local versus Central Government

In both waves of the panel we asked whether central government or local councils were more to blame for local financial difficulties.

We can regard blaming central government as consistent with a local election voting preference for Labour—first, because Labour is ideologically more sympathetic to high-spending local authorities and second, because in 1985–6 central government was Conservative while a majority of district councils were Labour-controlled. A four-way tabulation of local election preferences in November and May by attribution of blame in November and May shows that over 85 per cent of those with consistent attitudes and preferences in November held on to both in May (defining consistency as *either* prefer Labour and blame government *or* prefer Conservative and blame councils—see Table 16.1).

Only 73 per cent of inconsistent Conservatives (i.e. Conservatives who blamed the government) held on to their contradictory views through to May—and 20 per cent of them switched away from a Conservative preference.

On the Labour side the changes amongst those with inconsistent attitudes were far more dramatic: only a third of them continued to combine a Labour preference with blaming the local councils. Over half changed their attitudes about blame, though almost none switched their preference to the Conservatives.

Amongst those with an Alliance voting preference in November we are reluctant to describe any as consistent or inconsistent since

Table 16.1. Resolution of inconsistencies between local election voting preferences and attitudes towards the blame for local financial difficulties

	Attitudes and preferences in May					
	% Held on to both attitude and party	% Changed attitude	% Changed party*	% Changed both*	% Switched to Alliance	
November Position:						
Consistent Con.	86	9	0	3	2	100%
Inconsistent Con.	73	6	4	3	13	100%
Consistent Lab.	85	5	2	0	9	100%
Inconsistent Lab.	36	54	1	0	9	100%

	Attitudes and preferences in May		
	% Stayed with Alliance	% Switched to Con.	% Switched to Lab.	
November Position:				
Alliance with Con. attitude	80	12	8	100%
Alliance with Lab. attitude	72	4	24	100%

Notes:
1. Based upon tracking individuals' changing attitudes and preferences through from Nov. 1985 to May 1986.
2. The 'Conservative attitude' was to blame the councils, the 'Labour attitude' was to blame the government.
3. 'Consistent' means that in Nov. an individual's party preference and policy attitude were both Labour or both Conservative.
4. Party changes in the columns marked with an asterisk, mean changes to the opposite party: i.e. Conservative to Labour or vice versa.
5. Because of rounding, the figures in each row may not sum to 100% exactly.

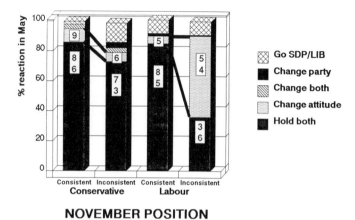

NOVEMBER POSITION

Fig. 16.1. Blame and party preference (*see Table 16.1*)

Alliance policy was less sharply perceived. About three-quarters held on to their Alliance preference through to May. However, amongst Alliance respondents with a Conservative attitude (i.e. blaming councils in November) more switched to the Conservatives than to Labour. Conversely amongst Alliance respondents with a Labour attitude (i.e. blaming central government in November), six times as many switched to Labour as to Conservative.

So how should we summarize these reactions to policy attitudes and party preferences? Over the six months leading up to the local election it does seem as though policy attitudes influenced the voting intentions of former Conservative and Alliance respondents. But amongst Labour respondents the balance of causal forces went decisively in the other direction—they stayed loyal to Labour and, if necessary, changed their policy attitude to bring it into line with their party preference.

It could be argued that this analysis should have been restricted to districts with Labour-controlled councils, to avoid the partisan ambiguity involved in blaming councils where the councils were actually Conservative. We did repeat the analysis, restricted to districts with Labour councils. The results were similar to those in Table 16.1; patterns were even sharper, but on a reduced sample size that might be a sampling artefact—so we present Table 16.1 as a *minimum finding* which is confirmed and even exaggerated by further analysis.

Taxes versus Services

We repeated this analysis using attitudes to tax-cuts rather than attitudes towards blame for local financial difficulties. Attitudes to cuts in taxation and services were remarkably weak, indeed almost non-existent influences upon party preference. Whether tax-cut attitudes were consistent or inconsistent with party voting preferences, large numbers of respondents changed them (i.e. their tax-cut attitudes) between November and May. Inconsistent Conservatives were particularly likely to change their tax-cut attitudes to bring them into line with their voting preference. The same could not be said of inconsistent Labour respondents who, by and large, merely retained both their Labour preference and their desire for tax-cuts.

Policy inconsistency on tax-cut attitudes had very little effect at all: it seemed to encourage about 6 per cent of Labour and Conservative respondents to switch their voting preference away from their initial party, but it was much more likely to produce a change in tax-cut attitudes.

However once again (though less on attitudes to tax-cuts than on blame) Alliance respondents with Labour policy attitudes were more likely to switch to Labour and those with Conservative policy attitudes were more likely to switch to the Conservatives (Table 16.2).

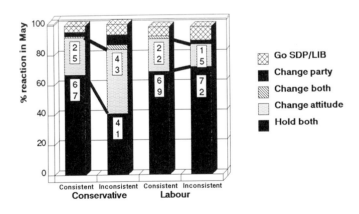

NOVEMBER POSITION

Fig. 16.2. Tax-cuts and party preference (*see Table 16.2*)

Table 16.2. Resolution of inconsistencies between local election voting preferences and attitudes towards tax-cuts

	Attitudes and preferences in May				
	% Held on to both attitude and party	% Changed attitude	% Changed party*	% Changed both*	% Switched to Alliance
November Position:					
Consistent Con.	67	25	3	1	4	100%
Inconsistent Con.	41	43	7	3	7	100%
Consistent Lab.	69	22	0	2	6	100%
Inconsistent Lab.	72	15	3	0	9	100%

	Attitudes and preferences in May		
	% Stayed with Alliance	% Switched to Con.	% Switched to Lab.
November Position:			
Alliance with Con. attitude	83	9	9	100%
Alliance with Lab. attitude	69	8	23	100%

Notes:
1. Based upon tracking individuals' changing attitudes and preferences through from Nov. 1985 to May 1986.
2. The 'Conservative attitude' was to cut government spending, the 'Labour attitude' was to maintain or increase government spending.
3. 'Consistent' means that in Nov. an individual's party preference and policy attitude were both Labour or both Conservative.
4. Party changes in the columns marked with an asterisk, mean changes to the opposite party: i.e. Conservative to Labour or vice versa.
5. Because of rounding, the figures in each row may not sum to 100% exactly.

Party Identification

Finally we looked at those whose party identification and local voting preferences in November were inconsistent. As we saw in Chapter 11 such people were few in number and scattered over a range of different inconsistencies, which makes further analysis difficult. However, if we take the most frequent inconsistency—that is, a Labour or Conservative identification but an Alliance preference for a local election—we find that two-fifths hung on to their inconsistent attitudes, another two-fifths brought their local preference into line with their party identification, and somewhat less than one-fifth changed their party identification to bring it into line with their local preference.

Cross-lagged Regressions

Cross-lagged regression analyses confirm the findings of these four-way cross-tabulations on the resolution of inconsistencies. In cross-lagged regression we use attitudes and preferences in the previous November to predict attitudes and preferences at election time in May. That is one way (not the only one) of determining whether attitudes have more effect upon voting preferences than vice versa. For these regressions we recoded voting preferences to treat an Alliance preference as midway between a Conservative preference and a Labour preference.

In all the cross-lagged regressions the most powerful forces were simple continuities—attitudes in November predicted attitudes in May, while voting preferences in November predicted voting preferences in May. However, there were also substantial cross-influences between blame and voting preferences, and between party identification and voting preferences, but *not* between tax-cut attitudes and voting preferences (see cross-lagged regression diagram).

Voting preferences seemed to have about as much influence upon party identification as party identification had on voting preferences. Voting preferences had twice as much influence upon attitudes to blame for financial difficulties as these attitudes had upon subsequent voting preferences. Between tax-cut attitudes and voting preferences the estimated influences were very small and statistically insignificant. Moreover, tax-cut attitudes were also unstable as well as merely unpredictable.

NOVEMBER   MAY

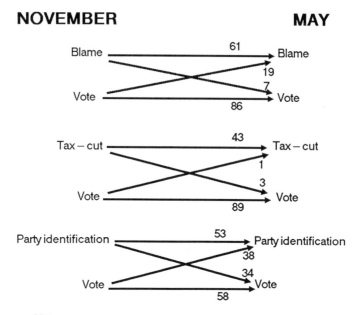

Notes:
1. Vote = vote preference for a local election
*2. The figures shown are standardized regression coefficients,
also known as "beta weights" or "path coefficients". Except in
very peculiar circumstances they cannot exceed 100. They are
fully comparable with each other and so measure the relative
strength of the various influences.*

Fig. 16.3. Cross-lagged regression analyses of the influences between policy
attitudes and voting preferences

This may help to explain one of the paradoxes of recent analyses of
national election behaviour in Britain. Throughout the 1980s opinion
polls have shown support for an increase rather than a decrease in
taxes and services but still the Labour Party has not prospered, while a
right-wing Conservative government committed to cutting taxes and
services has been re-elected twice. Our evidence suggests that voters'
responses to standard tax versus services questions are both unreliable
and unimportant as a guide to future political behaviour: tax-cut
attitudes in November were a poor predictor of tax-cut attitudes six
months later (hence *unreliable*) and failed utterly to predict voting
preferences six months later (hence *unimportant*).

17 Conclusion: The Quality of Local Democracy in Britain

Democracy involves more than elections. None the less, the Layfield Committee described local elections as 'the essence of local democracy'.[1] But *what* do local elections do for democracy? And, *how well* do they do it? In answering these questions we need to adopt both a local and a national perspective, for many would argue that the most important feature of local democracy is its contribution to national democracy.

What Do Democratic Elections Do?

Let us start with a quick check-list of some of the functions of democratic elections.[2] These include:

(1) Providing representation for different opinions, social groups, and parties.
(2) Offering a choice between rival political leaders and policies.
(3) Giving the winners a mandate to govern and conferring legitimacy on both the government and the political system— legitimacy both in the eyes of the electorate and in the eyes of powerful internal or external actors who might be inclined to overrule the government or even overturn the wider political system.
(4) Educating the electors about the political process, and about current political issues; and, at the same time, educating political leaders about the concerns of the electorate.

The first two items on this list might be described as 'bottom-up' functions that help to give the electorate a choice; the third might be described as a 'top-down' function that helps elected officials accumulate enough authority to govern effectively; the last describes an exchange of information and influence between governors and governed.

In the context of national elections in Western democracies this list is not controversial. Commentators may disagree about how well particular elections in particular countries perform these tasks, but few would pretend that any of them were not proper functions for national elections. By contrast, some of these functions may be regarded as inappropriate for local elections. The Widdicombe Committee itself suggests that local authorities do not derive a local mandate from their electorate.[3]

There is disagreement, therefore, not only about the functions that local elections *do* perform, but also about the functions that they *ought* to perform. That brings us to the question of the purpose of local government itself. If we can define the proper functions of local government then we can deduce the proper functions of local elections, and evaluate their performance accordingly.

What Should Elected Local Government Do?

As Elcock points out,[4] the British system of government includes a wide range of decentralized agencies—Regional and District Health Authorities, Regional Tourist Boards, Regional Arts Associations, Regional Water Authorities—most of whose members are appointed by central government ministers. In addition many central departments, especially the Department of Employment, the Department of Health and Social Security, and the Department of the Environment, have extensive local or regional structures. Many of the appointments to these boards and committees are intended to represent local interests and opinions and, despite holding office by ministerial appointment, they often have some discretion and do indeed oppose or resist ministerial policies. A comprehensive system of *elected* local government covering the *whole* of Britain is less than 100 years old. Yet already many of the important responsibilities assigned to it have been lost again by transfer to central government, to non-elected bodies, or even to private sector companies. Clearly, elected local government is not the only way of running things locally.

For the last half-century, two important characteristics of British local government have been that it is *elected* and that it is *multi-purpose*. During this period, Britain no longer had the system of elected special-purpose boards for schools (ILEA excepted), roads, or poor-relief that still existed in the USA—though the Thatcher Government proposed to reinvent them by transferring power away from all-purpose local authorities to parents' committees as well as various non-elected boards. Those who argue the case for all-purpose, elected local government claim that this system provides:[5]

(1) efficiency;
(2) responsiveness;
(3) participation; and
(4) pluralism.

Local government is said to be *efficient* because it has a depth of local knowledge that central government lacks and because, as a multi-purpose authority, it can play a co-ordinating role better than any single-purpose agency like, for example, the Health Service.

It is said to be *responsive* because it is aware of local needs and opinions and, as an elected body, it has the motivation to respond.

However British local government is far from being truly local. By international standards British local governments are very large: the Greater London Council (abolished 1985–6) covered about seven million inhabitants, while Strathclyde Regional Council covers half of Scotland, and even the district councils typically serve large populations. Local needs and opinions are much more local than that and the electoral process, by itself, cannot ensure sensitivity to very local concerns, though the political culture of electoral democracy may encourage a respect for the electorate and a suspicion of bureaucracy.

Thirdly, elected local government automatically encourages *participation* at two levels; participation by the electorate in voting, and more complex participation by activists, candidates, and elected officials. In practice, it also provides opportunities for direct influence by individuals and pressure groups through consultation, local lobbying, and a massive amount of co-option—though this kind of access could equally well be provided by non-elected bodies.

Finally, and most important, local government is said to contribute to *pluralism*. Pluralism means a system with many centres of power and decision. This may encourage technical experiment and innovation. J. S. Mill argued that variety and diversity were good in themselves, reflecting freedom and choice which were, for him, ends in themselves. But he also argued that there should be 'experiments in living . . . (so) that the worth of different modes of life should be proved'.[6] Local government experiments were particularly valuable because the costs and damage of failure would be limited while success could be copied by other local governments. (The contrast with central government's experiments with economic theories should be obvious!) Byrne quotes as examples of local government innovations the 1847 decision by Liverpool Council to appoint the first Medical Officer of

Health; decisions by London and Birmingham Councils later in the century to develop the first council housing; and more recent local experiments with free bus travel and special housing for pensioners. Variety is technically expedient.

But even more valuable than its contribution to innovation is pluralism's function as a bulwark against totalitarianism and tyranny. When Lord Butler was Home Secretary he told the House of Commons, 'I am quite convinced that it would be wrong for one man or one Government to be in charge directly of the whole police of the country. Our Constitution is based on checks and balances.'[7] Of course, Britain does not have a constitution nor a specially designed system of 'checks and balances'—hence Lord Hailsham's description of Britain as an 'elective dictatorship'.[8] If we follow Lord Butler's line we are expecting local government to substitute for the *lack of a constitution* and for the *lack of an institutional system of checks and balances*. This idea is not so implausible as it at first sounds, since the Widdicombe Committee notes[9] that when Lord Salisbury set up the first nation-wide system of elected local government in 1888 he intended the new local authorities to 'diminish the excessive and exaggerated powers' of central government. The Layfield Committee referred to local government as 'spreading power . . . by providing a large number of points where decisions are taken by people of different political persuasion' and 'providing a safety valve . . . to accommodate pressure or dissatisfaction before they build up to major proportions'.[10]

The idea of pluralism pre-dates democracy and even today it does not depend upon elections. Pluralism, in contrast to totalitarianism, requires the acceptance by central goverment that alternative views are legitimate, that opposition is not disloyalty or stupidity, and that other power centres within society should be tolerated if not welcomed—and certainly not destroyed. Hampton mentions the House of Lords and the trade unions contributing to a pluralist national polity in much the same way as local authorities. He might well have added the churches, the mass media (especially the BBC), and the universities—though all of these exert intellectual and moral influence rather than direct decision-making power.

Perhaps we need to emphasize once again that *British local government is not local* in the same sense as in most other countries—exceptions such as Paris and New York notwithstanding. British local governments cover large populations, partly because they have been designed for efficient service provision rather than as community forums. At the same time Britain conspicuously lacks both a system of constitutional checks and balances and a system of regional government. This combination of circumstances means that British local government also has to perform (well or badly) much of the role of American States or German Lander in preserving pluralism and resisting total uniformity. British local government would not be nearly so important for the health of British national democracy if we had a system of devolved government for Scotland and the regions of England.

But given the scarcity of pluralistic institutions in Britain, we have to assess the quality of local democracy both in terms of its performance *within the locality* and in terms of its contribution to the *national political system*.

Some writers dismiss the concept of local democracy completely. Thus Midwinter and Mair state: 'There is a problem with the concept of local democracy. We are doubtful if this ever was an accurate concept in the descriptive sense, even in the simpler society of the 19th century. Rather we would see local government as an important aspect of national democracy.'[11] The Widdicombe Committee, however, sees local government's contributions to local democracy and to the national political system as 'interlocking and complementary'.[12] Certainly, if local elections did legitimize local councils in the eyes of central government then pluralists at least would agree that they strengthened both local and national democracy—albeit in different ways. Conversely, it is difficult to see how local elections can contribute towards national democracy if they do not contribute to local democracy, since the prestige, authority, and legitimacy that they command in the national political system must depend to a large degree upon their performance within the local political system.

Central Government's Attack on Local Government

Throughout the 1980s local democracy in Britain has been on trial. Its viability has not been accepted and its existence has not been guaranteed. Following Hayek and others, recent Conservative governments have espoused a stridently libertarian rhetoric. But it has been as much populist as liberal: it has emphasized the freedom *of the individual* but not the freedom *of intermediate organizations of individuals*. It has supported the freedom of individuals to participate *as individuals* in the market-place but not their *freedom of association* in either geographic or functional interest groups. Despite Hayek's own claim that 'nowhere has democracy ever worked well without a great measure of local self-government' and his firm rejection of 'the deadly blight of centralisation',[13] both the Heath and the Thatcher Governments have gloried in strong leadership as much as in individual liberty, and their tolerance towards obstructive local or functional organizations has been strictly limited. Toleration of opposition, and especially of organized opposition, may be the hallmark of liberalism, but in 1972 they abolished Stormont, the devolved system of government for Northern Ireland; in 1979 they opposed, and then repealed the legislation to set up devolved Assemblies for Scotland and Wales; in 1985 (with effect from 1986) they abolished the Greater London Council and the metropolitan county councils for the West Midlands, Merseyside, Greater Manchester, West Yorkshire, South Yorkshire, and the Tyne and Wear area. They curbed the power of the trade unions, attacked church 'interference' in social affairs, and imposed a severe financial crack-down on the universities—especially in non-technical subjects. In the winter of 1986–7 they attacked the impartiality of the BBC, which the Prime Minister accused of being to the left of Gorbachev, and they defended an unprecedented night-time police raid on the BBC's Scottish headquarters in Glasgow.

It is a poor record for self-professed libertarians, but it has been justified on two grounds: first by the familiar populist and totalitarian argument that nothing must stand in the way of central government with its overriding national mandate; second, by the allegation that individual freedom was, or would be, restricted by these intermediate organizations. It was alleged that Stormont tyrannized Catholics in Northern Ireland; that permanent Labour majorities in Scotland and Wales would tyrannize middle-class taxpayers; that London and the metropolitan county councils tyrannized their ratepayers; that the union leadership and activists tyrannized rank-and-file union members; and that church leaders and journalists were at least unrepresentative, even if they could exert no more than moral and intellectual tyranny.

The Widdicombe Committee outlined its view of the constitutional position of British local government thus: 'In Great Britain, Parliament is sovereign . . . all current local authorities are the statutory creations of Parliament and have *no independent status or right to exist*.' The Committee added that while 'Central government is not itself sovereign . . . in practice [it] is drawn from the political party with a majority in Parliament'[14] and effectively exercises parliamentary sovereignty.

Some Scots might point out that under the 1707 Treaty of Union, local government in Scotland was guaranteed 'in all time coming' but the courts might be reluctant to uphold that view. And for the rest of Britain, very few would dispute Widdicombe's statement of the constitutional position: central government, acting through Parliament, has an unfettered legal right to determine local government's responsibilities, control its performance, reform it, and even abolish it. Consequently 'the future viability of local government therefore depends both on its external constitutional place within the wider political system, and *on its internal conduct*':[15] without a *right* to exist, it must *justify* itself by performance.

One relevant aspect of performance is efficient management of local services. On that basis alone local authorities might justify their continued existence, though the term local *government* might then be inappropriate: 'if local government is strong on the delivery of services but weak in the extent to which it provides for local democratic expression, it ceases to be sufficiently distinct from local *administration*'.[16] Thus the viability of continued local government in the full sense of the term depends upon its *performance in terms of democracy* rather than in terms of managing services. The problem is whether local democracy can perform in such a way as to merit the title democracy and at the same time perform in a way that is acceptable to a central government with, in the words of one senior judge, 'totalitarian' tendencies.

British central government has a general theoretical commitment to democratic ideals. Hence the Widdicombe Committee was instructed to make recommendations concerning the conduct of local government business with a view to 'strengthening the democratic process'.[17] At the same time central government has a very clear idea about what constitutes good and bad local decision-making. The 1979 Government was elected on a programme of cutting taxes and public expenditure. Unfortunately, it was not easy to cut local government expenditure and central government was driven to impose ever-greater controls to achieve that end—grant-related assessments, targets, penalties, and rate-capping. In England and Wales it took powers to prevent local governments setting a supplementary rate half-way through the year and in Scotland it went further and took powers to force local authorities to make mid-year refunds to their ratepayers.

No one could pretend that such measures improved local democracy. They were a negation of the very idea of local democracy. But if local democracy produced the 'wrong' decisions by local councils then there were only three options open to central government:

(1) It could accept that 'wrong' local decisions were the essence of local democracy and therefore tolerate them in the interests of a pluralistic national democracy.
(2) It could accept that 'wrong' local decisions were the essence of local democracy and abolish local democracy in the interests of 'correct' decisions.
(3) It could reject the view that 'wrong' decisions rose from a well-functioning local democracy, treat them as an aberration caused by defects in the operation of local democracy, and search for ways to remedy those defects.

Recent governments have been too ideologically motivated and too self-righteous to take the first option, of toleration. They have gone a long way towards taking the second option by abolishing some elected councils, controlling the decisions, or transferring responsibilities away from those councils that remain. But that option involves the exercise of naked central power which is unpopular with the public at large and disturbs those members of the government who do see some value in a pluralist national democracy.

The third option has great attractions. A reform that improved local democracy and produced local decisions more acceptable to central government would square the circle. A change in the basis of local taxation would allegedly make local councils more 'accountable' to their electorates and create pressure to keep local expenditure low. On the assumption (not necessarily valid) that central government will always want to keep local spending down, such a local taxation system would simultaneously improve local democracy and make local decisions more acceptable to central government.

The government's Green Paper *Paying for Local Government* claimed that the existing system of local finance lacked accountability and encouraged irresponsibility. Since there were differences between 'those who vote for, those who pay for, and those who receive' local government services, voters were encouraged to vote for high public spending which they themselves would not have to finance: non-ratepayers could vote to impose burdens on ratepayers and the local electorate as a whole could vote to impose burdens on industry and commerce. In the words of the Green Paper:

Local authorities' main income sources are non-domestic rates, domestic rates, and Exchequer (i.e. central government) grants. All of them are unsatisfactory.

—Non-domestic rates are paid by business and public institutions to whom local authorities are not directly answerable.

—Domestic rates are paid by a minority of local electors and vary in a way that now has little or no regard to the use made of local authority services. The burden of rates is carried on too few shoulders.

—Central government grants are calculated in a very complicated way that conceals the real cost of local services from the electorate.[18]

The ideological implications in these words are breathtaking. The proposition that business and public institutions should not pay taxes to an authority unless they have direct representation on it recalls the constitution of Regent Horthy's regime in pre-war Hungary. The complaint that taxes are paid by a minority and vary in a way that has little regard to the taxpayers' use of public services is a criticism of any society that combines political equality with economic inequality. As nineteenth-century politicians feared, if you let the poor vote then they may vote to tax the rich. What is perhaps more remarkable is that they have used their electoral power so sparingly in practice. But it is the very essence of free Western democracies that they combine political equality with economic inequality and therefore that they use taxation to moderate (but not eliminate) economic inequalities.

As for the comment on the complexity of central government grants, that is simply laudable but uncharacteristic self-criticism.

Yet while it is easy to pour scorn on the low intellectual quality of central government's arguments, there is still a need to examine the quality of local democracy since its long-term viability still does depend upon its own performance as well as upon the hostility of central government.

Local Elections and Local Democracy

We can assess the quality of local democracy by returning to the functions of democratic elections that we listed at the start of this chapter. They cover the ground associated with central government's attack on local government, and more. We can ask:

(1) *Are local elections representative?*—central government alleges undue influence by non-ratepayers.

(2) *Do local elections offer a choice?*—central government alleges that local governments tyrannize their localities.

(3) *Do local elections give winners a mandate to govern?*—some local politicians have claimed that they do, while central government (and the Widdicombe Committee) say not.

(4) *Do local elections educate* the public and the politicians about each other's concerns?

1. Are Local Elections Representative?

Turn-out in local elections is low—not much more than half the turn-out rate in parliamentary elections. So the potential exists for local election voters to be a very unrepresentative subset of the local electorate. Central government has implied that non-ratepayers could vote themselves free services at the expense of the ratepayers by turning out in greater numbers. But the whole accumulated wisdom of political science would imply exactly the opposite bias. Almost universally it is rich taxpayers who turn out to vote more readily than poor non-taxpayers.

What did the panel show? First, that there were higher tendencies towards turn-out amongst the old, the middle class, the highly educated (Table 7.1), those who sympathized with the police (Table 7.3), right-wingers (Table 9.4) and Conservative Party identifiers (Table 9.2); second, that the tendencies towards bias in local election turn-out were much less in the event than in anticipation—when it came to voting in actual elections rather than expressing an intention to vote in a hypothetical election, biases were attenuated or even eliminated (compare the columns headed 'November' and 'May' in the tables already cited, plus the whole of Chapter 9).

So the tendency—that is the psychological motivation—ran counter to central government's expressed fears, though in the event turn-out bias toward left or right, rich or poor, council tenant or house-owner was very small or non-existent. In particular ratepayers and non-ratepayers were almost equally likely to vote in local elections, with the merest hint of higher turn-out rates amongst ratepayers (Tables 7.4 and 9.5). Moreover, ratepaying was a psychologically meaningless variable because almost everyone thought of themselves as a ratepayer, irrespective of whether they were the spouse of a ratepayer or a ratepayer themselves, and irrespective of whether or not they enjoyed rate rebates (Table 2.1). Contrary to central government's fears that irresponsible non-ratepayers would take advantage of the opportunity to impose taxes on the ratepayers, the non-ratepayers not only failed to turn out in especially great numbers, they failed even to appreciate that they were non-ratepayers.

Apart from central government's worries, there are other respects in which local election voters might be unrepresentative however. One reassuring feature of local election turn-out was that despite the low overall level of turn-out there were few consistent non-voters. Low turn-out was produced by intermittent participation rather than by an electorate stratified into consistent voters and consistent abstainers. While three-fifths of respondents reported abstaining at one or other of two successive local elections, less than half that number reported abstaining at both (Table 6.5). If we had been able to extend the questioning over a sequence of three or more local elections, the numbers of consistent abstainers would have dropped still further.

Of course there was a natural bias between the interested and the uninterested. Those who had no interest in national or local politics, who did not discuss politics and did not read a local paper were less inclined to vote (Tables 7.2 and 7.4). The advent of an actual election reduced but did not eliminate turn-out differences between the interested and the uninterested (Tables 7.2 and 15.6).

Alienation from local *elections* naturally reduced turn-out. Those who felt that local elections 'did not decide how things were run in the area' or who felt they were 'too complicated' or that they encouraged politicians to make dishonest promises, had relatively low turn-out rates (Table 7.5). However the span of explanation here is very short: in form it corresponds to the music critic's fail-safe report that 'those who like this kind of music will find that this is the kind of music they like'.

But dissatisfaction with local *councils* did not have this effect. Dissatisfied electors were not cowed into withdrawal from the system. Those who blamed local councils for financial problems were at least as likely to vote as those who did not. Those who had contacted or even complained to local councillors and council offices were more likely to have high turn-out rates. And while dissatisfaction with the way councils were running things in May seemed to produce lower turn-out, dissatisfaction in November seemed to lead to higher than average turn-out six months later (Table 7.4). Overall therefore, there was very little turn-out bias due to either satisfaction or dissatisfaction, though those who were active enough to make an actual complaint seemed active enough to vote as well. In particular, there was no statistically significant evidence for Noelle-Neuman's 'spiral of silence' theory applying to local elections in Britain—the minority partisans in a locality were just as likely to turn out and vote as were supporters of the locally dominant party (Table 13.6).

2. Do Local Elections Offer a Choice?

For elections to offer a meaningful choice, political scientists usually suggest that they need parties to structure the choice; relevant policies and issues to give the choice a content that goes beyond personalities; and a sufficiently marginal or fluid division of partisanship to allow a real possibility of throwing out one lot of rogues and installing another.

Parties have a long history of involvement in British local government: 'By 1890, it would indeed be difficult to find any great English town . . . with a municipal council elected on other than party lines.'[19] By the 1980s party-structured local government extended much further than the 'great towns'. Our panel sample clearly perceived growing involvement by political parties even if they professed to dislike it (Table 3.2). Using 1983 data, Byrne classified 98 per cent of London councils as party-structured, along with 92 per cent of county and district councils in England and Wales, 72 per cent of Scottish district councils and 50 per cent of Scottish regional councils. Moreover, the non-party councils were in sparsely populated areas; so well over 90 per cent of the electorate lived in areas with partisan councils.[20] Parties are therefore available to structure local election choice at the level of councils. Particular parties may not field candidates in some wards (or 'electoral divisions') where their support is very weak, but even at the level of wards party competition is extensive. In the 1985 county council elections the Labour Party contested 89 per cent of the electoral divisions, the Conservatives 85 per cent, and the Alliance 75 per cent. Candidates were elected unopposed in only 6 per cent of divisions.[21]

It is less obvious that support is sufficiently evenly divided or sufficiently fluid for the choice to be real in the sense that incumbent councillors and administrations can be defeated. On 1985 data, Byrne classified 31 per cent of councils as 'one-party dominant' with one party holding between three and four-fifths of the council seats, and another 14 per cent as 'one-party monopolistic' with one party holding over four-fifths of the seats. So almost half the councils appear, on this classification, to be so much under the control of one party that electoral choice is unlikely to imply electoral change.[22]

But swings in local elections can be large. So even large majorities at one time may not imply long-term dominance. Byrne himself points to the record of 20 large cities in England and Wales. Labour controlled 17 of the 20 in 1965, only one in 1970, but 16 in 1973.[23] The Widdicombe Committee highlighted results within Greater Manchester Metropolitan County Council. There were 106 seats. Labour held 64 in 1977 but was reduced to a mere 23 in the election that year before surging ahead to win 78 in 1981.[24]

Comparing 1979 and 1985, Byrne shows that there was single-party control in 70 per cent of British local councils in 1979 and 68 per cent in 1985. Labour controlled 21 per cent in 1979 and 29 per cent in 1985; the Conservatives controlled 47 per cent in 1979 but only 35 per cent in 1985.[25] So the number of local authorities firmly in the pocket of one political party was limited, though not small.

What was the content of choice in terms of policies and issues? The evidence is mixed. Two-thirds of our panel read a local weekly paper (Table 2.1) and as many claimed that their local vote was influenced by local issues (Table 2.5). A third of the electorate said that in local elections, unlike parliamentary elections, they voted for the candidate rather than the party. And those who claimed to vote on local issues or for the local candidate rather than the party were indeed much more likely to cast a vote that did not reflect their national party identification (Table 11.7). The weight they attributed to local issues and candidates varied sharply over time however (Table 4.3). Respondents were not, therefore, divided into local and nationally orientated strata: instead, they had a frequent, but unreliable, tendency to claim a local orientation in voting choice.

On the other hand, they declared little interest in local affairs. Two-thirds said they had 'not much' interest in local politics or even 'none at all', while over half said they 'rarely or never' discussed local politics (Table 2.2). Levels of interest and discussion were much higher for national politics, and respondents overwhelmingly named central government rather than local government as having the responsibility for the issues they themselves regarded as most important (Table 2.2). Significantly, their willingness to blame local rather than national government for local financial problems correlated more strongly with their rating of central government's performance (Table 4.9) than with their rating of local government's performance (Table 4.8).

Overall this suggests that local candidates and issues were of some importance but not a lot. At the same time, people felt that local candidates and issues should be important and they overstressed their own local orientations when describing their voting choices, though not when describing their interest in local politics or the abstract 'importance' of issues. People wished that local politics were more interesting and dealt with matters of greater importance.

We found that over four-fifths of the electorate voted in accordance with their national political preferences when (and if) they voted in local elections (Tables 11.7 and 11.8). Whether that seems a high or a low figure depends upon prior expectations. Clearly local choices are *not totally* dependent upon national choices; equally clearly they are fairly strongly related to national preferences. Given the partisan split in local votes shown in Table 11.3 then random choices in national and local elections, without any differences in the overall distribution of partisanship, would have produced 36 per cent with the same choices at national and local level. A 36 per cent coincidence would indicate nothing but chance, no real connection between national and local choice. The actual figure of 84 per cent coincidence between national and local preferences was thus exactly three-quarters of the way between the minimum figure of 36 which would indicate nothing more than the random coincidence and the maximum of 100 which would indicate total coincidence.

Midwinter and Mair none the less argue that even if there were no difference at all between local and national voting intentions, local elections would still have a valid content:

we find it *un*surprising that over 80 per cent of local voters voted exactly in accord with their national party choice . . . we would find it very surprising if people with right-wing values and attitudes should vote for a left-wing candidate on the basis of his personal characteristics . . . the nationalisation of local politics could be more simply interpreted as the growth of partisan politics in local government.[26]

Thus Midwinter and Mair argue that local elections have a valid content even when they reflect no more than general ideological or partisan values. People in one part of the country may feel that the Labour Party has the correct approach to political and economic problems and so give it their support in both national and local elections. In other areas they might feel that way about the

Conservative Party. These local party choices have a certain democratic validity irrespective of whether they coincide with the local people's choices for parliamentary elections. In a country as small as Britain, more surely in a country as small as *England*, the bases of political choice are not likely to vary much from area to area. Local choices, therefore, may not be based upon unique conflicts internal to specific localities, yet they remain a valid local choice. If people in a particular local authority area feel more comfortable with a particular party while other areas support different parties then there is a democratic argument that they should be allowed to do so. Essentially this is the case for devolved regional government. It is less applicable to local government since the powers of local government are so limited as to make the partisanship of local councils little more than symbolic. But it is more applicable to local government in Britain than elsewhere simply because, as we pointed out earlier, British local government is not truly local and has to do duty for the non-existent regional tier of government found in other countries.

Midwinter and Mair's argument is less persuasive when viewed in a temporal rather than a spatial context. Mid-term swings have long been a feature of British politics. Half-way through a parliament central government appears to lose support in opinion polls, parliamentary by-elections, and local elections. There is an argument for saying that a local council should be under Labour Party control because people in that locality are Labour partisans. But there is not nearly so strong an argument for saying that local councils elected in a particular year should be Labour just because the local election coincided with the mid-term of a Conservative-controlled parliament. Indeed, it is tempting to argue that different parties' controlling councils in *different areas* contributes to the freedom-preserving chaos of pluralism while different parties' controlling councils elected in *different years* contributes only towards the meaningless, useless, irrational chaos of adversary politics and mindless opposition: that it makes sense to have local councils represent areas opposed to the central government of the day, but not to have local councils that automatically and routinely oppose central government simply because they were elected in the mid-term. If we accept that argument then remedies are available: local councils could be elected at the same time as central government (as in 1979) and with a term of office equal to that of central government; or, less radically, local councils could be elected by thirds (i.e. with one third of councillors retiring at each local election) as is the practice in the metropolitan district councils at present (and, for example, in the US Senate).

Election by thirds averages out the effects of time and biases councils neither towards or against central government. It preserves spatial variation while suppressing temporal variation—which meets Midwinter and Mair's suggested representation of local political differences without giving undue representation to mid-term anti-government feeling. On the other hand, elections for whole councils in the mid-term bias councils against central government and are a recipe for amplified opposition; while coincident local and national elections would bias councils towards central government and be a recipe for more agreement and less antagonism between them.

The Widdicombe Committee recommends that all councils should shift over to the Scottish system of whole councils elected for four-year terms that take no account of the parliamentary election cycle. By accident therefore, they sometimes produce results biased towards central government, sometimes against. If we were to accept Midwinter and Mair's argument that the content validity of local elections rested not on the internal politics of a locality, but on its right to express a particular local attitude towards national politics then election by thirds would make more sense. But an extreme pluralist might argue that local councils should be elected on a whole-council basis and always in the parliamentary mid-term: that would ensure the maximum partisan difference between local and central government!

3. Do Local Elections Give Winners a Mandate to Govern?

A mandate to govern is a recognized entitlement to govern. One important question about recognized entitlements is this: *who* recognizes? The range of actors who might give or withhold their recognition depends upon the circumstances. In the case of British local government three actors are most relevant: the courts, the central government, and the mass electorate.

The Widdicombe Committee bluntly states the position of the courts and of central government: 'there is no validity in the assertion that local authorities have a local mandate by which they derive authority from their electorate placing them above the law.'[27] Midwinter and Mair state that the first principle of British local government is the '*ultra vires* principle . . . local government is a creature of parliament and may only act within the specific powers set by it'.[28] Not only is it illegal for councils to do what the law expressly forbids, it is equally illegal for councils to do anything which is not expressly allowed by parliamentary law—in technical jargon, councils have no 'general competence'. Failure to abide by these principles can and does lead to fines, bankruptcy, and even imprisonment for local councillors.[29] The courts do not accept that local elections give any special authority to local councils; so they have *no legal mandate in the eyes of the courts*. Central government often uses the language of 'partnership' which implies some recognition of a local mandate, but it has increasingly moved towards treating local councils as irritating and inefficient agents of central government: so local councils have *no political mandate in the eyes of central government*.

The public take a different view. Many of our survey findings suggest that local government has a remarkably *strong popular mandate in the eyes of its electorate*—that is, the public think that local councils should have the right to take decisions even though that right is denied them by central government and the courts.

It would be wrong to think of this popular mandate, as politicians so often do, as a mandate for specific policies. Although two-thirds of respondents said their vote was influenced by local issues (Table 2.5), relatively few could name specific local issues that affected their vote (Table 2.2). But none the less there was strong popular support for the ideal of responsible local government.

The weakest aspect of this support was the low level of interest expressed in local politics (Table 2.2) and the low level of turn-out (Table 5.1). Moreover, the atmosphere of a local election failed to raise the level of interest in local politics while it (slightly) raised the level of interest in national politics (Tables 14.1 and 14.2). None the less, the public expressed a high level of confidence in local elections ensuring accountability (Table 3.1).

On the whole, people were satisfied with the way local councils ran things, much more satisfied with local than with national government (Table 3.5); and they tended to blame central government for the problems of local government (Table 3.5). They were generally satisfied with specific local government services: less than a fifth were critical of any specific service other than street-cleaning (Table 3.3). Moreover the public took a broad view of the proper scope of local government activities. One-fifth opposed local council grants to voluntary organizations but only one-tenth opposed council involvement in job creation schemes and a mere 2 per cent opposed council provision of rented housing (Table 3.4).

When they were questioned explicitly about local government autonomy, people were evenly split on their perceptions of whether local or central government had more say in local decisions, but they were very much in favour of less central control and totally opposed to appointed boards replacing elected local councils (Table 3.6). We should remember that switching powers and responsibilities from elected local councils to appointed boards has exactly the same effect as replacing elected councils with appointed boards. Overall, only 12 per cent wanted more central control of local government, 48 per cent wanted no change, and 37 per cent wanted less central control (Table 3.6).

We have already discussed one aspect of the allegation that local councils tyrannized their inhabitants—namely, the extent of permanent one-party rule. Now we can return to the question again and ask whether local partisan minorities were crying out to central government for protection from tyrannical local councils.

Naturally, those who lived under a council controlled by their opponent's party were less satisfied with the local council—but 71 per cent still said their council was running things 'fairly well' or 'very well'. These (local) minority partisans tended to have more contact with council offices and less with councillors. They were much more likely to endorse a non-party system of local government. They were more likely to blame the local council for its financial problems, and less likely to blame central government. But despite all of this, they were scarcely any more favourable to increased central government control of local government (Table 12.6).

Labour partisans opposed (Conservative) central government control irrespective of whether they lived under Conservative or Labour councils; Conservative partisans supported more central government control irrespective of whether they lived under Labour or Conservative councils—though they were somewhat more in favour of central control if they lived under a Labour council (Table 13.5). Scottish Conservatives opposed central control, shire-county Conservatives were marginally in favour, while London and metropolitan Conservatives were most in favour of more central control (Table 13.2).

There is little evidence here of many local minorities crying to central government for relief from local council tyranny. Instead Conservative partisans seem to be giving some support to their own party in central government, especially if they live in London and the metropolitan counties. But even so, the degree of support for more central control was limited: less than 29 per cent of Conservatives living under Labour councils, or under London and metropolitan councils wanted more central control—most wanted nothing more dramatic than the status quo.

If local councils were tyrannizing local partisan minorities, only a small minority of the minority appears to have thought so. Labour councils were the most unpopular, especially with Conservative minorities who lived under them; but 63 per cent of these minority Conservatives still said their local Labour council was running things 'very or fairly well', only 29 per cent wanted more central control and 4 per cent wanted less (Tables 13.4 and 13.5).

4. Do Local Elections Educate the Public and the Politicians about Each Other's Concerns?

This question can be posed in terms of both national and local politicians. Let us begin with national politicians. Judging by central government's obsession with local expenditure and rates, local elections have not succeeded in educating the public very well about the concerns of national politicians. In 1985 and 1986 only a tenth of our panel respondents quoted local rates as an important influence upon their vote.

Conversely, public support for local autonomy and public opposition to the use of appointed boards has not been reflected in central government action. Central government politicians have certainly been unresponsive to the attitudes and opinions of the local electorate as a whole.

But perhaps we should expect a Conservative government to be responsive to the attitudes of Conservative electors, rather than the electorate as a whole. It seems that major changes in local government —abolition of the London and metropolitan councils, introduction of the new community charge or 'poll tax', and the switch of responsibilities from elected councils to appointed boards or private sector companies— were designed in part to meet the concerns of Conservative electors, especially those who lived under Labour councils. In particular, the poll tax seemed to be a response to the impact of rating revaluations on Conservative voters in Scotland. If so, central government has misunderstood its own supporters and grossly over-reacted to a vociferous minority. We have seen that the large majority of Conservative partisans, even in London and the metropolitan areas did not support increased central government control and were at least 'fairly' satisfied with their local councils. According to our panel, the poll tax was no more popular with Scottish Conservatives than with English (indeed, on our small sample, it was actually less popular amongst Scottish Conservatives—see the poll-tax tables in Appendix III). There seems no evidence here that it met the particular concerns of Scottish Conservatives. In the parliamentary election of 1987, the Scottish Minister responsible for the poll tax lost his seat and the area of affluent owner-occupation most closely associated with agitation over rates revaluation, Bearsden, also unseated the Conservative incumbent.

The primary role of local elections in educating national politicians seems to be as a large-scale super opinion poll on the general popularity of central government. Prime Ministers have regularly used overall local election results as a guide to the wisdom of calling an immediate general election—notably in 1970, 1983, and 1987. But there is little evidence that they get much more information than that out of local elections. If they do, they ignore it, and respond to their own central concerns.

What do local elections teach the public? According to the Widdicombe Comittee:

In their earliest, and somewhat paternalistic, form arguments about participation were essentially based on the *educational* value of local government as a *training ground for democracy*. Such arguments were developed in 19th century England, particularly by J. S. Mill who saw the principal value of local self-government as raising the political capacities of the people.[30]

Mill stressed that 'local government educates both the citizen and future national political leaders to the practice of good government'.[31] Hill states that Mill 'justifies local government as political education . . . as such it is the prime element in democracy, and has an *intrinsic value regardless of the functions it may carry out*'.[32]

No doubt British local government does teach some lessons about democracy. *But what lessons?* When Mrs Thatcher was questioned in the late 1970s about whether the trade unions would let her govern should she be elected, she replied that elections would be a 'sham and a fraud' if the elected government were prevented from implementing its policies by powerful veto groups. It is difficult to disagree. Elections *are* a sham and a fraud (though frauds can be useful) if they do not confer decision-making authority upon those elected. Thus the 'intrinsic value' of an election cannot be separated from the 'functions the elected government may carry out'.

Local government and local elections do educate thousands of local councillors and the general public in the barren technicalities of local administration. At election time our panel became significantly better informed about the names of their county and district councils, the names and parties of their local councillors, and the name of the party that controlled their local council (Table 2.3). But these are mere technicalities. Local politicians conduct widespread canvasses of the electorate at local election time, and they pore over the results, usually attributing more significance to local personalities, campaigns, and issues than they merit. But our panel shows that the election did *not* increase public interest in local politics, nor public discussion of local politics, nor the feeling that local councils had responsibility for issues of importance (Tables 2.2, 14.1, and 14.2), nor public perceptions of local autonomy (Tables 3.6 and 14.4).

With increasing central controls imposed upon local government, with a local government system tightly bound by statutes enforced by fines and imprisonment for offending councillors, we might expect the lessons taught by local elections to be that local elections are irrelevant to local affairs (even if they send a message to central government); and that democracy requires *both* free elections for the electorate and decision-making discretion for those elected.

Despite this, our panel agreed by a large majority that 'the way people vote in local elections is the main thing that decides how things are run in this area' (Table 3.1). However there are many indications that this was a statement of democratic aspirations rather than perceptions. The electorate were evenly divided as to whether local or central government had most say in setting local rates and services (Table 3.6). They thought that a vote against the council would be one of the least effective ways of preventing the council taking a wrong course, and the most effective would be an approach to parliament through their MP (Table 2.4). And an overwhelming majority indicated that the political issues of importance to them were matters for central, not local, government (Table 2.2).

So the public were well informed about the limitations of local democracy in terms of both its scope and its freedom of action. At the same time, they wanted less central control and were totally opposed to appointed boards instead of elected councils (Table 3.6). They knew that local democracy was limited, but they wanted more. Instead of rejecting local elections as a 'sham and a fraud' the public were firmly attached to the limited amount of local democracy that they enjoyed, aware of the limitations, but critical of central government and central control rather than alienated from local democracy. For the public, local democracy was defective rather than fraudulent; their expectations were not high and their disappointment was not intense.

Notes

1. Layfield Committee, *Report of the Committee of Inquiry into Local Government Finance. Cmnd 6453* (London: HMSO, 1976).
2. For a fuller discussion see M. Harrop and W. L. Miller, *Elections and Voters* (London: Macmillan, 1987). ch. 9.
3. Widdicombe Committee, *Report of the Committee of Inquiry into the Conduct of Local Authority Business. Cmnd 9797* (London: HMSO, 1987), 46.
4. H. Elcock, *The Importance of Being Local* (Aberdeen: Political Studies Association Conference, 1987).
5. See Widdicombe Committee, *Report*, 47–56; W. Hampton, *Local Government and Urban Politics* (London: Longman, 1987), ch. 1; T. Byrne, *Local Government in Britain* (Harmondsworth: Penguin, 1986), ch. 1.
6. J. S. Mill, *On Liberty*, ed. M. Warnock, (London: Fontana, 1962) 185, cited by A. C. Tuxill, *Self and Other-Regarding Actions: The Proper Assignment of Local Authority Functions* (Aberdeen: Political Studies Association Conference, 1987).
7. Quoted by H. Elcock, *The Importance of Being Local* (Aberdeen: Political Studies Association Conference, 1987).
8. 'Elective Dictatorship' is the title of ch. 20 in Lord Hailsham's *The Dilemma of Democracy: Diagnosis and Prescription* (London: Collins, 1978).
9. Widdicombe Committee, *Report*, 48.
10. Layfield Committee, *Report*, 53.
11. A. Midwinter and C. Mair, *Rates Reform: Issues, Arguments and Evidence* (Edinburgh: Mainstream, 1987), 22.
12. Widdicombe Committee, *Report*, 47.
13. F. A. Hayek, *The Road to Serfdom* (London: Routledge, 1944, 1976), 174–5, quoted in part by T. Byrne, *Local Government in Britain* (Harmondsworth: Penguin, 1986), 7.
14. Widdicombe Comittee, *Report*, 45.
15. Ibid. 56.
16. Ibid.
17. Ibid. 45.
18. Green Paper, *Paying for Local Government. Cmnd 9714* (London: HMSO, 1986).

19. J. Redlich and F. W. Hirst, *A History of Local Government in England*, ed. B. Keith-Lucas (London: Macmillan, 1958, 1970), quoted by T. Byrne, *Local Government in Britain* (Harmondsworth: Penguin: 1986).

20. T. Byrne, *Local Government in Britain* (Harmondsworth: Penguin, 1986), 109.

21. T. J. Karran and H. M. Bochel, *The English and Welsh County Elections 1985* (Dundee: University of Dundee, 1986).

22. T. Byrne, *Local Government in Britain* (Harmondsworth: Penguin, 1986), 107.

23. Ibid. 117.

24. Widdicombe Committee, *Report*, 168.

25. T. Byrne, *Local Government in Britain* (Harmondsworth: Penguin, 1986), 108.

26. A. Midwinter and C. Mair, *Rates Reform: Issues, Arguments and Evidence* (Edinburgh: Mainstream, 1987), 151.

27. Widdicombe Committee, *Report*, 46.

28. A. Midwinter and C. Mair, *Rates Reform: Issues, Arguments and Evidence* (Edinburgh: Mainstream, 1987), 18.

29. See for example, W. Hampton, *Local Government and Urban Politics* (London: Longman, 1987), ch. 10, for recent examples of all these misfortunes. Since his book was published former councillors in Liverpool have been fined a third of a million pounds and their houses and other possessions will be seized and sold if they cannot pay.

30. Widdicombe Committee, *Report*, 49.

31. J. A. Chandler, *Justifications for Local Government* (Aberdeen: Political Studies Association Conference, 1987).

32. D. M. Hill, *Democratic Theory and Local Government* (London: Allen and Unwin, 1974), 23, quoted by W. Hampton, *Local Government and Urban Politics* (London: Longman, 1987).

Appendix I   The Panel Design

This book is based upon an analysis of a two-wave panel of 745 respondents interviewed in late November 1985 and again in May 1986. Sampling and field-work were carried out by NOP Market Research Limited of London. The interviews in November 1985 were funded by the Widdicombe Committee; the interviews in May 1986 were funded by a grant from the Economic and Social Research Council to the author.

The First Wave (November 1985)

The survey was based upon a random sample in 112 sampling points. Scotland was over-sampled by a factor of 3.33 in order to produce sufficient numbers there to permit separate analysis. The sampling points were selected from those used for NOP's Random Omnibus Survey. They were drawn from all constituencies in Great Britain (except Orkney and Shetland, and the Western Isles) by a process of multiple stratification. In England and Wales a systematic half of the 163 sampling points was selected while in Scotland all 17 sampling points were selected, plus an additional 13. In each constituency a ward was selected and 17 names drawn systematically from the register (21 names in the Greater London Council area).

At each sampled address residents were asked if there was anyone living there aged 18 or over who was not on the electoral register. A list was compiled of these non-electors and one of them selected for interview according to a random process. Thus in some cases two interviews could be conducted in the same household.

The questionnaire was developed by NOP, the Widdicombe Committee staff, their research adviser Ken Young, and the author. It was tested on a pilot survey of 24 interviews. Four interviewers worked on this pilot survey and each attended personal briefing and debriefing sessions.

Interviewing for the first wave began on 23 November and continued until December with 112 interviewers working on the survey—one in each sampling point. At least 4 calls were made at each address before it was abandoned as a non-contact. Other than the non-electors as discussed above, no substitutes were taken.

Ten per cent of all addresses were subject fo field quality control checks, which revealed no more than minor levels of interviewer error.

In total, 1,145 interviews were conducted and this represents an overall contact rate of 63 per cent. Details of the contact rate are shown overleaf:

Electors sample:
Names issued	1,935
Dead wood (vacant, died etc.)	238
Effective sample	1,697
Interviews with electors	1,028
Contact rate (1,027/1,697 × 100%)	61%

Non-electors sample:
Non-electors located	146
Interviews with non-electors	117
Contact rate (117/146 × 100%)	80%

Overall sample:
Available for interview	1,814
Interviews	1,145
Contact rate (1,144/1,814 × 100%)	63%

The Second Wave (May 1986)

Local elections took place throughout Scotland, London, and the metropolitan districts of England on 8 May 1986. On the same day there were also elections for all councillors in a very few shire districts and for one-third of councillors in the approximately 40 per cent of shire districts of England and Wales that had opted for 'election by thirds'.[1]

For this second wave of the survey all the 1,145 successful interviews from the first wave were reissued to the field. Interviewing began on 15 May and continued until 24 May. At least 4 calls were made at each address before it was abandoned as a non-contact. No substitutes were taken.

The questionnaire used in the second wave was drawn up by the author. It was based upon the questionnaire used for the first wave with a few additions and a few deletions. Wherever possible the wording of the original questions was retained, but questions about local election voting were altered to reflect actual behaviour (in those places where elections actually occurred) rather than just intention.

In all, 745 interviews were obtained. This represents a recontact rate of 68 per cent. Details of the recontact rate are shown below:

Names issued	1,145	
Dead/moved	56	
Available for interview	1,089	100%
Interviewed	745	68%
Refused	122	11%
Away during second wave	45	4%
Not available	116	11%
Other	61	6%

Coding

Coding frames were drawn up from the first 100 replies to each open-ended question in the first wave. After these had been agreed with the Widdicombe

Committee's research adviser, questionnaires were coded according to these codes. No new open-ended questions were used in the second wave.

Contextual Data

Further data were added for each interview as follows:

(1) The ward, constituency, and conventional geographic region in which the respondent lived.

(2) An indicator of whether the respondent lived in Scotland, Inner London, Outer London, a metropolitan county, or a shire county. In the text the term 'region' is applied to this categorization.

(3) The party in control (if any) of the county council in November 1985.

(4) The party in control (if any) of the district council in November 1985.

(5) The largest party in a county council where there was no overall control (November 1985).

(6) The largest party on a district council where there was no overall control (November 1985).

The above data were supplied by NOP, relying in part upon Department of the Environment sources. Classification of respondents as living in a place with or without àn actual election in May 1986 was based upon a question put to respondents in the May interview.

Analysis

For each respondent, information from the first and second wave interviews, plus the relevant contextual data, were merged. The over-sampling of Scottish electors was compensated by applying weights to make the (weighted) Scots come to 9.45 per cent of the total (weighted) sample. All results in this book are from such weighted analyses.

Notes

1. For a fuller explanation of these complex arrangements see Widdicombe Committee, *Report of the Committee of Inquiry into the Conduct of Local Authority Business. Cmnd 9797* (London: HMSO, 1987), 165–6; and T. Byrne, *Local Government in Britain* (Harmondsworth: Penguin, 1986), 95.

Appendix II How Representative Was the Panel?

As we noted in Appendix I the panel consists of 745 respondents who were each interviewed twice—once in November 1985 and once in May 1986. This panel was a subset of the full random sample of 1,145 respondents interviewed in November 1985. This book is based entirely upon the panel. Since almost a third of the original respondents were not included in the panel there is a danger that the panel may not be a representative subset of the original sample. However only a tenth of the original respondents refused and the rest of the failures to recontact were involuntary and thus less susceptible to bias.

We can measure the representativeness of the panel very easily however, by comparing the answers given in November 1985 by the 745 panel members, with the answers given then by the full 1,145 members of the random sample (which, of course, includes the 745 in the 1,145). As we shall see, the panel was remarkably representative of the full random sample from which it was drawn. Panel members were *very slightly* more interested and informed about local affairs and *very slightly* more inclined to vote, but otherwise they were fully representative.

Let us classify the panel as showing negligible bias on a question if the frequency of each possible answer amongst panel respondents is within 2 per cent of its frequency in the full random sample. On that very tight definition, there was *no panel bias at all* on:

Age
Sex
Employment status
House tenure
Education
Social class
Ratepaying
Length of residence
Party identification (both direction and strength)
Satisfaction with county and district coucils
Blaming central or local government for financial difficulties
Voting for the candidate rather than the party (either in local or parliamentary elections)
Voting on local rather than national issues in local elections
Preferring elected councils rather than appointed boards
Perceiving central government control of local councils

Approving central government control of local councils

Assigning the responsibility for important political issues to national or local government

Assigning pressure for local job creation to the council or the MP.

It is a long list and it underscores our main point that the panel was so representative of the full random sample that we could simplify the analysis in the text by restricting it entirely to panel respondents—which then has the added advantage that comparisons between November and May waves compare like with like, the same 745 respondents each time.

Panel respondents were *very slightly* more interested and informed about local politics however. The biases were small, but they include those shown in Table A.1.

Table A.1. Panel bias

	% amongst full random sample of 1,145	% amongst panel sample of 745	Panel bias
Know:			
county name	52	55	+3
district name	70	73	+3
councillor's name	29	31	+2
councillor's party	53	58	+5
'Great' or 'fair' interest:			
in national politics	51	54	+3
in local politics	33	36	+3
'Often' or 'occasionally' discuss:			
national politics	58	61	+3
local politics	42	46	+4
Did not vote:			
in 1983 General Election	18	15	−3
in last county election	41	39	−2
in last district election	39	37	−2

Note: All figures based on answers given to questions put during the first wave of interviews in November 1985.

Appendix III The Poll Tax

In 1987 central government legislated to change the basis of local government taxation in Scotland and began moves towards a similar change in England and Wales. These changes were prompted by the reaction of some ratepayers to the 1985 revaluation of properties in Scotland, one of whose effects was to switch the burden of local taxation from industry to domestic ratepayers.

In the 1980s approximately 30 per cent of local government revenue came from rents and charges, 30 per cent from rates, and 40 per cent from central government grants.[1] Rates were a tax levied on the value of domestic, commercial, and industrial property. Rather less than half the rates income comes from domestic rates in England and Wales, and only a third in Scotland.[2] Because the Scottish property revaluation in 1985 changed the ratio of industrial to domestic values, it shifted the rates burden on to domestic ratepayers. Until the government took emergency action (by means of a special subsidy) it appeared that revaluation would by itself reduce industrial rates by 25 per cent and increase domestic rates by 17 per cent—leaving commercial property rates unchanged.[3] MORI opinion polls in that year showed that only a fifth blamed local government in Scotland for the domestic rates increases that year, 46 per cent blamed central government cuts in grants, and 33 per cent blamed revaluation. Labour supporters mainly blamed central government, Conservatives mainly blamed revaluation.[4] From that time onwards, systems of local taxation were a matter of public debate in Scotland but much less so in England and Wales.

Our panel was asked its preferences on systems of local taxation in the May 1986 wave of interviews. However, it should be remembered that by the spring of 1986 the Scottish public was much more exposed to debate and argument about the merits of alternative systems than the English and Welsh.

The question put to the panel was:

There have been proposals to replace the rates by a new residents tax. Under this system each adult would pay the same amount. So the tax on your household would not depend on the rateable value of the house, but it would depend upon how many adults live here. Which would you prefer—rates, or a residents tax?

The wording and timing of such questions is important. Other questions at other times might produce different results but this seems a reasonably neutral question put at the outset of the debate (at least for the majority of our respondents, who, of course, lived outside Scotland). With this question we found 38 per cent in favour of rates, 48 per cent in favour of a poll tax and 14 per cent with no opinion on the matter. (Since 1986 the English electorate has been more exposed to arguments about the poll tax and English opinion seems to have swung against it. By November 1987, Gallup reported that opinion throughout Britain divided 57 per cent against the poll tax and only 30 per cent for it. Gallup's figures are intriguingly close to those we found for Scotland in 1986. Familiarity seems to have bred contempt.)

It is interesting to see how the percentage in favour of a poll tax varied across different groups of people. In some cases we found strong patterns where they might be expected; in other cases patterns were surprisingly weak.

Table A.2. Who wanted a poll tax? (May 1986)

| | % who favoured: | | |
	Rates	Poll tax	DK
All British respondents	38	48	14
Those who think of themselves as:			
Conservatives	29	61	10
Labour	45	36	19
Alliance	41	54	5
Young (under 35)	46	42	13
Middle-aged (35–55)	43	44	13
Old (over 55)	24	59	16
House-owners	33	53	14
Council tenants	53	32	15
Class AB (managerial)	33	57	11
Class C1 (clerical)	31	57	12
Class C2 (skilled manual)	44	45	12
Class D (unskilled manual)	50	34	16
Unemployed	52	28	20
Self-described ideology:			
Left	44	44	12
Centre	41	46	13
Right	33	57	10
Blame financial crisis on:			
Council overspending	32	60	8
Lack of government grants	45	40	16
Want more taxes and services	41	49	10
Want to cut taxes and services	38	53	9
Rates:			
Do not pay	29	46	25
Pay in full	38	50	12
In Scotland	54	26	20
In England and Wales	37	50	13

We asked a lot of questions about party support and voting intention. No matter which index of partisanship is used, Conservatives were much more in favour of the poll tax than Labour supporters—61 per cent of Conservatives but only 36 per cent of Labour supporters wanted a poll tax.

And there were strong demographic patterns. Only 42 per cent of the young, but 59 per cent of the old favoured the poll tax; so did 53 per cent of house-owners but only 32 per cent of council tenants; and 57 per cent of the managerial 'AB' class but only 34 per cent of the unskilled working class. Only 28 per cent of the unemployed wanted a poll tax.

We found some relationship between broader political attitudes and attitudes to the poll tax: 57 per cent of those who described themselves as being on the right of the political spectrum wanted a poll tax but only 44 per cent of those on the left; 60 per cent of those who blamed council overspending for local financial difficulties wanted a poll tax but only 40 per cent of those who blamed central government.

On the other hand there was little or no relationship between poll tax attitudes and attitudes to the tax versus services question; nor attitudes to central control of local government; nor ratepaying itself. This last point needs emphasis. Central government argued that many local electors were not liable for rates and were therefore financially irresponsible. The Department of the Environment claimed that only two-thirds of the electorate paid rates in full. However our survey shows that almost everybody *thinks of themselves* as a ratepayer. And even when we probe to find out whether they get rebates or not, those who actually do not pay rates do not have very different attitudes to the poll tax.

Table A.3. Which Conservative and Labour partisans wanted a poll tax? (May 1986)

| | % who favoured poll tax amongst: | |
	Conservative supporters only	Labour supporters only
All respondents	61	36
Young	46	37
Middle-aged	58	29
Old	73	44
House-owners	63	41
Council tenants	(68)*	29
In Scotland	(53)	15
In England and Wales	62	39

* % figures in brackets based upon less than fifty interviews.

Attitudes to the poll tax seem to be dominated by political partisanship. But it turns out that demographic variables had a genuine influence on poll tax attitudes even amongst supporters of the same party. Young Conservatives were 27 per cent less favourable to the poll tax than old Conservatives. Conversely, Labour-supporting owner-occupiers were 12 per cent more favourable to a poll tax than Labour council tenants.

Finally, support for the poll tax ran at 50 per cent in England and Wales but only 26 per cent in Scotland, despite (or because!) of the fact that the measure was imposed on Scotland first.

Perhaps Scots Conservatives were specially keen on the poll tax? Alas, there were so few Conservatives in Scotland that survey statistics become somewhat unreliable (because the samples are so small). But for what it is worth, our survey suggests that Scots Conservatives were less favourable to the poll tax than English Conservatives (and Scots Labour supporters were similarly less favourable to the poll tax than English Labour supporters).

Notes

1. T. Byrne, *Local Government in Britain* (Harmondsworth: Penguin, 1986), 197.
2. A. Midwinter and C. Mair, *Rates Reform: Issues, Arguments and Evidence* (Edinburgh: Mainstream, 1987), 107.
3. A. Midwinter, C. Mair, and C. Ford, 'Rating Revaluation Revisited' in D. McCrone (ed.), *Scottish Government Yearbook 1987* (Edinburgh: Edinburgh University, 1987), 36.
4. A. Midwinter and C. Mair, *Rates Reform: Issues, Arguments and Evidence* (Edinburgh: Mainstream, 1987), 168.

Index